SCREENING STRANGERS

NEW DIRECTIONS IN NATIONAL CINEMAS

Jacqueline Reich, editor

SCREENING STRANGERS

MIGRATION AND DIASPORA IN CONTEMPORARY EUROPEAN CINEMA

Yosefa Loshitzky

INDIANA UNIVERSITY PRESS
BLOOMINGTON & INDIANAPOLIS

This book is a publication of

Indiana University Press
601 North Morton Street
Bloomington, Indiana 47404-3797 USA

www.iupress.indiana.edu

Telephone orders   800-842-6796
Fax orders   812-855-7931
Orders by e-mail   iuporder@indiana.edu

∞The paper used in this publication meets the minimum requirements of
the American National Standard for Information Sciences—Permanence
of Paper for Printed Library Materials, ANSI Z39.48-1992.

Manufactured in the United States of America

Library of Congress Cataloging-in-Publication Data

Loshitzky, Yosefa.
Screening strangers : migration and diaspora in
contemporary European cinema / Yosefa Loshitzky.
p. cm. — (New directions in national cinemas)
Includes bibliographical references and index.
ISBN 978-0-253-35453-2 (cloth : alk. paper) —
ISBN 978-0-253-22182-7 (pbk. : alk. paper)
1. Motion pictures—Europe. 2. Identity (Psychology) in motion
pictures. 3. Minorities in motion pictures. 4. Immigrants in
motion pictures. 5. Culture in motion pictures. I. Title.
PN1993.5.E8L58 2010
794.43'6526912—dc22
2009032137

1   2   3   4   5   15   14   13   12   11   10

Dedicated to the memory of my parents,

Moshe Loshitzky
and
Doba (Dora) Loshitzky (Eisenberg)

CONTENTS

ACKNOWLEDGMENTS

I wish to thank The Leverhulme Trust for awarding me a generous grant to work from January 2004 to March 2005 as a Leverhulme Trust Visiting Professor in the Programme of MA in Film Studies at University College London (UCL). Unfortunately (as I explain in the Afterword), due to health problems I could not make the most out of the grant, and my public Leverhulme Lectures (which constituted the basis for this book) had to be cancelled. I wish to thank especially David Forgacs, who applied for the grant on my behalf and has been very supportive and understanding during the difficult times that I have been through. I would like also to thank the Institute of Germanic and Romance Studies (IGRS), School of Advanced Study, University of London, where, from February 2003 to April 2005 I was a Visiting Research Fellow. During my fellowship period I had the opportunity to present my work in progress and use the excellent Senate House Library of the University of London. I wish to thank Jo Labanyi and Judith Still, the former directors of the IGRS, and Naomi Segal, the current director, for supporting the international conference "Fortress Europe and Its 'Others': Cultural Representations in Film, Media and the Arts," which I initiated and organized and which took place at the University of London on April 4–6, 2005. I would like to thank all the other sponsoring bodies of the conference: the British Academy; School of Social Sciences, Media and Cultural Studies, University of East London; the journal *Third Text*; and the Italian Institute in London for their generous support. I also wish to thank all the participants of the conference (which, as I explain in the Afterword, I could not physically attend) for their interesting contributions. In particular, I would like to acknowledge the excellent lectures of the keynote speakers: Iain Chambers, Thomas Elsaesser, Ian Hancock, David Morley, Mica Nava, Judith Still, Lisa Schuster, Luisa Passerini, and Saskia Sassen. I would like also to thank Jennifer Langer from Exiled Writers for arranging performance by refugee/exiled poets Yang Lian, Ziba Karbassi, and Sahira Hussain, and Rosemary Lambeth from the IGRS for her kindness and excellent administrative support. The conference led to the publication of a special issue of *Third Text* (November 2006) on "Fortress Europe: Migration, Culture and Representation." I would like to thank the editors, Rasheed Araeen, Ziauddin Sardar, and Richard

Appignanesi, for providing this important forum for critical debate, as well as for the honor of being invited to guest-edit.

I also wish to thank my students at UCL, King's College, and UEL, with whom I had lively and sometimes provocative discussions on migration and diaspora in European cinema. In addition, I would like to thank the following individuals for inviting me to give papers and lectures on this topic in various academic conferences, symposia, and workshops: Tzila Ratner, Jo Labanyi, Ross Forman, Timothy Mathews, Dimitris Papanikolau, Enrica Capussotti, Parvati Nair, Paul Levine, and the late Roger Silverstone (whom we all miss). I am also deeply grateful to Haim Bresheeth for his support; to Maggie Humm for being such a wonderful mentor, the epitome of professionalism, kindness, and intellectual generosity; to Ashwani Sharma for his bright ideas as well as for being such a supportive colleague; to Gavin Poynter for being the best and kindest "boss" I have ever had; to Susannah Radstone for being my first Virgil in London; to Don Flynn, a tireless activist for migrants' rights; to Fran Cetti, my Ph.D. student from whom I have learned so much about refugees and the security state; and to Kay Dickson, David Rodwick, and Lee Grieveson for their support while I was teaching at King's College (and after). Some prominent film scholars have read the prospectus and provided me with invaluable insights and encouragements. I would like to thank them all, particularly Susan Hayward, Dana Polan, Frank P. Tomasulo, Phil Powrie, E. Ann Kaplan, Mireille Rosello, and Dudley Andrew. I also wish to thank Dave McCall, Commercial Manager at the British Film Institute in London, for his help in selecting images. Special thanks go to Jane Behnken, Music and Humanities Editor at Indiana University Press, and to Jackie Reich, the editor of Indiana University Press's book series New Directions in National Cinemas, whose faith in my project and persistent support brought this book into being. I also thank Alex Trotter for doing the index.

Some of the material used in this book has already appeared in print in somewhat different form. A modified and much shorter version of chapters 1 and 2 appeared under the title "Journeys of Hope to Fortress Europe," *Third Text* 20, no. 6 (November 2006): 629–34, in the special issue on "Fortress Europe: Migration, Culture and Representation." A slightly different and much shorter version of chapter 4 appeared under the title "The Post-Holocaust Jew in the Age of Post-colonialism: *La Haine* Revisited," *Studies in French Cinema* 5, no. 2 (2005): 137–47.

SCREENING STRANGERS

INTRODUCTION

SCREENING STRANGERS IN FORTRESS EUROPE

The Europe I have in mind will not be a "shrine of memories,"
but an idea, a symbol, a spiritual power center, just as to me the
ideas of China, India, Buddha, Kung Fu are not pretty memories,
but all that is most real, concentrated, and substantial.

Hermann Hesse, in correspondence with Thomas Mann

IN Thomas Mann's monumental novel *Doctor Faustus* (1947), written during his American exile, the protagonist, Adrian Leverkuhn, as the modern Faust, embodies the moral dilemma and culpability of the German nation. Mann writes: "It stands wholly and entirely at the service of the regime which brought us into this war, laid the Continent literally at our feet and replaced the intellectual's dream of a European Germany with the upsetting, rather brittle reality, intolerable, so it seems to the rest of the world, of a German Europe."[1] This German Europe described in *Doctor Faustus* came to be known as Fortress Europe (*Festung Europa*). By 1944, Hitler's Europe had become a seemingly impenetrable fortress, protected in the west by what was later termed the Atlantic Wall, perhaps the most massively fortified military position in history and a formidable obstacle for the Allied war planners.

Today's Europe, led by a coalition of former enemies—Germany, France, and Britain, and still haunted by the shadow of World War II and the Holocaust—likes to view itself as the "New Europe," free of its dark past and liberated from its traditional racism. Several politicians, public figures, intellectuals, and researchers have even declared the "end of nationalism" in Europe and the emergence of "post-Europe." Old Europe's grand narrative is collapsing, they intone, but out of this collapse a new and better Europe is emerging. This book examines, through an exploration of some contemporary European films, whether, indeed, this utopianism is flourishing in contemporary Europe seemingly "flooded" by waves of migration and "tainted" by "colored diasporas" in the midst of its formerly "white" capitals. It asks what counterforces (in the form of racism, xenophobia, and ultra-nationalism) are working against this utopian vision of borderless Europe currently experiencing massive migration, which is seen by some as "the greatest challenge facing all European governments,"[2] and what forces are working to make this utopia feasible.

Although Europe, as a geopolitical entity and as an ideological concept, has historically evolved through a process of absorbing, hybridizing, and assimilating different people from diverse ethnic, religious, and national groups, European countries have tended to view migration as challenging and threatening to their territory, identity, and ways of imagining themselves and others. In contrast to Jürgen Habermas's identification of Europe not as a nation-state in the sense of having a common descent, language, and history, but as a civic community that volunteers to have a collective expression in actions throughout Europe,[3] Fortress Europe increasingly erects racial, ethnic, and religious boundaries. At the same time that Europe is encouraging the expansion of the EU, it is also defining and closing its borders to the "others." Andrew Geddes argues that European countries, unlike settler societies such as Australia and the United States, have tended to view international migration rather nervously, as a threat.[4] Liza Schuster, noting the function of this phenomenon, points out that in the post-Cold War era "asylum seekers provide the sense of threat that underscores the protective function of the state . . . as well as proof that these states are liberal and deserving of their citizens' loyalty."[5]

The idea of "screening" migrants, of differentiating between the "indigenous" population and desired and undesired migrants, is still influenced by popular and racist myths according to which immigrants bring disease and pollution to the body of the nation (and the continent) and therefore need to be screened and contained. The process of screening practiced by the "host" society (which very often is more hostile than hospitable) is to screen the "good immigrant" and expel the "bad" to the literal and metaphorical "dumping grounds" of "the rest" of the world. Both the penalty system and the state and supra-state apparatuses built to solve the problem of "human waste" are driven by the desire to screen the "good migrant," to separate her/him from the "bad/undesired stranger." This instrumental approach to human lives explains the prominence of the screening metaphor in elite political discourse on migration, as well as in media and public responses to it.

Through practices of assimilation, absorption, and integration, which are in accordance with the models of citizenship adopted by each European nation-state—*ius sanguinis* (law of blood), *ius soli* (law of the soil), and *ius domicile* (law of residence)—it is hoped that the good migrants will be digested by the national and European body. Even racial mixing, or miscegenation, which has become one of the landmarks of the European metropole, and London in particular, can also be seen as a practice of screening and controlling, a way of assimilating the inassimilable. These "screening strategies," executed by the European national and supra-national bodies, exemplify what Zygmunt Bauman—following Claude Levi-Strauss' anthropological observations in *Tristes Tropiques*—views as the two pervasive "methods" of dealing with the presence of strangers. The first solution is to eat the strangers up, so that symbolically the "strangers are ingested into the national body and cease to exist as strangers." The second solution is to expel them, "either from the realm of the state's power or from the world of the living."[6] These conscious and unconscious, deliberate and unintentional practices of containing the flux of migrants express the symbolic dynamic of screening "strangers" in Fortress Europe, the political process through which Europe's major political agents/actors (state governments, the transnational EU, the media, the public) aim to preserve, perpetuate, and retain what they view as the "essence" of European culture and identity, which entitles its bearers to benefits and privileges that cannot be accorded to others.

The problem of "human waste" and the need to recycle it marks, according to Bauman, the shift from the welfare to the penalty model, manifested through new and innovative ways and modes of recycling refugees.[7] One such innovation was the famous proposal raised by David Blunkett, the former Home Office Labour minister, to "dump" failed asylum seekers and "illegal immigrants" in the peripheral zones of Europe (the "garbage" countries), or even better to "offshore processing centre outside Europe." The idea, of course, is to push refugees from the metropolitan centers of power, and to relegate them to their "natural" place, the wasteland of poor and underprivileged people disguised in Tony Blair's high-moral-ground language as "regional protection zones" and denounced by the UN "as dumping refugees on poorer countries."[8] The highly sophisticated yet unofficial penalty system designed to deny "failed asylum seekers" basic rights and support is obviously another state mechanism (currently harmonized by the European community) to solve this problem of "human waste." In Britain, the Nationality, Immigration, and Asylum Act of 2002 denies accommodation and basic support to those who fail to claim asylum as soon as seventy-two hours after entering the country. This has led to a flood of high court applications. The fifth asylum bill since the early 1990s removes benefits from failed asylum seekers, including families with children, who refuse to cooperate with their deportation.

The problem of human refuse also explains the prevalence of the cultural metaphors of the doctor, hospitals, and medical discourse in European cinema dealing with migration, as my analysis of many of the films discussed in this book shows. The highly evocative metaphor of screening is currently affiliated with five different discourses: (1) the discourse of cinema, or screen media, (2) the discourse of psychoanalysis (the screen dream), (3) medical discourse,[9] (4) the post-9/11 screening of potential terrorists by airport security that is based on "racial profiling" and driven by "white paranoia,"[10] and (5) the introduction of compulsory identity cards in the UK and elsewhere to enable screening using new biometric technologies "to establish identity and to check movement at borders."[11] The screening metaphor reflects the rise of the surveillance society and the emergence of Panopticon Europe, the New Europe obsessed with controlling its geographical and cultural borders, which is a recurrent theme in many of the films discussed in this book.

The historical and mythical layers embedded in Western European attitudes toward screening the "other" and the "stranger"[12] are currently being reinforced by growing resistance to the flow of migrants and refugees from non-European and Eastern European countries, as well as to Pan-European trends toward unification of the continent. This resistance has been expressed most vocally by the far-right populist parties and movements, but also in more restrictive immigration and asylum laws throughout the liberal democracies of Western Europe.[13] Contemporary Europe's new "others" are migrants and refugees from poor countries, particularly from Africa and Asia. These others, as this book shows, have replaced the "classical others" of Europe, the Jews and the Romanies (the Gypsies), who, as the two oldest minorities in Europe, were viewed as "the other within," associated with the East, and marked for extermination and total annihilation by the Nazis.[14]

Contemporary Europe, in the words of David Morley, can be regarded "as an entity whose primary identity is still implicitly defined in both religious and racial terms."[15] Until recently the term "European" has retained in the popular imagination its associative affinity with Christianity and whiteness despite the fact that Europe's population has been "hybridized," "creolized," and "colored" by waves of nonwhite, non-Christian migrants throughout its history.[16] Today as well, Europe's traditional resistance to nonwhite migrants, its racial selectivity, is tainted by religious tones. Post-9/11 and -7/7 anti-Muslim sentiments characterize the current European zeitgeist, feeding and nurturing the emergence of a new cultural racism, very often disguised as a war against terror and crime. Capitalizing on growing European xenophobia and Islamophobia fed by fears of terror and anxieties about Europe being "swamped" by undesirable immigrants, European society routinely conceptualizes migrants as criminals and as a security issue and subjects them to procedures that effectively classify them as criminals and terrorists. According to Don Flynn, the criminalization is embedded in the legal process itself.[17] Teresa Hayter, who advocates an open-borders approach toward migration, argues that refugees "are being criminalized by deliberate government policy. The words 'asylum seeker' and 'illegal immigrant' are constantly bracketed together."[18] Martin Thomas observes that from 9/11 on, in a dramatic reversal of the basic principle of civilized law, the "proof of criminal charge is a redundant complication"—at least as far as foreign refugees are concerned.[19] As I show in chapter 2, *Dirty Pretty Things* (Stephen Frears, UK, 2002) subverts this dominant xenophobic discourse. White London's dirty business (left to be carried out by the non-English) becomes a metaphor for the criminal exploitation and annihilation of the humanity of the other, of globalization's refugees.

The discourse regarding immigrants and particularly asylum seekers has been shaped, especially in Britain, through four major phases. The first phase, the pre-9/11 discourse, was mostly characterized by the criminalization of asylum seekers and immigrants, and attempted to explain the rise of crime in the UK (and also in France, where it contributed to the rising power of far-right nationalist Jean-Marie Le Pen). The second phase is the post-9/11 stage, in which the immigration debate has been framed into a new discourse of "the war on terror." This discourse implies quite openly that asylum seekers are terrorists or at least provide the breeding nest for them. The third phase was the period preceding the attack on Iraq during which the discourse of disease, epidemic, and plague was prevalent. The asylum seekers were presented as well poisoners, invoking echoes of the classical antisemitic discourse regarding Jews and Romanies as those who bring the plague, infecting and contaminating the local "indigenous" population (see chapter 1).[20] The post-7/7 period signifies a new phase in the war against migration, especially in Britain and France. The suicide attacks on the London underground, as well as the riots in France's *banlieues*, shift the focus of danger from the boundaries to the center, from the global periphery to the global metropolis. The fortified cities of Europe and the West—be they London (see chapters 1, 2, and 5), the Paris of *La Haine* (Mathieu Kassovitz, France, 1995) (see chapter 4), or even the Rome of *Besieged* (Bernardo Bertolucci, Italy, 1998) (see chapter 3)—replicate through their internal divisions the global power relations existing between the West and the rest. The growth of the postcolonial diaspora from within transforms the strategies of thinking and imagining the post-imperial. The first- or second-generation migrant may hold British or French citizenship, eat fish and chips or baguettes, but he is still the dangerous "stranger," "alien," and "foreigner."

Fortress Europe, Diasporas, and Globalization

A particularly interesting aspect of contemporary migration to Europe is that classical countries of emigration such as Italy, Spain, Ireland, Greece, and Portugal have themselves become desired destinations for migrants from the third world. Furthermore, even new members of the EU (the accession members), the newcomers to the "European club," have been not only sending migrants to Western Europe but are also receiving migrants themselves. One can see today, even in a white-blond country like Poland, a growing African diaspora. This new phenomenon is the result of globalization processes. Emergent forms of cultural transnationalism forged by labor migration from the poor periphery of the globe to the rich metropolitan centers of the world constitute new "ethnoscapes" at the urban centers of the West.[21] The rapid growth of "liminal political spaces"[22] in a postcolonial world that has become a site for voluntary travel (tourists, travelers, pilgrims, immigrants, occupational transnationals) as well as involuntary travel (refugees, asylum seekers, displaced populations, transferred populations resulting from "ethnic cleansing," foreign workers, the homeless, undocumented migrants) has resulted in the recent emergence of new diasporic polities in the metropolitan centers of the West, particularly in Western Europe. This global character of international migration results, as Stephen Castles and Mark J. Miller argue, in "the intermingling and cohabitation of people from increasingly different physical and cultural settings."[23]

Since the 1980s, scholars from different disciplines have tried to theorize the new kind of social space which has been created in our world—through the growth of crisscrossed economies and cultures—in terms of globalization. According to many scholars of globalization, the status of structures "in a world where capital, production, and peoples are in constant motion" and "interpretations and reversals between the different worlds"[24] result in hybridity is all the more conducive for the emergence of diasporas. As "the nation-state is no longer taken for granted as the global unit of political organization,"[25] the postcolonial subject "is comprehended in terms of hybridness or 'in-betweeness', he is not contained any more within fixed categories or binary oppositions."[26] What Benedict Anderson called in 1994 "the postmodern Exodus" or "post-1930s nomadism"[27]—namely, the massive migration to the metropolitan cores—creates, according to him, two types of political consequence in our rapidly changing world. The first consequence is "the recent emergence in the United States and other older nation-states of an ethnicity" out of which the "ideological program of multiculturalism"[28] has appeared. In Europe, this tendency is manifested through an "ethniciza-tion" process—or "neo-tribalism," to use Philip Schlesinger's derogatory language[29]—in which racism is a very strong element. The 1990s Balkan war in the former Yugoslavia and the continuing ethno-religious-national conflicts in Kosovo are the prime examples (see discussion in chapter 2 in particular). The second consequence of globalization is the emergence of what Anderson calls "long-distance nationalism,"[30] in which migrants in the prosperous West support extremist nationalism back home. In the post-9/11 world, this support for nationalism has been shifted and transformed into support of resistant and subversive transnationalism in the form of a Muslim *umma* (the world Muslim community) and the so-called globalist Islamist terrorism, fundamentalist world Jihadism, and so on.

Global space, as Michael Peter Smith claims, is "a space of flows." The boundaries of the nation-state "no longer correspond to the social spaces . . . borderless people inhabit. The blurring of once taken-for-granted boundaries differentiating states, ethnicities, and civil societies is producing new spaces of daily life, new sources of cultural meaning, and new forms of social and political agency that flow across national borders."[31] This new social space of deterritorialized people produced by transnational migration has created, as Hamid Naficy observes, people who are not, or do not want to become, fixed in any identity: "By their status as liminal hybrids and syncretic multiples, they form a global class that transcends their original or current social and cultural locations."[32] Consequently, contemporary Western Europe's metropolitan centers have become hybrid spaces of class, ethnicity, nationality, and internationality of a "third world space" within the first world.[33]

Arif Dirlik notes that "Third Worlds have appeared in the First World and First Worlds in the Third. New diasporas have relocated the Self there and the Other here, and consequently borders and boundaries have been confounded. And the flow of culture has been at once homogenizing and heterogenizing."[34] World cities have thus become hybrid sites of real and imaginary travel. The growth of post–World War II world cities, those megacities which attract global migration that both "internationalize" and "ethnicize" them, is part of a larger process (see chapter 2). Currently, as many scholars observe,[35] the West, particularly Europe, is dominated by two simultaneous but contradictory processes: the rise of particularism on one hand and universalism in the form of growing globalization on the other. As forms of transnationalism, diaspora and exile constitute domains of political and cultural otherness that challenge the nation-state and its claim to the exclusive representation of some "essential" collectivity, which manifests a national "self." The fact that the formation of exilic and diasporic "others" is currently on the rise, on a global and historically unprecedented scale, makes that "otherness" all the more menacing to the western liberal nation-state.

The Cinema of Fortress Europe

A complex phenomenon like today's "Europe" cannot be described or experienced as a whole but only as a site of negotiation over identity. The media and the arts have become a new site of articulation of Europe's new sociocultural space, shaped and negotiated by the experience of displacement, diaspora, exile, migration, nomadism, homelessness, and border crossing, challenging the traditional notions of "Europe" and "Europeanness." The growing migration to Europe and the emergence of large diasporas at the heart of the European metropolitan centers further enhance the questions of "Where is Europe? Whose Europe?" These questions challenge the imaginary and imagined borders and boundaries erected and fortified by Europe in an attempt to construct itself as a coherent and unified geographical, political, and cultural entity. Yet, as Liza Schuster argues, while the possibility of protecting and demarcating culture has been challenged by many scholars and public intellectuals, for many, culture remains something that needs borders. Such "culture," when invoked as a justification for border controls, serves two linked functions: reinforcing political control and legitimizing racism.[36] Recent events in Europe, such as the 7/7 bombings in London, the March 11, 2004, Madrid train bombings, the November 2005 riots in Paris (*Intifada des banlieues,* see chapters 4 and 5), the slaying of the maverick filmmaker Theo van Gogh by a second-generation radical Muslim of Moroccan origin, and the global row over the Danish cartoons depicting the Prophet Muhammad, only foreground and enhance the severity and seriousness of this crisis.[37]

This book, responding to this crisis of European cultural identity, goes beyond the specific national context of film production in Europe, and discusses how the issues of migration and diaspora are challenging the conflicting, and sometimes conflating, ideas of post-Europe, Fortress Europe, post-Holocaust Europe, New Europe, post-nation Europe, and transnational Europe. It asks how the films dealing with migration and diaspora challenge European identity, particularly traditional notions of Europeanness, and how they subvert or/and reinforce hegemonic and counter-hegemonic attempts to construct and deconstruct European identity. Most of the films discussed in this book were made by symbolic representatives of the host/receiving societies, rather than by the "strangers" in their midst whose work constitutes part of "minority discourse," traditionally based on ethnic autobiography and autobiographical fiction.[38]

The films of the "minority discourse" mark a shift in the politics of representation of others and strangers in European cinema. No longer made by representatives of the host and/or dominant culture, these films are created by members of the minority community itself and they constitute a form of social document without being a documentary in the traditional sense. Furthermore, as a form of self-representation, these films are free from xenophobia, as well as from the idealization or exoticization that often characterize films made by "outsiders." They are experimental diasporic films using basically Western film forms to speak from non-Western culture to a mixed audience. As hybrid films they perform the disjunction typical of ethnics in a state of cultural transition and reveal the process of exclusion by which nations and identities are formed. Moreover, as ethnic films they are also diasporic films, a form of otherness that poses cultural and political challenges to the hegemony and homogeneity claimed by the nation-state. At times explicitly and at other times implicitly, these films introduce the possibility of a multicultural, multi-ethnic, and multi-religious Europe, free of the fear and hatred of the other. The "problem of the other" in these films is presented from within, from the point of view of the other himself/herself, negotiating whether and how to maintain his/her identity within a dominant culture.

My choice to discuss mostly hegemonic rather than minority/diasporic/ migrant films is related to my attempt to explore the crisis of European identity through the emerging dominant discourse of anxiety regarding its new strangers and others within. Nowhere are these anxieties better articulated than in cinema, which both reflects and constructs societal attitudes, because, like architecture, cinema is one of the most public arts. Furthermore, as Europe's recent and less recent history is tainted with unprecedented acts of racism, the investigation of this topic demands further research into the heart of darkness (or rather whiteness) itself through the study of cinema, one of the core representations of European culture. It is also important to point out that European cinema's preoccupation with issues of otherness, much like the phenomenon of migration itself, is neither new nor exclusively contemporary. The use and abuse of archetypes of the other and the stranger were also at the center of early classical European cinema, especially in works associated with German Expressionism, the "haunted screen" of "shadow cinema" which, according to Siegfried Kracauer and Lotte Eisner, anticipated the emergence of Nazism.[39] Figures such as the robot, the Golem, the somnambulist, the vampire, and the homunculus have appeared in the classics of German Expressionist cinema like *The Golem* (Paul Wegener, Germany, 1914, 1920), *The Student of Prague* (Stellan Rye, Germany, 1913), *The Cabinet of Dr. Caligari* (Robert Wiene, Germany, 1919), *Metropolis* (Fritz Lang, Germany, 1926), and others. These images epitomized European archetypes of the stranger and the other which were often associated with the threatening presence of the Jew, the Gypsy, and the Bolshevik as symbols of the menacing East. More explicit racist images were later manufactured by Nazi cinema in films such as *The Jew Suss* (Veit Harlan, Germany, 1940) and *The Eternal Jew* (Fritz Hippler, Germany, 1940), which became "Nazi classics" in the service of a regime of racial annihilation. Although this book focuses on new European cinema, from the turn of the twentieth century to the beginning of the twenty-first century, and the political consequences of its depiction of issues pertaining to diasporic communities, migrants, and ethno-religious identity, it also explores the historical roots of this politics of representation. The primary focus of the book, however, is on the experience of being threatened by the other (the migrant, the refugee, the non-European, and Eastern European) as represented, articulated, and debated in contemporary European cinema.

The present book, drawing more on a cultural studies reading of films than on a specifically cinematographic analysis, is not a historical and ideological in-depth study of the overall corpus of European cinema about migration and diaspora (a task beyond the competence—let alone expertise—of any individual scholar), but an attempt to discuss the projection and negotiation of European identity through an analysis of films that constitute unique sites of struggle over identity formation and meaning, and further open and broaden the public space for debating this issue. This book does not set out to survey all the films made in Europe on migration and diaspora, nor even all the major films on the topic. Rather, it represents a compromise between the breadth of cultural products available and the depth of their analysis. The aim is to cover significant shifts, central anxieties, and ambiguities. The book does not discuss more recent films on the topic, most of them released while the first draft was being prepared.[40]

Screening Strangers investigates in-depth images of otherness reproduced by European cinema as part of the continent's struggle with the question of identity, including notions of fluidity and contingency, that is, identity and counter-identity as formed in particular historical circumstances. The book thus attempts to suggest a complex and unique view of European society and its struggle to forge a collective identity at the expense of plural identities. The volume's exploration of cinematic texts on the one hand and its drawing, on the other hand, on current developments in contemporary critical discourse on racism, nationalism, transnationalism, globalization, and ethnicity attempts to "transcend" conventional critical analyses of European society and culture and break new ground for a more "rounded" view of a culture undergoing a difficult process of constructing and deconstructing identities.

The chapters in this book all deal, in different ways, with the question of European and post-European identity in crisis experienced under the "pressure" of migration, globalization, and terror. Each chapter highlights a distinct theme that constitutes the core of the public discourse on the European immigration debate. Some of the issues raised in this debate are more subtle, concealed, and covert because they are taboo in post-Holocaust Europe, such as the topics of race and racial mixing (miscegenation). Rather than being easily recognized as part of an overt racialist discourse, they are dislocated and disguised as part of a discourse on culture, social cohesion, integration, shared values, common heritage, and other similar rhetorical figures. Other issues, such as terror, crime, and faith-religion, though seemingly more openly discussed, are relegated to the discourse on security, conveniently used to silence critical and dissenting voices.

Chapter 1 addresses prominent cultural motifs, metaphors, and tropes in a number of significant cross-border and journey films. The chapter shows how the films of this genre project and represent both the physical and sociocultural landscapes of Europe, which have been significantly altered as a result of migration and diaspora. I argue in this chapter that by portraying the difficulties and hardships experienced and endured by refugees and migrants on their way to the Promised Land (the host country in Europe) and by concentrating on the refugees' lived experience, this genre challenges and subverts contemporary media and public discourse on migrants which dehumanizes and criminalizes them. Chapter 2 demonstrates how contemporary European cinema has used the European city, and particularly the European capital, as the stage for the drama of the current "exodus" to Europe, while chapter 3 focuses on one city, Rome, as portrayed in Bernardo Bertolucci's *Besieged* (1998), an example of a European film about miscegenation, which is occupied with highly charged master/slave dialectics and constitutes a form of social document about the ambivalence embedded in the attitude of the European host society toward racial mixing.

Chapter 4 expands on previous discussions of Mathieu Kassovitz's *La Haine* (France, 1995) by concentrating specifically on the construction of the image of the Jew, Europe's historical "other" and "stranger," within the film's representation of a multi-ethnic, multiracial, and multi-religious trio. By shifting the boundaries of the debate on *La Haine* from the *banlieue* genre to the relationship between what I call the "post-Holocaust" French Jew and the postcolonial context which characterizes the condition of contemporary France, the chapter offers a new perspective on the relationships between Europe's "old" and "new" others. Chapter 5 elaborates and expands on Giorgio Agamben's thesis regarding the centrality of the camp as the fundamental biopolitical paradigm of the West, through a discussion of three films (what I term the "camp trilogy"): *In This World* (UK, 2002), *Code 46* (UK, 2003) and *The Road to Guantanamo* (UK, 2006), all made by one of Britain's most prolific and controversial directors, Michael Winterbottom. It is within the post-9/11 climate of fear that these films have been initiated, produced, and received. Each of the films in this trilogy introduces a different representation of the idea of the camp and the real and symbolic space it occupies in what Naomi Klein perceptively describes as "disaster capitalism" based on the shock doctrine.[41] In considering the connection between Europe's migrant populations and the camp, this concluding chapter shifts and expands the focus of the book from the European migration debate to the broader questions of the post-Holocaust world, anchoring the "lessons" of the global debate on migration, crime, and terrorism in this dark chapter of European history.

The chapters in this book follow not only the prominent themes of the European immigration debate and their articulation in cinema, but also the physical and ideational trajectory of the migration to Europe itself. While chapter 1 traces the beginning of the migratory route in the borderless, lawless, liminal zones and landscapes of Fortress Europe, chapter 2 discusses the second stage in the migration narrative, the arrival at the city, the migrant's fantasized Promised Land. Chapters 4 and 5, on the other hand, deal with the reverse ideological journeys of the second generation. The centrality of the Balkan, as a metaphor for the fragility of multiculturalism, is interwoven into the narratives of the films and the chapters alike, whether they take place in post-imperial Paris or in post-imperial London, Europe's most global city. Even chapter 3, which focuses on Africa as the new "Sick Man of Europe," constitutes an ironic historical twist to the Balkans, Europe's former (?) "Sick Man." Likewise, chapter 4, which focuses on France, frames the Republic's resistance to migration and multiculturalism as a time bomb threatening to Balkanize Europe. The "Muslim Question" (which is also central to the "Balkan Question") is at the center of chapter 5. Although the "Muslim Question" (in an ironic historical twist of the "Jewish Question" discussed in chapter 4) has come to haunt the European zeitgeist, this "question" is still inseparable from the issues of race and color due to the fact that most of the world's Muslims are nonwhite. While both chapters 4 and 5 deal with European anxieties about the new other within, chapter 5 focuses in particular on the fears of the Muslim, perceived as "the enemy within," collaborating and conspiring with "the enemy without," the "axis of evil" of migrants, terrorists, and the poor in the post-9/11 discourse. As readers will realize, this book offers diverse and controversial readings of the European "immigration debate," as it is represented in various films, in the hope of engaging its readers in an ongoing, provocative, yet productive discussion.

I

JOURNEY/ OF HOPE
TO FORTRE// EUROPE
CROSS-BORDER AND MIGRATORY FILMS

The long-standing dream that Europe would one day be
borderless has for many turned into an angst-ridden scenario
embodying insecurity and threatened identity.

Kate Connolly

IN this chapter, I attempt to address some of the prominent cultural motifs, metaphors, and tropes in some significant films of the contemporary migrant and diasporic European cinema. This cinema has become a recent site of articulation of Europe's new sociocultural space, shaped and negotiated by the experience of displacement, diaspora, exile, migration, nomadism, homelessness, and border-crossing, "putting in flux the idea of Europe itself."[1] Today's "Europe" is a phenomenon that can no longer be described or experienced as a coherent whole, save as a site of negotiation over identity.

In recent years, Europe's multicultural struggles have become a prominent topic in European cinema. This cinema clearly utilizes issues related to ethno-religious diasporas, racism, and migrant culture in order to reflect, negotiate, and construct a new image of the "Old World." Europe, as represented in these films, is no longer predominantly white and Christian, but a multicultural, multi-ethnic, and multi-religious domain. My discussion of these topics attempts to show how the new European cinema projects and represents both the physical and sociocultural landscapes of Europe, which have been significantly altered as a result of migration and diaspora. The tropes and motifs that I discuss cross the national borders of their narratives, contexts of production and sociopolitical circumstances, and thereby transcend the traditional understanding of "national cinema," which is produced within the fixed boundaries of the nation-state and is thought to reflect its imagined collectivity. Conversely, the new transnational European films that deal with migration and diaspora—many of them multinational co-productions—are part of an independent, hybrid, transnational cinema which, in the words of Hamid Naficy, "cuts across previously defined geographic, national, cultural, cinematic, and meta-cinematic boundaries."[2] Three evolving genres of films about immigration can already be traced in the emerging diasporic and migrant cinema, each referring to a different stage in the migratory tour/route, what might, ironically, be called the *grand tour* of the migrants, namely: the migratory journey from the homeland to the host country and sometimes back home. A fitting name for the first genre might be "Journeys of Hope," although very often they turn into journeys of death, as in the emblematic Swiss film *Journey of Hope* (*Reise der Hoffnung*) (Xavier Koller, Switzerland, 1990). By portraying the hardships endured by refugees and migrants on their way to the Promised Land (the host country in Europe), the films of this genre challenge and subvert contemporary media and public discourse on migrants which dehumanizes and criminalizes them.[3]

The second genre might be called "In the Promised Land" (see chapters 2, 3, and 4) and includes films such as *Beautiful People* (Jasmin Dizdar, UK, 1999), *Besieged* (*L'assedio*) (Bernardo Bertolucci, Italy, 1998), *Nordrand* (*Northern Skirts*) (Barbara Albert, Austria-Germany-Switzerland, 1999), *Dirty Pretty Things* (Stephen Frears, UK, 2002), and many others that investigate the encounter with the host society in the receiving country. These films usually revolve around such issues as racism, miscegenation, cultural difference, and economic exploitation. They focus on the process of immediate absorption in the new country, portraying a reception of the migrants by the host society that in most cases is more hostile than hospitable.

The third genre deals with the second generation and beyond (see chapters 4 and 5). It explores the processes and dynamic of integration and assimilation and their counterparts, alienation and disintegration. The films in this category, best exemplified, perhaps, by the French genre of the *beur* and *banlieue* film (see chapter 4) as well as by some of the British films on the black and Asian diaspora in the UK,[4] deal with the experience of the second generation, children of migrants who are still marginalized and oppressed by the host society. These films raise questions about the status of ethnodiasporas in relation to the national body. Are ethno-religious diasporas an integral part of the national body, or are they foreign to it? Do they threaten or transcend it so as to constitute a transnational body? Ultimately these films raise questions about the politics of belonging and non-belonging and the cultural identity of the "New Europe." This chapter focuses on the first genre, the journey films in, of, to, and even from Fortress Europe.

The Traumatic Landscapes of Fortress Europe

The city is the setting, backdrop, and principal stage of drama for the majority of the migrant and diasporic films. The prominence of the city in the cinemascape of Fortress Europe reflects the centrality and importance of the city in the migratory process and in the migrant experience. Because most contemporary migration to Europe is economically motivated, it is only natural that the city, with the economic opportunities it has to offer and its growing diasporas, is the main magnet for migrants in search of a better life. Yet since the city is usually the migrants' final destination, its appearance in the films is most often preceded, in reality as well as in these films, by journeys through the more varied landscapes of Fortress Europe. Moreover, because the journey motif constitutes one of the most abiding *topoi* of literature and film worldwide, the literal trip in the landscape becomes a metaphorical voyage necessary for the construction of a new world, a new self. These excursions thus become explorations of new identity, individual as well as collective.

The cinematic landscapes of Fortress Europe which these films use as a backdrop for their journeys in time and space are typically trauma-saturated rather than healing landscapes. *Journey of Hope,* for example, one of the first major films about migration to Europe and which won the 1991 Academy Award for Best Foreign Language Film, takes place in the Swiss Alps, which in this film became the geographical and symbolic icon of Fortress Europe (though Switzerland is not a member of the EU).[5] The film tells the story of a Kurdish Turkish couple, Haydar Sener (Necmettin Çobanoğlu) and Meryem (Nur Surer), who start their journey of hope from a small village in the mountains of southeastern Turkey in September 1988. They have decided to take their 7-year-old son Mehmet Ali (Emin Sivas), who is the brightest of their eight children, following the grandfather's (Selahattin Firat) suggestion to the couple that "he is a fresh seeding to grow roots in the new soil of your future" and the one "who will save the family."[6] The family has sold its livestock and farmland in order to finance the trip to the supposed Swiss Paradise of milk and chocolate. Their first stop after leaving their Kurdish homeland is Istanbul, where they are stowed away on a freighter to Genoa. Once in Italy, they are taken to the mountains by traffickers/smugglers and left to fend for themselves in the snow and cold as they make their way toward Switzerland. Their journey of hope now turns into their worst nightmare. Meryem breaks her leg in the freezing mountains, the child dies of cold, and Haydar is arrested by the Swiss authorities on charges of neglecting his son. The film ends as the couple awaits deportation back to Turkey.

The film mobilizes a mythical and epic journey about the expulsion of refugees from the Swiss Eden in an attempt to stop the exodus of poor migrants in search of the European Promised Land.[7] A traditional space of luxury and privilege for wealthy Europeans since the end of the nineteenth century, Switzerland, the "Paradise beyond the mountains," as Haydar describes it, remains sealed, closing its heavenly gates to the poor "invaders" from Asia. The different modes of transportation that carry the family along their journey, buses, trains, lorries, ship, and private car, expose, as Hamid Naficy observes in his discussion of accented films, the dialectical relationship between "the inside closed spaces of the vehicles and the outside open spaces of nature and nation."[8] These vehicles thus become mobile prisons within a foreign landscape. The film begins with Ali, the child, playing a dangerous game, lying still on the railway tracks under a roaring train. The menace associated with trains is carried over to the Milan train station at which the family arrives at night. The deserted and empty station is an image of alienation, displacement, and rootlessness. It is a non-place, which could be anywhere.[9] A Turkish man, the only other living soul to be seen, approaches the family. Recognizing them as fellow travelers and co-patriots he says, "We are all going north, aren't we?" thus invoking the North/South divide at the heart of globalization and migration. When later he lends money to Haydar to pay for the extra fee charged by the traffickers, he tells the grateful family: "Exile brings people together." His kind and warm words create an emotional space of solidarity and humanity on the background of the deserted station.

The most enthusiastic traveler in this journey of hope is the child, Mehmet Ali, for whom the journey is an exciting adventure. This is his first excursion into the world beyond the remote, dry, and rugged mountain landscape of his birthplace, so different from the landscape of the lush green Alps crowned with white snow peaks as they appear on a postcard sent to Haydar's family by an uncle who immigrated to Switzerland. The child communicates easily with the people they meet throughout the journey. Meanwhile, the people in the various European countries that they traverse on their route to Switzerland, whose languages the family does not understand, also find it easier to communicate with him than with his parents. The child (as in many migratory situations) becomes the mediator between the migrants and the "indigenous," the outsiders and the locals, the "Asians" and the "Europeans," the past and the future. When he dies, therefore, the future dies with him. It is the death of hope.[10]

The Hybrid Matrix of Memory: Jewish and Muslim Refugees

The multiplicity of languages employed in *Journey of Hope* (Kurdish, Turkish, Italian, Swiss German), as well as the shift from one language to another, is typical of exilic cinema and represent the in-between state of the migrant who shifts from one linguistic code to another or experiences this shift simultaneously. This linguistic journey demonstrates the transnational dimension of the migratory process as well as the transnational aspect of Europe itself. The multilayered linguistic code employed in the film is reverberated in the iconic religious palimpsest which the film creates. Although the Kurdish family is Muslim, the director grafts Judeo-Christian iconography into the religious matrix in order to visually portray their plight to a non-Muslim audience through familiar and recognizable symbolism. For example, the three family members recall the Christian holy family with Meryem the mother invoking Maria, and the father carrying in his arms the frozen, "crucified," dying child, echoing the famous *Pieta* image. The child also recalls the biblical son Isaac, sacrificed on the altar of his father's migration fantasy.

If the journey of hope to Fortress Europe is a journey in search of a new life, it also involves discarding the old life. As such, the journey in the foreign landscape is also a journey of forgetting, a passage where identity is lost yet where the prospects for gaining a new identity are dubious. One of the most interesting scenes in *Journey of Hope* occurs when the migrants lose their suitcases while wandering in the Alps. The suitcase, as Hamid Naficy observes, is "a contradictory and multilayered key symbol of exilic subjectivity: it contains souvenirs from the homeland; it connotes wanderlust, freedom to roam, and a provisional life; and it symbolizes profound deprivation and diminution of one's possibilities in the world."[11] In fact, in this scene, the Turkish trafficker who leads the refugees through the mountains presses them to throw away their suitcases, telling one of the refugees, a devout Muslim dressed in traditional clothes and carrying an exceptionally heavy-looking suitcase: "You are making a fresh start—why carrying your suitcase with you?" Shortly afterward the suitcase of this religious Muslim (who, like Haydar, is later captured by the border police) is seen falling into the deep Alpine canyon as its contents—copies of the Qur'an and other sacred Muslim books—are scattered, lost and forgotten forever in the inhospitable landscape of the wintry Alps. Books—the basis and cradle of civilization—are reduced, in this scene, to objects that constitute obstacles to the survivalist refugees. For the less religious refugees, indeed, the heavy books and the suitcase are an obstacle to survival; but for the Muslim devotee, this suitcase is a repository of Islamic civilization, a container of personal memory and Muslim identity.

In light of the growing "Muslim Question" in Europe, this symbolic suitcase becomes a prophetic icon of the status of Muslims in Fortress Europe. The loss of the suitcase is the loss of identity, memory, and home, whereby the journey becomes one of despair instead of hope. Massimo (Dietmar Schonherr), the Italian guide who walks the family through the Alps, tries to convince Haydar to "leave the suitcase." "It's all we have," Haydar responds. But when his son freezes, the father drops the last suitcase and instead carries his child in his arms. The shift from carrying the suitcase to carrying the dying child is an image of double loss, the loss of the past (whose metonymy is the suitcase) and the loss of the hope for a better future (the son). This shocking image of Europe's "Muslim Problem" is emblematic of the heavy toll paid by migrants in their search for hope: the loss of their cultural and religious identity and memory. The suitcase might be seen as *the* prop of the twentieth century, a century which has experienced massive exodus of displaced people, refugees, and transferred populations. Most notably, the suitcase has become a dominant and recurring motif in Holocaust iconography, inspired by the piles of suitcases (among piles of other objects such as shoes and eyeglasses) taken from the Jews in the death camps and sorted out by slave laborers to be sent to the Fatherland for recycling and reuse by the German war machine.[12]

From this overwhelming scene, the film cuts to a shot of a full moon over icy cold white mountains, recalling the famous shocking montage of the cut from a shot of a moon "slicing" a cloud to a shot of the eyeball slitting in Salvador Dali and Luis Buñuel's *Un Chien Andalou* (Andalusian Dog, France, 1928). A Swiss border control unit is seen patrolling the area, using powerful flashlights and binoculars to catch border-crossing activities. On the background of this icy, hallucinatory landscape, the Swiss flag appears, waving in the icy stormy air like an apparition. On the sound track, the wind howls gruesomely, joined by the terrifying barking of the patrol dogs, and a cold blue halo hovers over the mountains. These sonic themes, much like the images of the refugees with their shabby and battered suitcases, invoke the iconography of the Holocaust. Implicitly, they conflate the memory of World War II's Jewish refugee with the contemporary Muslim refugee, creating a junction where the Holocaust Jew (and even his precursor, the mythical figure of the Wandering Jew) and the contemporary Muslim merge into what I call a "hybrid refugee." This enriched matrix of past and present icons of victimhood and persecution opens up the possibility of seeing the contemporary European policy of enforcing its fortress as the point of departure in forging a new attitude toward migration to the New Europe. *Journey of Hope* can thus be read as rethinking the status of contemporary migrants and refugees to Europe in light of the Holocaust. Moreover, it casts a shadow over the past of Switzerland, its collaboration with the Nazis under the guise of neutrality, and its continuing callousness toward the new refugees.[13]

On Swiss Hospitality and the Kindness of Strangers

The Swiss "Paradise beyond the mountains" turns into a nightmare in the Alps. Switzerland becomes a menace and its snow-covered mountains turn into a visual metonym of Fortress Europe, recalling the stories of Jewish refugees, who during the Holocaust tried to escape to "neutral Switzerland." (Today, particularly after the Swiss banks affair, the revelations that the banks were a major conduit for Nazi plunder during World War II and held onto assets belonging to Holocaust victims, there is an awareness that the Swiss not only collaborated with the Nazis but actually benefited from them.)[14] In the context of the film, the famous Swiss neutrality is revealed as cruelty, a demonstration of indifference to the plight of the poor and suffering. This dispassionate state cruelty is reflected and echoed by the wintry Swiss landscape: cold, freezing, and indifferent to human suffering.

The cruelty of Switzerland, a wealthy country, is an official cruelty practiced and executed by the authorities. The mistreatment of the refugees in the film is never enacted by ordinary people, nor is it shown as grassroots racism or xenophobia; rather, it is part of the bureaucratic cruelty of the state apparatus and its symbolic representatives: the border police, the juridical system, and so on. By contrast, ordinary Swiss people, such as the lorry driver (Mathias Gnadinger), Massimo, the Swiss Italian guide who works with the traffickers, the man who takes Haydar and his dying child to the doctor, and the young woman doctor who helps the traumatized refugees and tells the representative of the border police ("I don't care who they are or where they are going . . . they will keep coming whatever you say") are represented as kind and humane. The kindness of strangers and the unkindness of the host, the receiving country/state, are at the midst of the migrants' tragedy.[15] Despite the transnational character of migration, the "faceless power" of the state, unmasked brilliantly by Zygmunt Bauman,[16] is still very effective. The good people are the human face of Fortress Europe, whereas the state apparatuses are the faceless agents of state power.[17] In *Journey of Hope* this division between bad and good applies not only to the Swiss but also to the Turks/Kurds. For instance, the Turkish traffickers prey on the vulnerable refugees, while the latter show considerable solidarity among themselves and support each other throughout their journey. Even the Turk who collaborates with the Swiss border control, using a megaphone to plead to the Kurds in their own language to give themselves up to the Swiss authorities, is ambivalent about his role in controlling immigration. He mediates between the refugees and the Swiss authorities, trying to appease both.

On Hotels, Hospitals, Hospitality, and Hostility

It is important to emphasize within this context of the discussion of migration to Europe, as well of other concerns addressed by this book, the special symbolic space occupied by Switzerland in the European but also in the wider global consciousness (and conscience). As Thomas Mann explained in *Doctor Faustus,* his seminal novel on the original Fortress Europe as envisioned by Nazi Germany,[18] "Switzerland, neutral, many-tongued, affected by French influence, open to western airs, is actually, despite its small size, far more 'world', far more European territory than the political colossus of the north [Germany], where the word 'international' has long been a reproach, and a smug provincialism has made the air spoilt and stuffy."[19] It is this air of cosmopolitanism that also made Switzerland the birthplace, the home, and the base of many international organizations and transnational bodies such as the International Red Cross, the Palais des Nations (headquarters of the defunct League of Nations, and today the European home of its successor, the UN), and CERN (the European Organization for Nuclear Research), as well as the place where important international treaties and conventions were legislated, such as the Geneva War Convention, the Universal Declaration of Human Rights, and the Geneva Refugees Convention.

In the popular imagination, Switzerland has been for many years associated with cuckoo clocks (despite the fact that they originated in South Germany), chocolate, peace, neutrality, prosperity, and wealth—the real promised land of Europe. It is therefore even more shocking for the spectator of *Journey of Hope* to find out that the only place in all of Switzerland where the Kurdish refugees are shown hospitality is the Alpine spa hotel, temporarily turned into a hospital. Perhaps the most interesting motif that appears in most films of the migrant and diasporic genre is the theme of the hospital, which in many films (*Journey of Hope, Beautiful People*) becomes the only haven for the refugees and, paradoxically or not, the only hospitable space in an otherwise hostile environment. The theme of hospital/hotel reaches one of its ironic/tragic climaxes in *Dirty Pretty Things* (see chapter 2), where the hotel (introduced as a micro-cosmos of the invisible London and the engine of global capitalism) is itself turned into a hospital, first by the greedy, ruthless "butcher," Senior Juan, and then by Okwe, the African "illegal migrant," a professional doctor who struggles to survive in London. The many references in these films to the themes of disease and cure not only enhance the symbolic association between refugees and asylum seekers and health/sickness, but also foreground (though in a very subtle way) many debates in Europe about immigration from the third world (see chapters 3 and 4).[20]

When the authorities interrogate Haydar, whom they hold responsible for his son's death, they ask him, "What made you come?"—to which he answers, "Hope." And indeed hope, or rather the fantasy of hope, is what motivates Haydar, an archetypal poor migrant driven by the desire to better the life of his family. The theme of hope reaches the height of its visual expression in the film when Haydar is seen on the background of the arid mountain landscape of his Kurdish homeland, returning home after buying some very expensive Swiss chocolate in the town closest to his village (which nonetheless is a full day's walk from his home). Haydar's fantasy of the "Paradise beyond the mountains" is, at this final moment of grand illusion, illuminated by a spectacular rainbow, the biblical and epic symbol of hope.[21] Hope (for a better life for themselves and their children) is indeed what Fortress Europe denies the so-called economic migrants banging on its doors. "Bogus asylum seekers" and similar derogatory names are the labels attached to these poor migrants, whose hope for new life is delegitimized by political and media discourse because it is motivated by economic desire and not by "genuine persecution." Because of Fortress Europe's delegitimization and criminalization of economic migration in its war against the poor (who are themselves the victims of globalization), the traffickers in the film instruct the poor Kurdish migrants to declare themselves "political refugees" when they hand themselves to the Swiss authorities in order to avoid immediate deportation.

Swiss Postcards

The most dramatic part of *Journey of Hope* takes place in the spectacular scenery of the Alps, a landscape that has always had an aura of romantic mystery. Spanning 700 kilometers through seven different countries, the Alps lie in the middle of Europe. In the Middle Ages, so many pilgrims crossed them en route to Rome that the Alpine passes, as Fergus Fleming explains, became multicultural melting pots, attracting travelers from as far away as Iceland and bandits from as far as Palestine.[22] The Alpine landscape, which from the end of the nineteenth century has been a healing landscape for Europe's wealthy with its health resorts and spas, and a recreational haven for the

Figure 1.1. Dreaming of Switzerland, the "Paradise beyond the mountains," in Xavier Koller's *Journey of Hope*. Haydar Sener (Necmettin Çobanoğlu) against the background of the arid mountain landscape of his Kurdish homeland, illuminated by a spectacular rainbow, the biblical and epic symbol of hope.
COURTESY OF THE BFI

well-to-do to enjoy skiing in the winter and hiking in the summer, becomes, in *Journey of Hope,* the modern "killing fields" of the continent.

The transcendental grandeur of the Swiss Alps lends itself to postcard imagery, the ultimate use of commodification by the tourist discourse. Spectacular vistas, stunning Alpine views of majestic mountains, and dramatic valleys and tranquil lakes all make the Alps, particularly in Switzerland, the most magnificent scenery in Europe, fulfilling our idea of the picturesque. Jean-Jacques Rousseau's famous walks in the scenic mountains near Geneva and Lake Leman have been immortalized in his *Confessions.* They provided the literal and philosophical-metaphysical background for his treatise on education and the setting for the ideal social contract.

Indeed, the migration fantasy of Switzerland harbored by Haydar's family—the "Paradise beyond the mountains"—was actually built around a postcard sent to them by an uncle who emigrated to Switzerland. This postcard of a sweeping view of the Swiss Alps, which was partially eaten by their goat while still in Turkey, fills the whole frame of one of the shots in the opening scene of the film, foregrounding the power of seduction held by representation. The postcard motif, which runs throughout the film, deconstructs and subverts the picture-postcard image of Switzerland, bred from generations of paintings, photographs, postcards, and calendars, and underscores the important role of mass-produced representations in generating fantasies that become driving forces in global geographical mobility.[23]

The Wild West of Eastern Europe

Spare Parts (Damjan Kozole, Slovenia 2003) is one of the few films in the cross-border/journey genre that focuses on the traffickers rather than on the refugees.[24] The film takes place in the European wilderness, the mountainous border zone between Eastern/Central Europe (Slovenia) and Western Europe (Italy). This landscape becomes Europe's Wild West, a liminal zone dominated by smugglers, traffickers, criminals, and stateless refugees. The wild, harsh landscape, used as the backdrop for the refugee drama, also bears a silent witness to the tragedy of the traffickers themselves, who, like the refugees, are the victims of globalization and the New Europe. Their victimization is embedded in the post-Berlin Wall, post-communist landscape of pollution, nuclear waste, over-industrialization, smoke, and smog that cause the death from cancer of both the older trafficker Ludvik (Peter Musevski) and his wife.

The traffickers in *Spare Parts* are portrayed not necessarily as "born" criminals but as the products of the sociopolitical processes that prevail in the new post-Berlin Wall Eastern Europe (privatization, decline of social services, and so on). The inhuman immigration and asylum policy of the "liberal" West European states is likewise portrayed as no less of a significant factor in the brutalization of the traffickers. During the border crossing from Slovenia to Italy, the trafficker boss tells his young "pupil," Rudi (Aljosa Kovacic): "Compared to what is done on the other side of the border—Italy—we are tourist guides." The gradual process of dehumanization that the traffickers undergo is best illustrated by the young protagonist's rite of passage from innocence to the harsh adult world of the super-masculine traffickers.

The problem, the film suggests, is not the illegality of the trafficking but the inhuman policy/system that criminalizes the refugees and those who traffic them; the system is the real criminal. This recalls *Dirty Pretty Things*, which also inverts the criminalization trope, placing the blame on the system that creates and perpetuates crime (see chapter 2). "I pity those people who dream about Europe," says one of the human traffickers in the film, challenging the cruel and unrealistic migration fantasy that nurtures and drives the exodus of refugees to Europe. This new Europe, the film implies, is perhaps even worse than the old, racist Europe. Its brutality and cruelty are, accordingly, played against the backdrop of a no-man's land, a harsh border-crossing zone beyond the boundaries of civilization.

Little Britain

Pawel Pawlikowski's _Last Resort_ (UK, 2002), a film about a young Russian woman, Tanya (Dina Korzun), who arrives in England with her 10-year-old son (Artiom Strelnikov), also challenges the mask of the New Europe through its deconstruction of the "Englishness" of the English landscape. Instead of meeting her fiancé as planned, Tanya finds herself in a detention center for asylum seekers in Stonehaven (shot at Margate, Kent), a deserted and dreary seaside resort, a bleak cement desert dotted with empty vodka bottles. A sign over the ghostly, desolated amusement park next to the high-rise populated by asylum seekers reads "Dreamland Welcomes You" in a sort of mock mimicry to the inscription at the base of the Statue of Liberty, the entry point to America and popular mythic symbol of the immigration fantasy.

Tall watchtowers loom over the detention center, exercising the controlling gaze of panopticon Europe. The high-rise slum, where the asylum seekers are imprisoned, is the postmodern European Tower of Babel housing, where refugees from all over the world live, speaking many languages. Ironically, the refugee zone, as described by the director (who grew up in communist Poland), resembles a communist-style detention center.[25] Tanya is assigned a dingy flat in a communist-grey apartment complex and is informed that she cannot leave it for the months it will take to process her case. "This city," Tanya says, "is like punishment for some mistake that I made." Tanya, along with the other asylum seekers, discovers that they are virtually imprisoned in the town. The real town of Margate thus becomes a paradigm for the desolate English sea resort town turned penal colony, with borders patrolled by police dogs and kept under surveillance by television cameras to control people designated as criminals by the immigration authorities. The image of the town established by director Pawlikowski is that of a ghost town dominated by filmic images of desolation: the mostly deserted amusement arcade, the gloomy sea, the seagulls, the broken carousel, the shabby houses, the empty bottles of alcohol, and the busy telephone call boxes (in the age of the mobile phone) crowded by asylum seekers.

Last Resort, like _Dirty Pretty Things,_ exposes the other England, the invisible England. It shows fortress England with its post-Orwellian devices of control and surveillance. _Last Resort_ unveils the apparatus behind the idea of Fortress Europe, its mechanism of control and punishment aimed at turning

Figure 1.2. Tanya (Dina Korzun), a young Russian woman, and her son (Artiom Strelnikov) are rescued from the Babylonian tower of the detention center by Alfie (Paddy Considine) in Pawel Pawlikowski's *Last Resort*.
<small>Courtesy of the BFI</small>

its back on outsider strangers (including those fleeing persecution who have the right to protection under international law), forcing the outsiders to resort to the last means of survival: the world of crime. The other, "Little Britain," of *Last Resort* is portrayed, as mentioned, by a foreign director, whose camera captures the other side of Englishness and English hospitality. Yet, as in *Journey of Hope,* the inhospitality is attributed only to the anonymous, bureaucratic, and faceless state apparatus and not to ordinary people who can be decent and welcoming. In *Last Resort,* for example, Tanya, the damsel in distress locked in the Babylonian tower of the detention center, is eventually freed by Alfie (Paddy Considine), the gentle, working-class hero of the film.[26]

Even the sea, a vast expanse of borderless space, a traditional symbol of freedom embodying the counter-image of border-controlled Fortress Europe, is associated in this film with a force of containment.[27] The sky, like the sea, is always dark grey, creating a feeling of a boundary signifying the end of the world, a place from which there is no escape.[28] This identification enables the paradoxical location of the detention center, the prison of the undesired migrants near the sea with false promise of freedom and escape. Eventually Tanya and her son, helped by Alfie, will indeed escape by sea and the boat will be their first means of transportation in their return journey of hope.[29] "That a Polish film-maker should see the Isle of Thanet as a suitable location for a drama of exile, surveillance, containment," *Sight & Sound* critic Iain Sinclair rightly wonders, "is an intriguing cultural marker."[30]

The Refugee Gaze

Related to the deconstruction of the visual rhetoric of the urban and natural landscapes of postcard Europe is the dialectical relationship played out in these films between the respective gazes of the refugee, the tourist, and the spectator. As most of these films involve journeys and travel, they have the potential for producing a virtual tourist's experience by turning the film's spectators themselves into voyeurs of the exotic, acting as tourist brochures promoting "authenticity" and "idealized typicalities of the other."[31] Michael Winterbottom's *In This World,* for example, takes place along the historical Silk Road, as well as in some of Europe's most glamorous capitals. Yet the camera's gaze identifies with the refugee's gaze, the gaze of the survivor, for whom the "exotic" landscape or the historical landmark is not a beautiful spectacle to be consumed and admired, but a space that needs to be penetrated, traversed, and survived, and that in most cases is inhospitable and hostile. In some of these films, such as *In This World* and *Journey of Hope,* the camera's gaze deliberately deprives the spectator of the scopophilic "touristic" pleasure, subordinating his or her gaze to the perspective of the refugee, the gaze in pursuit of survival.

In This World, a film that follows the journey of teenage Jamal (Jamal Udin Torabi) and his cousin Enayat (Enayatullah) from a refugee camp in Afghanistan along the Silk Road toward Britain, depicts the pair of youngsters traveling in pickups, buses, and an airless container through landscapes of primal beauty: deserts and rocks, debris-littered roads at sunrise, and Kurdish mountain passes in darkness. However, they scarcely seem to notice these spectacular landscapes. In only one of the scenes in the film do they enjoy the scenery. As they sit and admire the view of the snowy mountains of Turkey which they are about to cross on foot, Jamal says: "Look at the view, Enayat!" to which Enayat responds: "Look at the snow, it's nice." But as in *Journey*

Figure 1.3. A child refugee on the road. Jamal (Jamal Udin
Torabi) in Michael Winterbottom's *In This World*.
COURTESY OF THE BFI

of Hope, the two youngsters will soon discover that the spectacular snowy
mountains are deceiving; when they start crossing them, beauty will turn
into a struggle against death and detention.

In *In This World*, the dialectics of gazes is particularly complex. The
spectator's gaze (mimicking that of the tourist) is negated by the refugee's
gaze. In fact, one contradicts the other. While one gaze seeks pleasure (even
an involuntary one), the other seeks survival. The tourist's gaze searches for
difference, exoticism, and poetic stimulation of the eye. It is a consuming
gaze driven by the pleasure principle. By contrast, the refugee's gaze is indifferent to the spectacular landscape. For him or her, the landscape is an enemy
to be overcome. In contrast to both of these, the spectator's gaze oscillates between the two, the pleasure-seeking gaze of the tourist and the refuge-seeking

refugee's gaze. This oscillation between tourism and "poorism" is used in *In This World* as a distanciation effect, resulting in a Brechtian docudrama of alienation.

This complex dialectic of gazes creates the spectator's moral dilemma in many of the cross-border films, and in *In This World* in particular: Is the spectator entitled to derive pleasure from the refugee's suffering? Consequently, the spectator of the refugee's journey film is transformed into the reflective/analytical spectator in the Brechtian tradition. In *Journey of Hope,* the child, Mehmet Ali, possesses the tourist gaze. After all, the figure of the tourist is only a mature replica (or some would argue, caricature) of a child in search of pleasure and excitement. Tourism is based on a temporary disavowal of one's "real" life; it is an escape into the fantasy of childhood's freedom, the pre-adult pleasure in "discovering the world." Tourism, much like cinema, is based on the suspension of disbelief. For a limited period of time the reality principle is suspended and the pleasure principle is in absolute control. An example of this is when the kind lorry driver who traffics Haydar's family to Switzerland, and the child, Mehmet Ali, are seen, while in Italy, simultaneously taking snapshots of each other licking ice cream. For a moment, they all pretend to be tourists rather than "illegal immigrants" and traffickers. They perform the tourist's ritual: taking photos and refreshing themselves with gelato. At that rare moment of grace, the refugees disavow, deny, or perhaps revolt against the harsh reality that robs them of their basic humanity, including their entitlement to the simple pleasures of life, those taken for granted by the innocents abroad.

It is interesting to note that in many of the journey films the narrative is seen, fully or partially, from the point of view of the innocent: a child in *Journey of Hope, Last Resort,* and *In This World,* and an adolescent in *Spare Parts.* The child in *Last Resort,* like the child in *In This World* and *Journey of Hope,* is street-wise and smart. His worldliness relative to his mother and the resulting role reversal underscore children's roles as well as the price they pay in the family's cultural transition. He is the first to integrate and find friends who create their own multicultural gang/clan and whose oldest female member and presumed leader is a Romany (Gypsy) girl. They smuggle goods (especially gadgets), drink and get drunk, and peep into the porn industry. The child, recognizing the futility of his mother's migration fantasy, reproaches her, "You drugged me all the way to the armpit of the universe," accusing her of being neurotic and delusional. He is also mature enough to warn his naïve mother against the pimps who attempt to lure her into acting in their cyber-porn network. In their first attempt to escape, it is he who leads them. The boy also teaches her English. His initiation into working-class Britain is mediated through Alfie, who functions as the mother and son's father figure. Alfie enlightens them about working-class "Englishness" and teaches the child "proper," i.e., working-class English.[32] In fact, the son treats the mother as if he were her father or husband, as when he caresses and comforts her after her humiliating experience with the pornographers. This theme—the pragmatic, down-to-earth, streetwise child and the naïve romantic and innocent parent—occurs throughout the genre, reflecting a reality in which refugee children prematurely become grownups due to the hardships that they endure, as well as agents of integration and assimilation into the receiving society.

In *Spare Parts*, however, the gaze of the innocent assumes an even more complex role. We see the narrative unfolding through the gaze of the young trafficker whose "growth" and transition from innocence (which means compassion, empathy with the plight of the other) to adulthood (which means lack of compassion, cynicism, lack of empathy) are signifiers of his assimilation into the world of the traffickers, and his reception by them as "a real man." The choice of the innocent's perspective, and particularly the child's point of view, creates an interesting angle. Instead of sentimentalizing the issue (as is the common strategy of Hollywood cinema), this portrayal sharpens the moral dilemma raised by these films. It demonstrates the destruction and corruption of innocence and the premature maturity forced upon refugee children turned into hostages of Fortress Europe.

One of the most iconic scenes of *Journey of Hope* shows the desperate, freezing refugees knocking on the double-glazed glass windows of a heated indoor swimming pool inside an Alpine spa hotel. The owner of the hotel is seen, through their gaze, swimming in the pool. Because of the pool's soundproof glass walls he cannot hear the refugees' desperate appeal for help. At this dramatic moment, the film creates a dissolve of two conflicting images, generated and exchanged between two different gazes, that of the poor, hungry, and freezing refugees who survived the harsh winter mountain storm, and the well-fed, overweight, white European "gatekeeper" bathing in the heated pool, seemingly deaf to the plight of the underprivileged and to their desperation. Perhaps this shocking image of reflective duality, of privilege mirrored by its counter-image, of a luxury spa hotel portrayed as a potential hospital or safe haven for poor and desperate refugees knocking on the glass walls of the space of the rich and comfortable is the ultimate iconic image of Fortress Europe, guarding its visible wealth and comfort against the dreams of non-Europeans in search of a better life. This image of "hospitality" denied is the image of the New Europe.

Figure 1.4. An iconic image of Fortress Europe. The desperate, freezing refugees knocking on the double-glazed glass windows of a heated indoor swimming pool inside an Alpine spa hotel in Xavier Koller's *Journey of Hope*.
COURTESY OF THE BFI

Globalization, Fantasy, and Fortress Europe

Contemporary journey films on and of Fortress Europe take us to the other side of globalization, in which people are trafficked like goods for currency. In setting themselves the task of accompanying the refugees on their journey, these films have sought to show the human qualities, the courage and stamina, of those described as "economic migrants," a term which, when set against that of "refugee," leads to an insidious distinction. The veritable cannibalism of the host society is already present in *Last Resort*. The poor migrants in the detention center are shown donating blood for a paltry sum, as the desperate, moneyless Tanya joins them. This iconic scene of virtual vampirism reifies the relationships between the migrants and their hosts. Aging Europe needs the "new blood" of the new migrants, cannot exist without it; but it is not willing to pay much for it, if at all. "Why don't you sell a kidney?" Alfie jokingly asks Tanya after he tells her that it costs 300 to 400 quid to get smuggled to London. *Last Resort* also provides a glimpse into the global face of the pornography industry, and particularly cyber sex, which preys on vulnerable refugee women. The pornographer, played by a real one (Ben Dover, in his first acting role), tries to convince Tanya to participate in cyber sex. She is typecast, due to her innocent face, in the roles of a nun and a naughty school girl. The safest sex, he boasts, is cybersex, which is globally consumed by "people from Saudi Arabia and Pakistan." The representation of the heartless exploitation of the vulnerable migrants in the Promised Land reaches its peak in *Dirty Pretty Things* (see chapter 2) with the stealing of their last resources, their internal organs.

The migration fantasy in these films is fed and nurtured by different means of manufacturing dreams and desires, from traditional postcards, posters, and amusement parks to images in cyber space. The only decoration in Tanya's bare flat in the detention center's Tower of Babel is a huge shabby poster of a pinkish sky dyed by the last red rays of a tropical sunset in a palm-lined beach on some fantasy island. The tropical deep turquoise of the sea looks very different from the cold and grey English sea. England, which was Tanya's dreamland island while she was still in Russia, has been replaced by a new postmodern camp aesthetic of a fantasy island, a new signifier in an endless chain of escape fantasies. Alfie, who is Tanya's and Artom's Virgil in the hell of "Little Britain," whose role is to rescue them from playing the role of the victim in the migration fantasy, removes this poster and paints the walls of the flat in blue. "I think this looks more like home," he tells Artiom just before Tanya comes back from the porn studio. From the flat painted in blue, still retaining the fantasy color of the sea, there is a cut to the guards patrolling the detention center with dogs. The blue dominates the palette of colors in the shot, recalling the cold blue of the border crossing scene (see above) in *Journey of Hope*.

The fantasy element is represented also through "Dreamland," the name of the amusement arcade where Alfie works.[33] Indeed, *Last Resort* is a narrative about a rescue fantasy, a rescue from the migration fantasy. Even Tanya's profession (she is an illustrator of children's books) is related to the world of fantasy. Toward the end of her mental, interior journey, Tanya realizes that she needs to return home to Russia: "I need to stop dreaming, I've been dreaming all my life. I need to go back and start my life." The moment of realization in the journey of self-discovery is also the moment when the migration fantasy collapses. Tanya realizes that she needs to start a new life in the old country, in her homeland and not in exile. And, indeed, her journey back home takes place in the tunnel with a light at its end.

Last Resort, critic Andrew O'Hagan argues, is "a film about journeys." O'Hagan notes the ability of the filmmaker and the cast "to connect the interior journeys of these characters to the British landscape of right now." The film, he argues, "has none of the anger and reproach of Ken Loach, and none of Mike Leigh's satire. Here is a new kind of film about modern Britain, one that shows the country in a different relationship to Europe, as a place of isolation and aloneness."[34] O'Hagan's celebratory reception of the film was echoed by other British critics. The film was generally perceived as a progressive intervention into the European and particularly the British debate about immigration and asylum.[35]

Yet, in my view, the film projects deep ambivalence toward contemporary migrants, sometimes even slightly tainted by covert racist tones. Tanya, the protagonist, with whom the spectators identify, is the only white "European-looking" woman in the detention center. She is a white woman in the midst of a faceless mass of dark-skinned asylum seekers. This is most evident in the scene when the asylum seekers are seen as, literally, dark shadowy silhouettes dancing and singing on the beach to Kurdish or Arabic music. It is very clear to the spectator that Tanya, the innocent white woman, is not part of this world of "real" asylum seekers, and one can feel her sense of alienation watching this "exotic" display of "oriental folklore." The scene conveys an impression of penetration into an alien territory. The accompanying sound track of Middle Eastern music creates an uncanny feeling of alienation, fear, and menace that seems to overcome Tanya and, likewise, the English spectator. The extensive use of Arab music in the sound track throughout the whole film can be seen as signifying alienation and cultural difference rather than a positive comment on Britain's increasing multiculturalism. Thus the return journey, the yearning for the old Russian home, can be seen as a rejection of growing British cultural hybridity perceived as a dark alienating presence.

Tanya is used by Pawlikowski as a mediator for the spectator's gaze precisely because she is white and middle class and seems not to fit into the stereotypical image, deeply rooted in the European popular consciousness, of the dark, poor, uneducated asylum seeker. This is presumably based on the assumption that it is easier for a white audience to identify with her ordeal, because, after all, she is "one of us." Implicitly the film seems to suggest that this drama of mistaken identity could have happened to any of you (you white people). However, the film's strategy turns out to be counterproductive: although it ensures the sympathy and identification of the British audience, it perpetuates the very stereotypes it is attempting to uproot. Furthermore, the film seems also to imply that because she is white and "European looking" she does not deserve to suffer. She does not belong to the universe of the detention center, a planet populated by dark young men (which may explain why she is rescued by an Englishman). It is also interesting to observe that the other dark male asylum seekers treat her with respect. They let her be the first on the queue to the telephone booth, and it is not clear if this is because they are humane and polite or because she is a white lady and therefore perceived as superior and entitled to privileges. The assumption that people identify with those who look like them, those who are not "racially and culturally different," and that it is therefore safe to assume that the white hero will gain more sympathy from a mostly white audience is completely subverted by Stephen Frears in *Dirty Pretty Things,* which is the first British film to present an African as a film hero (see chapter 2).

David Walsh offers a related critique of *Last Resort,* characterizing it as yet "another in an apparently endless stream of films advocating 'personal responsibility' and generally letting the social order off the hook." Instead of offering "some kind of exposure of the mistreatment meted out to immigrants and refugees in Britain and Europe generally," it resorts to personal drama. The film is not "a critique of British officialdom or an examination of the plight of refugees and immigrants at all, but instead is aiming its polemic against Tanya herself. She is the author of her own difficulties, it turns out." In *Last Resort,* he continues, the "harsher elements—police, bureaucracy, the unhappy state of the other refugees or would-be refugees in Stonehaven—having served their purpose of drawing us in, are gradually pushed to the film's margins and eventually vanish. What's left behind are the individual moral choices Tanya must make—to do pornography or not, to stay with Alfie or not, to pursue her vision of love or not."[36] As the director himself said, "*Last Resort* is not a passionate social plea. It highlights the refugee problem, but as an aside. A social realist drama about the misery of refugees would be much more dull. With a love story, you can hook the audience in—everyone can relate to falling in love. . . . I can't relate to the idea of making a drama full of social comment. For me, nothing is ever so straightforward."[37]

Ultimately, Pawlikowski's "characters who transcend the landscape," and his (very post-communist) aversion toward "social campaigning,"[38] use the "asylum/refugee problem" as a backdrop for yet another drama on white European angst. *Last Resort* ends with Tanya's journey toward light at the end of the tunnel which brings her back home. Her enlightenment, achieved by her involuntary journey through the maze of Panopticon Britain,[39] is based on her realization that there is no place like home. The real journey, by implication, should take place in one's own emotional and mental landscape rather than in foreign geographical and cultural landscapes. Thus, Tanya's metaphysical/psychological epiphany depoliticizes and de-historicizes the issue of migration and turns it into a matter of individual choice, a journey in search of self-fulfillment and self-discovery. The film's ending is therefore an additional indication that the film is a disavowal of the issues of forced migration and refugees and migrants as the victims of globalization.

Unequivocal Criticism of Fortress Europe: Damjan Kozole's *Spare Parts*

Like *Last Resort, Spare Parts* was made by an Eastern European (Slovenian) director. However, unlike Pawlikowski, a well-integrated British citizen, Damjan Kozole, who still lives in Slovenia, provides a unique and much more critical intervention in the European debate about immigration. According to Kozole, the special position of Slovenia as a hybrid of the Balkans and central Europe is apparently responsible for the less compromising approach taken by him toward Fortress Europe.[40] Unlike *Last Resort,* which uses the imagery of Panopticon Europe as a backdrop for white female angst, *Spare Parts* offers a very sharp critique of the New Europe and globalization. As in *Dirty Pretty Things,* the cannibalistic character of the New Europe is manifested through the human organs industry, which is based on the exploitation of vulnerable refugees. Ludvik, the former racing car driver, tells Rudi, an initiated trafficker he has taken under his wing, horror stories about what happens to the helpless refugees on their journey to Fortress Europe. On the Italian side, he says, "they drug them and take their organs for transplantation. One kidney is worth 15,000 Euro. . . . Most of these refugees will end up as spare parts," he concludes in his gruesome report recalling the horrors depicted in *Dirty Pretty Things.* The vision of "United Europe" in the form of "Fortress Europe," a legacy, ironically inherited from the Nazis, is bitterly criticized by Ludvik, the "master trafficker" who tells his young "pupil": "I pity them all. I pity all those who want to go to fucking Europe." United Europe, he explains to him, "was also Hitler's plan. He used tougher means to achieve it."[41]

Indeed, the New Europe is not free from racism either. One of the traffickers who does not participate in the forced sex with one of the black African refugees explains to his buddies: "I can't fuck niggers. They don't turn me on." The sexual exploitation of the women refugees is normalized by the traffickers, culminating in the irony that one of them, the most cynical and exploitative of the group, says: "Yes, all those who smuggle drugs should be killed. They all are criminals." The African child who dies from suffocation in the traffickers' airless car baggage is thrown into a river. Wearing a blood red coat, his young body floats on the water in a crucifix position, transforming him into the icon of the new brutal Europe. Yet the Muslim refugee from Albania who goes for the second time on the same route (on the first attempt he was caught by the Italians) shows the determination of the refugees to escape to Fortress Europe despite repeated "crucifixion" and the futility of the efforts to stop them, recalling the words of warning delivered by the woman doctor in *Journey of Hope.*

In many of the European migrant and diasporic films, "America" is a prominent motif (for further discussion see chapter 2). In *Spare Parts,* however, America is no longer identified with the traditional migration fantasy but rather with the hegemonic force of promoting inhuman globalization for which human trafficking and exploitation of vulnerable migrants (who are themselves the victims of globalization) is one of the major by-products. On different occasions, Ludvik expresses very explicit anti-globalization sentiments. When the young trafficker wants to go to McDonalds, for example, the older tells him bitterly, "I'll never go with the Americans even if they pay me." America, the film implicitly suggests, is the source of globalization and globalization is evil.[42] In yet another scene, the older and younger trafficker get closer to each other through a male-buddy ritual of heavy drinking soaked with anti-globalization rhetoric. They both conclude with the bitter, cynical assertion that globalization is a sewer and the whole world is one big shit.

These refugees, victims of economic and/or military globalization, are from all over the globe: Africa, Iran, Albania, and Macedonia, unlike the more homogenous group of refugees represented in *Journey of Hope,* who all hail from Turkey/Kurdistan. In this respect, *Spare Parts* reflects the process of the growing global nature of migration from the time of the making of *Journey of Hope* (1990) to that of *Spare Parts* (2003). The journey in *Spare Parts* is not only the passage of the refugees from the status of human beings to that of human spare parts, but also the journey of the young trafficker from innocence to "maturity." It is a father/son journey, in which the young protagonist follows his father role model, the "master" trafficker, and eventually, after his death, takes over his "job" and becomes the new boss, the new patriarch. The son becomes the father and the cycle of brutalization and dehumanization continues. The final shot of the film shows the now-new boss watching a motorcycle race while a younger, new aspiring member who wants to join the traffickers' club looks at him from below with an admiring gaze. This shot, which echoes the opening scene of Rudi's own initiation into trafficking, creates a kind of eternal repetition of the past and a sense of entrapment. The son cannot escape from his father or from the trap of trafficking.

The cycle of global exploitation is bound to continue, the film suggests at this climatic, sad moment. Globalization, and with it migration, exploitation, and dehumanization, will go on.

Subversive Journeys in/from the Promised Land

The return, as Miriam Cooke suggests, may be "even more difficult than the journey out, for it forces an irrevocable break with the world as it was before the journey. But it has created the conditions necessary for the construction of a new world, a new self."[43] The issue of the return journey, the trip back home, be it the geographical birthplace or the imaginary, symbolic, and mythic home that has always been longed for, is the subject of two films of Tony Gatlif, the Algerian-born son of Spanish Gypsies and the most prominent Paris-based Romany filmmaker: *Gadjo Dilo* (Crazy Stranger, France, 1997) and *Exils* (Exiles, France, 2004). *Gadjo Dilo* is the third of Gatlif's "Gypsy trilogy"; the other two are *Les Princes* (Princes, France, 1982)[44] and *Latcho Drom* (Safe Journey, France, 1993).[45]

Most of the cinematic representations of Gypsies, the most persecuted minority in Europe, have been made by non-Gypsy filmmakers and therefore usually reflect more on the cultures that produce them rather than any "authentic" Gypsy culture. In reality, as well as in the world of representation, Goran Gocic argues "the Gypsies are Europe's extreme vision of marginality," offering as such "one of the most persistent pictures of Eastern pagans in Western fiction. . . . Moreover, the Gypsies have remained one of the few mysterious, unspoken currencies of cinema, concentrated around identifiable stereotypes."[46] Dina Iordanova, in her study of Balkan cinema, argues that the Balkan Gypsy films evolve around the mechanism of "projective identification" whereby they are not meant to represent the Roma but to project concern about the "Balkan self." As the Roma "appear to mainstream society—marginal and poorly adapted but likeable for their vigour and non-traditional exuberant attitude—so the Balkans (would like to) appear to Europe," she observes, adding that "to a large extent, exploring the Roma serves as a means of self-representation, of admitting and reflecting on one's own marginality."[47] *Gadjo Dilo,* like Gatlif's other films, is an example of a "minority discourse" film (though not completely immune to charges of self-exoticization of the Roma people) and therefore it marks a shift in the politics of representation of the Roma, a shift from representation by the hegemonic culture/host society to self-representation.

The film tells the story of a young Frenchman, Stephane (played by French idol Romain Duris), who wanders the icy roads of Transylvania in torn shoes during a bleak winter in post-Ceausescu Romania searching for a Gypsy singer called Nora Luca. Nora, we learn, was the voice that so moved Stephane's father, who died mysteriously among the nomads in Syria. Stephane's quest to find Nora will help him, he believes, to find himself through the exploration of the musical memory of his father. On his journey, Stephane meets a Gypsy patriarch named Izidor (Isidor Serban), who treats him as a surrogate for his biological son who is in jail. He also meets a Gypsy woman named Sabina (Rona Hartner), with whom he falls in love. Eventually Stephane adopts the Gypsy way of life and is transformed from a Gadjo Dilo (literally "a crazy stranger/alien" in Romany) into a full-fledged member of the Gypsy community. After the Gypsy settlement is set on fire during a pogrom committed by the Romanians from the nearby village,[48] Stephane and Sabina set out on the road toward an unknown destination. What Stephane undergoes in the course of the film, then, is a psychological and cultural transformation from tourist to member, from outsider to insider, from a western ethnomusicologist to "native" Gypsy and from European "self" to Europe's "other." As such, the film is about identity-crossing from dominant/privileged to the voluntarily chosen identity of one of Europe's classical victims: the Gypsy who, along with the Jew, is historically the "other within" Europe, its ancient scapegoat, the "pariah people," in the words of Max Weber.[49] The Jews, writes Isabel Fonseca, "poisoned the wells; the Gypsies brought the plague."[50]

The transformative moment from self to other in Stephane's journey occurs when he performs a traditional Gypsy burial to the recorded Gypsy music and notes he has laboriously collected throughout his journey. The burial takes place after the pogrom, when he is on the road with Sabina, heading toward an unknown destination. Since the Gypsies have no recorded history and their culture is oral, it is only natural that Stephane will continue this tradition and destroy his "Gadjo" attempt at documenting and recording it. In his first encounter with the Gypsy villagers, they assail him with the same insults that they suffered throughout their long history as a persecuted minority: "Thief! Bum! Murderer! Crazy alien (Gadjo Dilo)!" Yet, with his symbolic act of burying the artifacts that signify his being an outsider to the community, he is transformed from a cultural voyeur, a collector of "exotic" relics, to a member of the live and vibrant culture he has set out to redeem. By electing to perform culture rather than preserve/record it, Stephane becomes a full-fledged member of his voluntarily elected Romany culture. Rather than exhibiting Gypsy music in the dead and stifling space of the museum, the heritage industry, or the world of scholarship, Stephane chooses to be a member of this thriving culture by fulfilling its performative aspect.

Gadjo Dilo employs a complex dialectics of gazes looking at the Romany community from both outside and inside, seeing it from the point of view of the "crazy stranger" who is the spectator's mediator into the heart of the "crazy" Gypsy culture, and then as an insider, after his heart is conquered and he is "converted" and accepted by the tight-knit Romany community. The world of the Gypsies captures Stephane's imagination as much as it captures the audience's. The fact that only Stephane, Sabina, and a couple of others are played by professional actors and the rest of the cast is composed of authentic Gypsies further enhances this dialectic of outside/inside and amplifies the film's unequivocal celebration of marginality. Often the relationships between the Gypsy and the Gadjo are informed by boundaries. The Gypsies represent those liminal zones that society represses, rejects, and feels it needs to eradicate in order to exist. Over the centuries society's attempts to deal with this threatening "other" have ranged from assimilationist policies (especially in communist Eastern Europe through enforced sedentary housing, wage labor, and so on) to xenophobic, racist abuse culminating in the *Porrajmos,* the Romany Holocaust.

Gadjo Dilo is a film about a mental and cultural journey back home, the "home" of the Romany people. Yet as the Romany people have no recognizable, official homeland, and the Roma have "inherently hybrid, transnational identities,"[51] this return is not confined to the geographical boundaries of a specific nation-state (Romania in the case of *Gadjo Dilo*) or even to a broader regional unit (Europe in the case of this film). Rather it becomes, following the historical tradition of the Roma people themselves, a transnational journey (as is evident in *Latcho Drom*) in search of a cultural and spiritual home where Romany life can proceed free of persecution.

In the context of the journey to Fortress Europe genre, *Gadjo Dilo* subverts the common formula which, habitually, presents Europe and particularly Western Europe as the desirable destination of the migrant, her or his promised land. The promised land in *Gadjo Dilo* is not a specific political unit, the nation-state, the European Union, or even America, which acts as the ultimate symbolic object of desire in the migration fantasy, but rather the journey itself, life on the road, permanent nomadism. The Gypsy life on the road is the Promised Land and the road itself becomes a metaphor of transnational home that transcends geographical and national boundaries but still maintains a strong cultural identity. Because Roma live in the present, they have no specific place or home other than what they create for themselves in the moment, on the road. They traditionally have no homeland except for roots in archaic India or mythic Egypt. Time in their tradition is experienced as cyclical and mythic, the moment being constantly re-created through the journey. Yet within the European context, and despite the internal opening of borders arising from the enlargement of the EU, the Gypsy, the Romany, is required to desert her/his mobile home (literally his/her caravan), to settle down and give up his/her freedom to wander and roam freely. Much like the Muslim migrant who is asked to throw away his old suitcase and adopt a new way of life, "suitable" to his settlement in the "host" society, so is the Romany forced to relinquish his nomadic lifestyle and comply with the confinements of the society/country which, in the best of worlds, agrees to tolerate him or her. As much as *Gadjo Dilo* is a film in search of Romany identity, it is also, in the tradition of the journey *topos*, a quest for individual self-fulfillment, a search for an identity, which is ultimately intimately connected to and insep-arable from the collective. Given the nomadic character of Romany culture, it seems only natural and suitable for its generic expression to be manifested by the journey film.

Consistent with its recasting of the Promised Land idea, *Gadjo Dilo* also plots out a migratory movement that runs against the grain of actual con-temporary migration. It proceeds from Paris to the periphery of the Balkans (Romania), from the metropolis to the margins and perhaps back again (after the pogrom, the couple is seen on the road and their next destination is not clear). The world-wise Parisian is fascinated by the Gypsies and feels that this is where he truly belongs. This is an ironic reversal of the idea of assimila-tion and integration, which is usually what is asked from (and in many cases forced upon) the Gypsies of Europe. As Anikó Imre writes in her discussion of what she calls "Screen Gypsies," there is "an unmistakable contradiction between the nation's need for tribal, nomadic, primitive Gypsies, who are essentially different-inferior to proper, 'European' national citizens, confirm-ing the latter's sense of superiority, and the simultaneous expectation that Gypsies fully assimilate."[52]

In his most recent film, *Exils* (*Exiles*, France, 2004), Gatlif pushes the theme of the return journey even further. The film, which won the best direc-tor award at Cannes in 2004, goes against the traditional migratory route of the Franco-Algerian community. While most Algerians leave for Europe and particularly France, the protagonists of *Exils*, Zano (played again by Romain Duris) and Naima (Lubna Azaba), are lovers heading in the opposite direc-tion. Zano suggests that they head off to Algeria, the land of his father, an

Figure 1.5. Romain Duris, a French idol, as Stephane,
the crazy stranger in Tony Gatlif's *Gadjo Dilo*.
COURTESY OF THE BFI

Figure 1.6. Sabina (Rona Hartner), the wild Gypsy
woman, in Tony Gatlif's *Gadjo Dilo*.
COURTESY OF THE BFI

anti-colonialist activist. Naima, also of Arab descent, agrees. As the couple heads down through Spain to North Africa, they become calmer and gentler as they draw closer to the spiritual wellspring of Arab culture. All of Gatlif's films deal with the life of Maghrebi (North African) Muslims in France or with Gypsies in Europe. Hence, they introduce the two major entities of European "otherness," the Romany and the Muslim, into the ongoing debate about European identity and its historical and cultural roots.

Manuel Poirier's *Western* (France, 1997), a road film that takes place in Bretagne (Brittany), France, is also a film about identity crossing which combines the search for individual fulfillment (perceived as a successful heterosexual love relationship) with a reflection on the politics of belonging and un-belonging in the New Europe. *Western* is a buddy film about two men who wander the roads in Brittany. One is Paco (Sergi López), a Catalan and shoe salesman for a French firm, whose company car and stock were stolen by Nino (Sacha Bourdo), a vagabond, a Russian of Italian background. Although Paco beats Nino up for stealing his car, the two men become friends. Paco and Nino wander around Brittany encountering different adventures, and eventually Nino, the one who is usually less lucky with women than Paco, marries a Breton woman, Nathalie (Marie Matheron), who has seven children from different men.

Western is a border-crossing film within the context of the emerging genre of the migrant and diasporic film because it is a journey film which already takes place in the Promised Land itself (France). It is a road film within the Promised Land and in between the genres of the journey film and the "host/home" film. Like *Gadjo Dilo, Western* deals with a myriad of migratory routes, from Russia to Brittany, from Catalonia to Brittany, and inside Brittany itself. Brittany here is, as Peter Baxter suggests, "a pre-modern backdrop for a fable of post-national identity,"[53] but also for the rise of regionalism in the Odyssey of European politics of identity and belonging. Unlike the urban ghettos, the *banlieues,* depicted in most French films about migration (see chapter 4) as the claustrophobic space of the urban, in *Western* migratory experience is exchanged for what the director called "un film sur la route" (a film on the road).[54] Yet this road film about Western Europe, unlike its American counterpart the western, is very region-based, and lacks the vast, borderless expanse of the American landscape.

The progressive tone of the film, and what seems like its openness toward the idea of a borderless, transnational Europe, is best illustrated by the end credits, which display the national flags of each cast and crew member and reveal that most of them, including Poirier, belong to more than one "nationality." Yet there is a possibility of reading the "immigration-integration

Figure 1.7. Nino (Sacha Bourdo), a vagabond, and Paco (Sergi López), a shoe salesman, in Manuel Poirier's European road film *Western*.
COURTESY OF THE BFI

model" propagated by this film as conforming to the ideal of the French Republic, if not to its new right.[55] *Western* can be seen as a paradigmatic film reflecting the old model and patterns of migration to France. The assimilation and integration into the Republic, of the old wave of migrants, mostly single men who came to work in France, particularly from Italy, Portugal, and Poland, from the end of the nineteenth century until the current migration wave, was, in most cases, secured through the female womb, the hospitality offered to the migrants by love, sex, and the promise of establishing a new family in the new motherland. Contemporary immigration to France, by contrast, is completely different. It originates mainly from the third world (and particularly from the former colonies of France in the Maghreb) and it is the whole family, rather than single men, coming to France. Consequently, this type of migration reproduces its own culture in the receiving country, resisting any attempt to melt into mainstream French society (for a further analysis see chapter 4).

Viewed from this perspective, the two "strangers" in *Western* are not really "strangers." Paco is from Spain (though he insists on his regional Catalonian roots, which have much affinity to French culture), the western frontier of Europe, and Nino is from Russia, its eastern frontier. Yet despite his Russianness, Nino is from an Italian background. The film ends with an image of the enlarged transnational family sitting for dinner. This family is composed of Paco, Nino, Natalie, and many children whose diversity of colors and ethnic features (reflecting their different fathers) appears to testify to a postmodern, post-national, recreated "Last Supper" deeply embedded in the French imaginary. And yet, rather than being an image of transnationalism, this is an image of "domestication," the domestication of the strangers and their digestion into the French national cuisine. Although the final image looks so multicultural, multiracial, and multi-ethnic, they all still eat from the same table, from one single bowl of soup in a typical French manner. From outsider strangers, Paco and Nino become assimilated Bretons. This transformation is made possible through the mediation of the feminine womb, the vehicle and channel for the fusion of the blood of the stranger with the blood of the "native." It is no wonder, therefore, that the name of the woman who is responsible for the transformation of Nino from outsider to insider is Natalie. And indeed, as her name which is related to nativity suggests, she is in love not necessarily with the men she meets but with the idea of pregnancy and giving birth. As such she becomes an allegory for the French nation, the French republic which can assimilate, absorb, and digest the strangers in its midst[56] and give birth to new sons of the Nation. The women in *Western,* a film with a strikingly American title deliberately given to a uniquely European film, resemble the women in the American western genre, who are employed as the agents of civilization, the catalysts of domestication and acculturation.

The idealized assimilation model depicted and articulated in *Western* occurs in the countryside, far from the nation's capital. But the "real" story of most of the migration to the European Promised Land is the story of the migrant's city, the city of migration, which is also the story of the next chapter, where we see that the allegory of an attempted integration on the road plays out as failure in the city, exposing the story of the promised land as mere fable. The real story of migration to Fortress Europe is the urban legend that the city is the migrant's Promised Land.

2

CITIES OF HOPE
THE CINEMATIC CITYSCAPES
OF FORTRESS EUROPE

City life is carried on by strangers among strangers.
Zygmunt Bauman

IF the history of Europe is, as Saskia Sassen argues,[1] the history of migration to Europe, and as most of this migration has ended up in Europe's big cities, then perhaps the history of Europe needs to be rewritten from the point of view of its cities rather than its nation-states.[2] Indeed, contemporary European migrant and diasporic cinema has used the European city, and particularly the European capital, as the stage for the drama of the current "exodus" to Europe. The European films about migration and diaspora are very compelling in depicting landscapes of postmodern alienation. They persistently deconstruct iconic images of the classical European cities that make for easily consumed picture-postcard views. The famous monuments and landmarks of these cities are either absent from the films or stripped of their traditional cultural capital, assuming the role of posticons in an impoverished urban fabric, a non-place. Many of these films are set in major European capitals whose urban landscape, particularly in their geographical peripheries and margins, has been transformed by migration and diaspora. Thus, for example, Mathieu Kassovitz's *La Haine* depicts an urban rebellion in a Parisian *banlieue* (see chapter 4), Bertolucci's *Besieged*—a cross-race and -class love story—takes place in Rome (see chapter 3), *Beautiful People* and *Dirty Pretty Things* take place in London, and *Northern Skirts* (*Nordrand*, Barbara Albert, Austria-Germany-Switzerland, 1999) takes place in Vienna. Yet instead of celebrating or invoking the commodified postcard image of these famous cities and their monumental landmarks, these films often not only deconstruct them, pushing the mise-en-scène to their geographical and symbolic margins and peripheries, but also turn them from globally recycled iconic images of fantasy and glamour into non-places. Furthermore, by locating the migrants in the midst of the European metropolis, these films truthfully represent the process of hybridizing the nation via migration, commenting visually and ideologically on the parallel processes of migration and miscegenation. The films thus echo Hardt and Negri's claim in *Empire* that circulation is "a global exodus, or really nomadism; and it is a corporeal exodus, or really miscegenation."[3]

Post-Empire Vienna and the Challenge to Germanic Nationalism: Barbara Albert's *Northern Skirts*

Although Vienna is the only European capital of a former empire that has shrunk in size since World War I, the processes of hybridization, migration, and diaspora have not escaped this formerly *fin de siècle* cosmopolitan city. *Northern Skirts*, whose plot takes place in 1995 in the bleak industrial northern outskirts of Vienna, is set against the backdrop of the war in Bosnia. The film centers around the intertwined stories of five young people of different ethno-national backgrounds (though they are all from Austria and the Balkans): Jasmin (Nina Proll), Tamara (Edita Malovic), Roman (Michael Tanczos), Senad (Astrit Alihajdaraj), and Valentin (Tudor Chirilia), who meet each other in Vienna and whose emotions, hopes, and anxieties are shaped in one way or another by the sociopolitical realities of the time, notably the war in the former Yugoslavia. The two women, who grew up in the same suburb (Nordrand)—Jasmin, a blond "white trash" queen from the projects who gives herself freely to the men around her, and Tamara, her former classmate, the Vienna-born-and-raised Serbian from Sarajevo[4]—meet in an abortion clinic. The three men, who repeatedly cross their paths, are Valentin from Romania, who constantly dreams and talks about making it big in America; Roman, Tamara's boyfriend, a soldier who has to guard the Austrian border from "illegal" foreigners; and Senad, a Bosnian refugee who manages to slip into Austria.

The political circumstances in Austria around the time Barbara Albert's film was released provide the context to her debut feature. The premiere took place seven weeks after a new Austrian coalition government was formed by the conservative Catholic People's Party and the xenophobic, far-right Freedom Party led by Jörg Haider. Haider's populist politics of defamation attempted to portray "foreigners"—refugees as well as first- or second-generation immigrants from Southeastern Europe and the third world—as a dangerous threat to the "Germanic-Austrian identity."[5] At the end of *Northern Skirts,* as if in reaction to the new government, the "invasion" of the young and gentle Balkan refugees into the heart of post-Imperial Vienna during the New Year's celebrations implicitly suggests that Austria should start to envision itself as an actively multicultural territory rather than a "pure" Germanic nation-state.[6] The film both recognizes and celebrates the fact that Vienna has again become a melting pot for the first time since the 1930s.[7]

The emerging coalition between the film's characters, each representing a different ethno-national-religious group (much like the coalition of minorities, the *black/blanc/beur* trio of *La Haine;* see chapter 4), gives us an idea of their shared social/political interests and challenges Haider's "us-versus-them" political rhetoric, hence both documenting and resisting Austria's new racism and its emerging forms of xenophobia. The militarist chauvinism and the thuggish machismo and brutality of the young Austrian males depicted in *Northern Skirts* do not represent Austria in a very favorable light. The irony is that the male refugees from the "barbarian" Balkan, Senad from Bosnia and Valentin from Romania, are very gentle and humane, the opposite of the young "indigenous" Austrian males. As such, the film reflects the rise of neo-fascism in Austria, and the ascendance of a new racism aimed mainly against migrants.[8]

The Cityscape of Fortress Vienna

Most of Albert's film is shot in the industrial outskirts of working-class northern Vienna, which is dominated by tower blocks that recall the cityscape of the *banlieue* in *La Haine* (see chapter 4). Vienna in *Northern Skirts* is portrayed as a very brutal, unappealing, non-place which, although it still serves as Central Europe's crossroads between East and West, in no way recalls its glorious past as the capital of the Austro-Hungarian Empire.[9] Barbara Albert herself grew up in the northern outskirts of the Viennese working-class district on the quiet side of the Danube referred to in the title. The Danube, which along with the Sava River also serves as a natural geographic border between Croatia and Serbia, and in the past demarcated the boundary between the Austro-Hungarian and Ottoman empires, has interwoven many cultures throughout Central Europe's stormy history.[10] Yet this history of cultural diversity, the legacy of the Austro-Hungarian Empire, is negated by contemporary Vienna as portrayed in *Northern Skirts*. The Vienna of *Northern Skirts* is a city populated by militaristic thugs and brutal and chauvinistic young men. Its freezing cold weather is inhospitable to foreigners. Even Vienna's famous landmarks, its monuments of imperial grandeur, and its coffee houses and famous cream cakes (obsessively consumed by Jasmin)[11] do not look seductive or glamorous.

A significant transition from the periphery of the Northern Skirts to central Vienna, the place of the famous Viennese landmarks, occurs at the end of the film—during the New Year's Eve celebrations (which with their explosions of fireworks, and general feeling of chaos, subversively simulate the "look" of a war).[12] On this occasion, the marginalized young migrants from Bosnia and Romania "invade," "contaminate," and mark the iconic spaces of Vienna much as the hybrid *black/blanc/beur* male trio from the *banlieue* in *La Haine* invades central Paris and its iconic landmark (the Eiffel Tower). Only at this point do the marginalized youth dance along with other Viennese to Johann Strauss's *Blue Danube,* invoking nostalgia toward the past glory of *Mittel Europa.* Austria, it is implied, can reclaim its special relationship with the Balkans, not through the outdated model of empire but through the embrace of post-national, post-Germanic multiculturalism.

Sexuality, Rape, Nationalism, and Class

Sexuality and gender in *Northern Skirts* are interwoven with nationalism and ethnicity. The variations on the male-female sexual encounters in the film reproduce the "ethno-national" and recall collective sexual traumas of the last Balkan war. The brutal sex that Jasmin experiences with the Austrian men assumes the form of a violent rape. Tamara's sexual experience with her Austrian soldier boyfriend, though less violent, is aggressive and devoid of mutual intimacy. By contrast, the relationship between Jasmin and the Bosnian Senad is more human and affectionate, and the love scene between Tamara and Valentin is not only gentle but romantic. The mixture of sex and violence in the film is a constant reminder of the sexual violence taking place in Bosnia and Croatia at the time the film was made, including the rape camps and other sexual atrocities that were committed against Muslim and Croatian women by the Serbs as part of their ethnic cleansing campaign aimed to implement the "greater Serbia" project on the ruins of Tito's Yugoslavia. The excess of violent sex in the film foregrounds the status of women's bodies as sites of conflict.

The sexual explorations of the young characters of *Northern Skirts* are also journeys in search of identity. Unlike developmentally normal identity searches, some of the characters, as victims of forced migration, face a quest that is consequently more complex and painful. Tamara and Jasmin meet in the abortion room. Abortion in this context can be seen as an act of taking control of their bodies and lives. In reclaiming their bodies, they defy the role of the victim, which they play most of the time. As Jasmin and Tamara wait for Roman to pick them up after the abortion, the first flakes of snow begin to fall. The sight of the new and fresh snow makes Jasmin extremely happy. She is seen swirling around, laughing loudly and indulging in a Dervish-like dance of liberation. Later at home, suffering from agonizing pain, she is seen holding a pink teddy bear. Jasmin, despite her promiscuousness, is still a frightened little girl. The small flat in Jasmin's home on the outskirts of Vienna is crowded and claustrophobic, imposing forced intimacy without any respect for privacy. The mother and Jasmin close their eyes to avoid seeing the ongoing sexual abuse of the young sister by the violent father. Jasmin turns her back to them and buries her face in the kitschy wallpaper of their room. The journey toward maturity is echoed by the film's narrative that follows the cycle of the seasons, the mythical cycle of life from birth to death. The film is about life terminated, by war and by abortion, but also about the renewal of life and the hope for new birth manifested by Jasmin's later decision (encouraged by Tamara's offer of help) to become a single mother and not to abort for the second time.

In *Beautiful People,* a small child who is in the midst of the killing fields of the Bosnia war zone says, "In America everybody is free." And indeed in most of the diasporic, migrant films America is presented as a phantom structure, an absent center of the immigrant's escape fantasy. In *Northern Skirts,* all the young characters want to escape from Vienna. Valentin's Polish friend, Yolanda, who works with him in a bar, migrates to Australia, while Valentin, who dreams to go to America, tells her that "America is better."[13] The axis of America versus Europe[14] is a recurrent motif in the diasporic migrant cinema of Europe, with America figuring into the text mainly through music (Valentin listens constantly to Romanian rap) and other modes of hip-hop culture such as fashion and dance, as is most evident in *La Haine* (see chapter 4).[15] Valentin is surrounded by American icons: the Barbie doll that he gives as a present to the daughter of his Russian employer, a crooked used-car dealer, and a van painted with a huge American flag. Although America is not the preferred destination for the other characters, they all want to leave Vienna, which seems to suffocate them. Tamara, on her way back home from her hospital job after Valentin leaves for Romania, fantasizes about breaking the window of the train to escape without regard to where; all she feels is that she needs to run away. Senad, the deserting soldier from Bosnia who does not speak German, tells Jasmin (in English) when they are walking in the frozen landscape in a Viennese wasteland: "I want to be somewhere else in the sun." The harsh winter in Vienna, much like the harsh winter snow in *Journey of Hope,* is inhospitable to the displaced, to those away from their native soil and in search of a home. All the youngsters in these films left their homes either due to war (political, "public" violence) or to domestic violence. Jasmin escapes from her violent family's home to another tower block where she tells Wolfgang, the brutal Austrian, that she likes staying at his place because it is a tower and "I would love to live in a tower." Like Tanya in *Last Resort,* the damsel in distress lies waiting in the prison tower to be rescued by her knight, except that in Jasmin's case her knight not only fails to rescue her but further abuses her. In fact, Jasmin's father locks her in the flat and she escapes through the window to Wolfgang, her other jailer. Later in the film she is seen with Senad playing and kissing near the suburb's tower blocks.

The feeling of being exiled from home and the longing for a new home is manifested in various ways. After hearing about the death of Alexander, her brother, in Sarajevo, Tamara and Jasmin look through photos from home, memories of home. The diasporic exilic mode of the film is also expressed by linguistic shifts between Viennese German, Serbo-Croat, Romanian, Polish, Russian, and English. The changing ethno-scape of Vienna, its emerging "diasporic" look, is also revealed through snapshots, glimpses of the camera, and the characters' gaze into the new "others" of the city. Thus, for example, when Jasmin is in bed with Senad in a big hall in a refugee center, a black man is seen watching them. Later, at the New Year's Eve celebrations in central Vienna, the camera turns its gaze toward a black man celebrating with other Viennese people. The four young foreigners in Vienna adopt global (Western) youth culture as a new virtual home, but there is still a place in their lives for the culture of their old homes. In the Yugoslavian disco that Tamara visits, the youngsters dance to the sounds of global youth music, but they end the night with ethnic folk dance from their Balkan home. Even Jasmin, a born and bred Viennese woman, is an outsider in her own city. Her "trashy" background turns her into an exile in her homeland, a butterfly in search of the sun (the butterfly motif appears at the beginning of the film on a background of children's paintings and later as a golden butterfly on Jasmin's sister's T-shirt).

Indeed, much of the film takes place in liminal, peripheral urban spaces, in between places like bus stops and wasteland urban outskirts. Vienna as portrayed in *Northern Skirts* is a place of transit, not a fixed home. This sense of the transitory is in fact grounded in the reality of Vienna's post-World War II history. After the war Vienna was a way station for refugees and displaced persons.[16] In the 1970s, it served the same purpose for Jews escaping the Soviet Union on their way to America; Austria, as Ruth Wodak notes, later played a significant role as "land of transit" for asylum seekers in the autumn of 1989, after the fall of the Berlin Wall. The fall, as Wodak observes, raised Austrians' fears of being "inundated" or "overrun" by foreigners (*uberflutet* and *uberrannt*), particularly by refugees from the East.[17] These fears were crucial in the rise to power of Haider's party and are very salient in *Northern Skirts.*

The Bosnia Within

Like many other diasporic, migrant films which show Balkan people in Western European capitals, or use the Balkans and Bosnia to challenge or support the project of multicultural Europe, *Northern Skirts* is obsessed with the question of Bosnia. Much like *Beautiful People,* the "Bosnia problem" is articulated in ethnic rather than religious terms. The "threat" posed by the Balkanization of Europe is presented as ethno-national rather than religious. It seems that during the 1990s European cinema was not yet ready to deal with the so-called "Muslim problem of Europe," or, perhaps, because of the pre-9/11 zeitgeist, yet unaware of the "problem." In *Northern Skirts,* the Balkan people (like Pero in *Beautiful People*) are represented as kind and civilized, strikingly different from the locals, the "indigenous" Austrians who are violent, brutal, rude, and aggressive. The two women's characters based on binarism of personalities also enhance this point. Whereas Tamara is dark, slender, responsible, and reliable, Jasmin is an overweight, rude, and psychologically unbalanced blonde. Her redemption is due in large part to the emotional and economic support that Tamara provides her. The story of their friendship becomes a utopian allegory about the potentialities of multicultural existence, and more specifically to the progressive potential of the legacy of the Austro-Hungarian Empire to resolve its conflict with the Ottoman Empire over the control of the Balkans. In Sarajevo, Tamara's hometown, World War I started with the shooting of Archduke Franz Ferdinand, the heir to the Austro-Hungarian Empire, as the Balkans was a war zone between the two empires, west and east, Christianity and Islam. "It is not Yugoslavia here," one of Vienna's residents tells the young Balkans who are harassed by the police after leaving the disco, thus placing the blame on the victims rather than on the violent police. *Northern Skirts* raises the question of where Europe begins and ends and what its borders are. It asks where the Balkans is located vis-à-vis Western Europe and vice versa. Ultimately it questions the arbitrary boundaries erected between east and west.[18]

After World War II, Vienna was split among the Allies until 1955, when Austria regained its independence and declared itself to be neutral in the bi-polar world of the Cold War.[19] The recent war in Yugoslavia, described by the media as the war in "Europe's backyard," was a shock for the European consciousness and conscience. Prior to the last Balkan war, Sarajevo was a tolerant, multi-ethnic city, not "as a result of a western ideology of multiculturalism . . . but as a historical reality where people of Serb, Croat, Muslim and increasingly mixed backgrounds and relationships shared the same lifestyle."[20] The trauma of shattering this long-lasting historical mode of Bosnia-style multiculturalism has imprinted itself on the thin skin of the New Europe, an imprint to which both *Northern Skirts* and *Beautiful People* are a testimony.

In Praise of Multicultural London?
Jasmin Dizdar's *Beautiful People*

Beautiful People's seven intertwined stories (all concluding with artificial happy endings) are framed by two comically violent Bosnians, one Croatian (Faruk Pruti) and the other Serbian (Dado Jehan). The non-Bosnian audience, obviously, cannot recognize who is Serb and who is Croat on the basis of either looks or names. The two men were neighbors in the same village in Bosnia and now continue their "tribal" war on a London bus and in the London streets, injuring each other so badly that they end up in a shared room in a hospital with a Welsh terrorist. Half the film's characters are British, representing the entire English class structure. They include Portia (Charlotte Coleman), a female doctor and daughter of an upper-class Tory cabinet minister, who falls in love and marries Pero Guzino (Edin Dzandzanovic), a Bosnian refugee; Griffin (Danny Nussbaum), a heroin addict from a lower-middle-class background, whose mates are English football hooligans (nationalistic, racist, xenophobic, and determined to keep England "clean"); and Jerry Higgins, a middle-class Scottish television war correspondent (Gilbert Martin). Jerry, like the middle-class British doctor Mouldy (Nicholas Farrel) who delivers a baby (named Chaos) to a refugee Bosnian Muslim couple in a London hospital, is involved in a troubled marriage and develops a case of "Bosnia syndrome."

A Bus Journey in London

Beautiful People opens on a London city bus and, in the words of Robin Wood, in "a microcosm of an embryonic multi-racial community."[21] An icon of Englishness and a locus of nostalgia, the red bus has mobilized in recent years a passionate campaign to be retained and not replaced by more modern and user-friendly buses. The people seen on the bus testify to the changing face of London as the multicultural capital of Europe, if not the world.[22] The bus is introduced to the spectator as a spatial enclave, a capsule of the other London (or London of the other). An outbreak of a violent exchange of verbal abuses, which very rapidly turns into physical violence between the Serb and the Croat from the former Yugoslavia, former neighbors in the same village, disrupts the façade of multicultural harmony that exists among the strangers on the bus. The violent fight between the two "barbarian Balkans" projects the leading metaphor of the film: the import of Balkan-style violence to the heart of the old Empire or, alternatively, as I demonstrate later, the mirroring of British violence through its projection onto the Balkan other. The bus driver reproaches the two fighting "barbarians": "This is London transport; we don't behave like that." He thus patronizes the migrants (echoing the racist remark "It is not Yugoslavia here," made to the Balkan youth in the Vienna disco in *Northern Skirts*). The driver's self-righteous and condescending tone, aimed at deterring the invasion of barbarism to the civilized center of the old Empire, sets the tone for the entire film. But the "barbarians" do not listen to the "civilizing-mission" rhetoric delivered by the English bus driver. To the contrary, they escalate their mutual aggression, spilling over the violence from the bus into the streets of central London, which are adorned by some of the city's most iconic tourist landmarks, such as the statue of Churchill and Big Ben. The film then cuts from this fast-moving, noisy scene, shot in the style of Emir Kusturiça's crazy Balkan comedy, to the civilized space of an elegant old-fashioned house of an upper-class English family, further enhancing the theme of the invasion of the Barbarians, from the public space of the city streets to the most fortified private space of upper-class Britons. The shift from the democratic turmoil and chaos of the bus to the tranquility of the traditional upper-class English fortress is made even more noticeable by the sound track. It is a shift from noise (the sound of "foreign language"—Serbo-Croat—and the boisterous, Balkan-Gypsy music track) to quietness. In the perceptive words of Robin Wood, "we are shifted abruptly from the violence and hectic energy of the chase/fight to the perfect calm (read stagnation) of a British upper-class breakfast."[23]

In contrast to Wood's celebratory review of *Beautiful People,* Robert Lightning argues that "Dizdar's 1999 film (set in 1993) about Bosnian refugees in London must be viewed in the context of current global conditions."[24] I would argue that at the time of my own writing on this film (February and August 2006) global conditions have become even more crucial to the understanding and re-reading of this highly controversial film. Furthermore, in light of the suicide bombing attacks on the London underground and bus number 30 on July 7, 2005, the film attains a disturbingly prophetic quality. The fear of the Bosnia within, of the "infection" of Western Europe by the barbarism and ethno-religious conflicts of the Balkans, materialized in the form of the London 7/7 bombing and the Paris November 2005 riots, as the critics of multiculturalism often suggest (see chapter 4). While, as Laura Barton argues, the bombing of the underground "was widely interpreted as an assault on the symbol of London . . . it was the wrecked number 30 bus—cheap, jolly, universal—that truly represented the capital's wounded spirit."[25]

A Gaze at the Balkan Within

The gaze of the people in the bus at the fighting Serb and Croat is emblematic of the playful but nevertheless painful dialectics of Britain-Bosnia that the film establishes. The passengers look amazed and shocked at this spectacle of violence and barbarism and the consequent disruption of the "civilized" space of the London bus. The passengers' gaze is the outsider's gaze, which also mediates the spectator's gaze. "Why do they fight?" they seem to be asking. At this moment of high drama, the film implies that the outsider will never understand the complexities, subtleties, and depth of the conflict, the pain of the other. To him/her, the conflict looks like a childish, silly fight: "You started first. No, you started first," the two Balkan men argue later in the hospital. "You stole my sheep; no, you burnt my house," they keep going on and on. The outside observer will also never be able to notice the minor differences between the Serb and the Croat (minor differences, according to Freud, are the origin of all conflicts).[26] To him/her, outside conflicts will always look foolish and infantile, incomprehensible to the civilized, mature mind.

Yet the gaze of the outsider is quickly turned into the gaze of the insider, and consequently the patronizing view of the barbarian needs to be revised. One of the passengers, a black man, gets off the bus and begins talking to his girlfriend on a mobile phone about the "amusing" fight: "There were two funny bloody foreigners on the bus who fought." He does not even manage to finish the sentence before he is attacked by three white racists, Griffin's friends, for whom the black Briton is also a "bloody foreigner," an alien to the English national body. The same incomprehension of others' wars, fights, hatred, and pains will later be exhibited by the English nurse in the hospital who, in order to pacify the quarreling Serb and Croat, shows them that in fact they have the same shoe size, implying that there is no real difference between them as far as she is concerned and therefore there is no reason for them to fight.

Dizdar also targets the state of the English nation and its icons of "Englishness."[27] In particular, *Beautiful People* is very critical of the English class system. None of the three traditional classes is left untarnished by the sharp observant eye behind Dizdar's camera. The English working class is shown as suffering from football hooliganism tainted with racism and ultra-nationalism. The film establishes parallels between violent Bosnian men contaminated by ethnic and religious hatred and violent British hooligans infected by nationalist football xenophobia, expressed through their hatred and hostility toward their Dutch competitors on the football field and the "fucking Europeans" in general. Griffin's friends say, "We go to Europe to fuck the Europeans to fuck the Dutch."[28] The middle class is not spared either. Dr. Mouldy's middle-class family is broken, and the BBC television reporter's family life is also in turmoil. Portia's upper-class Tory family is introduced as snobbish, hypocritical, and ignorant. At the dinner prepared by Portia's upper-class, ultra-conservative brother for Pero, her fiancé, the brother prepares venison, a traditional dish of the English countryside nobility. "It is barbaric," says Portia, echoing the image of the deer which first enters the spectator's gaze as a dead deer in the war zone in Bosnia, an innocent victim of a barbaric war. But Pero approves of it: "In Bosnia," he tells his hosts, "we eat everything." Later, when Pero plays the piano, the snobbish family looks at him in amazement. How can somebody from the Balkans, their facial expressions reveal, play classical music, the cultural pinnacle of a highly civilized society?

But Dizdar's most scathing criticism is reserved for the gaze of the western media and particularly the BBC.[29] Because first-world networks provide the filter for images of the world's "others" through the institutions of "foreign news," they are part of a global structure of postcolonial constituencies. Echoing traces of the "old rhetoric of Empire," foreign news contributes to the body of "knowledge" created in the West about its non-Western other. Many critics of Western media charge that this information is unbalanced, distorted, and focused on negative rather than developmental news, thus creating an image of the other as a "primitive space" of chaos, disorder, and constant violence. In the film, the BBC, with its lust for war pornography, wants to use Jerry's footage shot in Bosnia (which he refuses to hand over) for a sensational documentary piece entitled "Four Days in the Hospital of Hell." The BBC, Dizdar suggests, has turned Bosnia (as well as peripheries such as Somalia, Rwanda, Palestine, and others) into an ambivalent object of fascination/repulsion for Western eyes. But even Jerry, the BBC correspondent, who suffers from a surplus of identification with the victim, insisting on amputating his leg after the trauma of watching a Bosnian's leg amputated in the battlefield without anesthesia, is not immune to the film's critique and caricaturization. It exposes his identification with the Bosnians' suffering, his deviation from the BBC's so-called objective and non-biased war coverage, which he considers hypocritical. No matter how completely Jerry identifies with the victim, he will never be one. Unlike the Bosnians, trapped in the claws of the war, Jerry has the freedom to move in and out, to enter and exit the theater of war as he wishes. And indeed, the Scottish war correspondent, the bogus victim, when finally cured of his "Bosnia syndrome," reunites with his family and goes on vacation to Hawaii, an act epitomizing Western narcissism and cynicism in the face of suffering.

In the film's happy ending, Ismet, the Muslim Bosnian (Radoslav Yourou-kow), receives a camera as a gift from Dr. Mouldy. The idea behind the gift is perhaps a "correction" of the distorting gaze customarily aimed at the Balkan other by the Western media. The new gaze, the gift seems to suggest, should no longer be a pornographic gaze indulging in atrocities committed against the other, but a critical and compassionate gaze from within, signifying a transition from dominant representation of the other to self-representation, as well as to representation of the dominant by the other. Ismet, like Dizdar himself, will enjoy the exile's advantage of possessing a double perspective, a condition of permanent duality in which one's life becomes bound to the immanent duality of being an exile, of being at and outside one's "home."[30] This double perspective will help correct the politics of representation emanating from the relations of power between the metropolitan centers and the periphery. The transforming power of the gaze is also manifested by how Dizdar himself gazes at British society as a Bosnian, using the style of the Balkan Crazy comedy (a genre which has reached its peak of popularity with the films of Emir Kusturiça) to seduce and attract the Western audience.[31] By transplanting the Balkans into the Western metropolis, Balkan "craziness" (as well as the forms invented to express this "craziness") is challenged. "Who is the crazy one?" the films which use Bosnia as a metaphor ask. Problematizing these issues, *Beautiful People* challenges the established dichotomy of a civilized West versus an Oriental Barbaric Balkans and offers a new way to view the West and the rest.

The Bosnia Syndrome: A European Trauma

When Jerry and his wife are seen by two psychiatrists, one of them diagnoses his illness as the Bosnia syndrome. "What is the Bosnia syndrome?" Jerry's wife asks. "I've never heard of it." "It is an obsession with helping, doing good. You identify with the victim to the extent that you start seeing the world through the victim's eyes. In severe cases, the distinction becomes so blurred that you become the victim, and the victim becomes you."[32] But, she adds, "It is not as bad as the Gulf syndrome. It is curable." Jerry's Bosnia syndrome is part of the dialectics played by the film between the here (Britain) and the there (Bosnia). The gulf between the two is, on the one hand, enormous—politically, culturally, and ethnically—yet, as the film suggests, the two also mirror each other in a myriad of curious ways. The Balkans' "sacral nationalism," identifying religion and national identity as an exclusive tribalism, is mirrored by the class structure of British society and particularly by English working-class neo-tribalism manifested through football hooliganism, ultra-nationalism, and xenophobia. Griffin,[33] a white male from a lower-middle-class family who adopts the paraphernalia of contemporary white English working-class culture—drugs, violence, football hooliganism, and racism—is literally transplanted, parachuted into a real war zone, a war the existence of which he was not even aware. A black UN soldier tells him, "It is war, my friend." "What's war?" Griffin asks, attesting to the indifference shown by the English to the suffering even of fellow Europeans. Thus the English outsider, alienated and resentful toward anything European, is forced to become an insider in the war drama unfolding in Europe's midst.

In London, meanwhile, the film shows how representatives of the Home Office authorities deport a female black African asylum seeker from the neighborhood where Pero lives. Racism and hatred of minorities, the film implies, are not exclusive to the ethnically divided Balkan. They are practiced with brute force at the heart of the metropolitan centers of the West. Bosnia was a uniquely European trauma because of its relationship to both world wars. The war in Bosnia was the first genocide to take place on European soil since the end of World War II, and the siege of Sarajevo evoked bitter memories of the famous shot in this city which triggered World War I. The failure of the multi-ethnic Austro-Hungarian Empire was echoed again by the failure of post–Berlin Wall Europe. Bosnia and London, therefore, are part of the equation posed by *Beautiful People,* as are Bosnia and Paris in *La Haine* (see chapter 4). London is Bosnia, Paris is Bosnia and vice versa. These films suggest that in both places, violence, racism, deportation, and "ethnic cleansing" are practiced on a daily basis (the forced deportation of asylum seekers in London is an "administrative ethnic cleansing").

When Pero arrives at Portia's upper-class house for dinner, he tells her mother: "Thank you very much for your hostility."[34] The confusion between hospitality and hostility is best expressed in the space of the shared hospital room[35] of the three "others" in the film: the Serb, the Croat, and the Welsh terrorist.[36] The attraction of the hospital as a space of extremes, a liminal zone between life and death, has traditionally landed itself, in the realm of film, to the extremes of comedy and tragedy, which very often are fused into the hybrid form of the tragicomic. Yet the London hospital is only one of two hospitals in the film. There is another in Bosnia, the killing field of the Balkan war, the parallel planet to London and the rest of Europe where life carries on as normal. The Bosnian hospital is very different from its London counterpart. It operates in the midst of a war. The medical staff amputates limbs without anesthesia, creating a contemporary image of hell on earth. The parallels and dramatic differences drawn between the two hospitals enhance the trauma of Bosnia, reminding the New Europe not only of its tragic and barbaric past but also of the fragility of its prosperous present. The BBC's idea of using Jerry's footage to create a documentary on "Four Days in the Hospital of Hell" is based on actual hellish images—reports and fantasies of atrocity and depravity in the Bosnian war zone—reproduced and restaged by Dizdar himself and consumed by the spectators of his film, which was marketed as a British comedy.

Critique or Affirmation of Multiculturalism, British Style?

The main question to be raised regarding *Beautiful People* is whether or not it is critical or affirmative of Britain and its (failed?) multicultural project.[37] The ambiguity of the film's ideological stance and its moral vision is already embedded in its title. After all, who are the "beautiful people"? Are they indeed beautiful, and what does the notion of "beautiful" stand for? Further opening itself to suggestion, the title credit appears so that "People" first appears in capital letters onto which "beautiful," in lowercase letters, is then imposed.[38]

My reading of *Beautiful People* suggests that it establishes dialectical relationships between what looks like the binary oppositions of Britain and Bosnia in order to challenge rather than enforce this dichotomy. The "two hybrid nations,"[39] Britain and Bosnia, are not essential others but mirror each other in a variety of complex ways. It is therefore not, as Lightning argues, a film embedded with racial essentialism, but rather a film that questions and challenges traditional assumptions about racial categorizations and hierarchies. Robin Wood observes that the film "celebrates the *possibility* of a harmonious multi-cultural society whilst acknowledging very firmly the difficulties in the way of its formation."[40] The Welsh terrorist cannot understand why the Croat and the Serb fight. He cannot even distinguish between them. It does not occur to him that his separatist ideology, his struggle against the English, may appear incomprehensible to somebody from the outside. It may be argued that Dizdar implicitly criticizes the parochialism of the regional struggle for self-determination, the absurdity of nationalism and its tragic consequences, as suggested by both Griffin's racist ultra-nationalist gang and the war in Bosnia.

In *Beautiful People* the world of hybrid London, a new Babylon of nationalities, ethnicities, and religions, where "indigenous" Britons can also feel like aliens in their own land,[41] is ultimately embodied in the infant called Chaos, the baby of the Muslim couple delivered by Dr. Mouldy. This child, despite the traumatic circumstances of his origins (his Muslim mother was raped by a gang of Serbian soldiers), bears the hope of a new multi-ethnic, multinational, multi-religious Europe, once symbolized by Sarajevo. Bosnia, therefore, embodies for Europe both the utopian hope (ironically based on the past) of multi-ethnic coexistence, as well as the catastrophic potential inherent in a multi-ethnic and religious situation. And indeed, at the end of the film, Portia chooses to live with her new husband Pero, the Bosnian refugee, in a hybrid London neighborhood of migrants, asylum seekers, and refugees where *Halal*—meat permitted for Muslim consumption—is advertised on many shop windows. Migrants and refugees bring chaos to the "civilized" metropolis of the West, but chaos (as literalized in the baby's name) is not necessarily something bad. The "uncivilized" refugees from the former Yugoslavia hold the promise of redemption not only for the whole gamut of the British class structure, but for both Bosnia and Britain as well. If you leave the Balkans to the Balkans, they will kill each other, and if you leave the Brits intact, they are destroyed from within, from the heart of the British family itself. New life begins in and from chaos.

Upon the birth of Chaos, the doctor, whose own marriage has disintegrated, finds consolation in their joy as he invites the new family to live and find refuge in his own home, thus extending British hospitality toward underprivileged strangers. The new hybrid British-Bosnian family heals the damaged lives of all three adults. The Bosnians, offered a new hospitable home, are healed of their war trauma, and the generous host heals from the loss of his family through the new pleasures he discovers in healing the wounds of others and bringing hope to their new lives. Dizdar's conscious neutrality with regard to the Bosnian war, acknowledged in many interviews, turns the film into an equivocal celebration of unnamed hybridity, linguistically and conceptually epitomized by the name "Chaos" given to the forbidden fruit of the Balkan war.

Issues related to multiculturalism, assimilation, integration, social cohesion, and the emergence of new hybrid urban families are at the heart of this film. Bosnia, which came to symbolize for the so-called New Europe

Figure 2.1. Hybridizing Britain with Bosnia in Jasmin Dizdar's
Beautiful People. The wedding of Porcha (Charlotte Coleman), a female
doctor, the daughter of an upper-class Tory cabinet minister,
and Pero (Edin Dzandanovic), a Bosnian refugee.
COURTESY OF BFI STILLS SALES

the dichotomy of multiculturalism versus tribal ethnicism—materializing its
worst ghosts and nightmares and casting a shadow on its dream of creating a
transnational, multicultural, and multi-ethnic entity—plays a major role in
the overall ideological economy of the film. The European fear of the "Bosnia
within" (i.e., the Balkanization of Europe) is transformed in Dizdar's film
into a successful experiment in hybridizing Bosnia with Britain, the "Balkan" with "Europe," the "Savage Barbarian" with the "Civilized European."
The threat of Balkanization, the film suggests, cannot only be avoided and
evaded but even inverted. The Balkanization of London, the symbol of "Cool
Britannia," does not fragment the city or destroy it from within, but to the
contrary enriches and cross-fertilizes it. It heals the pathology emanating
from the disintegrating British family structure and brings new hope and a
fresh blood supply to British society, a society in the grip of a severe identity

crisis. This hope culminates in the film's final scene, where the middle-class British doctor Mouldy is happily dancing a Balkan dance with his newly adopted Bosnian Muslim family, Dzemilia (Walentine Giorgiewa) and Ismet. This image of a life-affirming dance performed by a British/Bosnian family in a shared home is the film's utopian image of the new post–Fortress Europe experiencing the pleasures and delights of multiculturalism.

In the Bowels of the Global City: Stephen Frears's *Dirty Pretty Things*

Salman Rushdie writes: "The most precious book I possess is my passport."[42] Rushdie's bold assertion epitomizes the tragedy of "illegal immigrants" in our increasingly globalized world, a tragedy at the heart of Stephen Frears's film *Dirty Pretty Things*. Embedded in this phrase is the irony that Rushdie, one of the world's best-known postcolonial writers, whom we would expect to cherish one of "the great books," cherishes instead a mere passport, the ultimate reification and control of identity produced by the bureaucratic apparatus of the nation and the supra-nation state. One can only deduce from Rushdie's words that if even a world-renowned writer feels defenseless without a passport, then how might an anonymous ordinary "illegal immigrant" feel?[43] *Dirty Pretty Things,* which deals with the lives of ordinary migrants and whose protagonist is an "illegal immigrant," can be viewed as a socially conscious film masked as noir entertainment and, in the words of the publicity material of the film, "a thriller with a political edge set amongst London's largely invisible community of illegal immigrants."[44] The film follows eight days in the lives of Okwe (Chiwetel Ejiofor), a Nigerian refugee (defined as an "illegal immigrant" by the British authorities), and Senay (Audrey Tautou), a Turkish asylum seeker, both employees of the London Baltic Hotel. As they try to survive in the capital, Frears exposes a system of oppression and exploitation of their invisible underclass by the economically powerful city of London, which is ultimately driven by greedy and devouring global capitalism.

Philip French, the film critic of *Sight & Sound*, observed that Britain's most established and respected directors—Mike Leigh, Ken Loach, and Stephen Frears—all made admirable socially conscious movies on current issues during the same year: Leigh's *All or Nothing* on depressed families on run-down estates, Loach's *Sweet Sixteen* on working-class teenagers lured into crime, and Frears's *Dirty Pretty Things* on the lives of illegal immigrants.[45] Frears's film intervenes with the prevalent public and media discourse that equates migrants and asylum seekers with criminals. *Dirty Pretty Things,* however, inverts the criminalization trope, placing the blame on the contemporary British attitude toward immigration and asylum that creates and perpetuates crime. The film thereby subverts and radicalizes the abusive British discourse on migration and asylum in order to criticize the attitude of the beautiful people (the Brits) toward the invisible migrants who do their "dirty work." London's dirty, behind-the-scenes space, its invisible global bowels, becomes a metaphor for the exploitation and annihilation of the humanity of the other, of globalization's refugees.

Frears's Metropolis

Foreigners in London have always been met with stereotyping and racial prejudice, but London is also a city that cherishes its noisy, colourful immigrants. If London is the engine driving the rest of the country, immigration is the fuel that runs the engine.

Raheel Mohammed, *Time Out London,* **2004**

To the outsider, London is a sightseer's theme park, a rich assembly of landmarks and historic buildings, where blue plaques chronicle the passing of time right back to the Middle Ages. But like any modern city, London is a paradox; its true-blue heritage is supported by tourist money and, in many cases, employs personnel from all four corners of the world, working within various changing shades of legality. Such people are the oil that keeps London running smoothly, and the further one delves into the city's economy, the more one finds these invisible people, the un-thanked labour we pass on the streets every day but whose stories remain unknown and untold.[46]

Indeed, London in *Dirty Pretty Things,* as the above quote from the publicity material distributed to the audience in a preview screening makes clear, is not a non-place but non-London, or at least non-tourist London. Not only are there no recognizable landmarks in the film, but there are no street names and the locations chosen are generic. Almost anywhere in London looks similar to the sites shown in the film. One of my students (a born and bred Londoner) said she could not recognize any of the places, as the Turkish shops, the open market, can be seen almost anywhere in contemporary London. Even the posh area near the hotel could be located anywhere in the city center, where Londoners do not live (unlike the tourists) but come for shopping or entertainment. The areas where ordinary Londoners live could also be anywhere in the city.[47] The way in which the film captures the urban space of sameness is what highlights the clear division in London's spatial economy, its architecture of difference. Indeed, there is a clear division in the spatial economy of the film between the elegant hotel area, designed for the consuming gaze of the tourist and the shopper, and the rundown shabby place where Senay lives (which recalls the foreigners' neighborhood in *Beautiful People*). The multicultural cityscapes of Frears's London—the church steeples, minarets, and temple roofs—are also not identifiable. This architecture of difference, which paradoxically creates an urban space of sameness ("generispace"), is the embodiment of the multicultural body of London itself, the real protagonist or hero(ine?) of the film.[48] Yet this London is the Other London, the London of the Other. It is underworld London, the city of the dispossessed, London of the wretched of the earth. This is the invisible London of the invisible people who do the dirty work and keep the lives of the beautiful people from Dizdar's film going on smoothly. This cinematic city is subterranean London, dark London, hell-like London, the city that the "indigenous" Londoners do not see or rather do not want to see.[49]

London and the life of its refugees, asylum seekers, and migrants are represented as hell. Philip French aptly describes Sneaky (Sergi López), the Spanish manager of the Baltic Hotel, as "a modern Mephistopheles, buying bodies and souls. This parallel is made quite explicit when the threatened Turkish girl tells him to 'go to hell.' He replies with a line from Marlowe's *Doctor Faustus:* 'This is hell.'"[50] The claustrophobia induced by this contemporary Hades[51] is enhanced by the fact that there are very few scenes in the film that take place outdoors. One of them, shot at an open Oriental market in one of the film's many unidentifiable London sites, is accompanied by a sound track with Arabic/Turkish music. This penetration of "the Orient" into the heart of the West has become one of the landmarks of contemporary European cities and is reflected in many of the diasporic films about Fortress Europe; a similar space of open-market "orientalism" is also on display in *Besieged* (see chapter 3). The other significant outdoor scene takes place near a cemetery when Okwe confesses his real identity to Senay and renounces her naïve understanding of love.

The role of the migrants in operating and maintaining the city is much like that of the workers, the slaves of the Moloch of capitalism, in Fritz Lang's *Metropolis* (1927). Like Lang's metropolis, Frears's neo-capitalist London is a hell, where the Moloch of globalization is worshiped through the nightshifts, the never-ending work, and the repetitive efforts to clear the mess produced by the city. As Paul Coates perceptively observes in his discussion of Lang's film, the Moloch that consumes the children "is also the city itself—the Berlin that swallowed up so many peasants and others driven or drawn there by economic necessity."[52] The consumption occurring seventy-five years later in postmodern London differs from that of modern Berlin mainly in that

London swallows into its bowels migrants from the four corners of the globe rather than from the "nation" alone. "The jagged cityscape of *Metropolis*," Coates observes, "does not promise a new world—its meaning is the reverse of the Manhattan skyline that is said to have inspired Lang."[53] Similarly, it can be argued that the multicultural cityscape of Frears's London does not promise a utopia, and there is much built-in doubt in the film about New York being a better place than London for globalization's refugees. It is not clear if the utopian image of America imprinted in Senay's interior landscape of fantasy will indeed be sustained and New York, the capital of global capitalism with the phallic assertiveness of its skyscrapers, will be better than London, its subservient capital with its global service economy.[54] Whereas Lang's *Metropolis,* viewed by many critics as proto-Nazi, concludes with a healed relationship between labor and capital, Frears's liberal critique of global capitalism leaves the contradiction unresolved. In *Metropolis,* as Coates observes, the working class is "unsexed by the machines that drain their libidinal energy," and the mechanical whore, the "bad" Maria, represents "the sexuality invested in the machine."[55] In *Dirty Pretty Things,* the slaves of the machine economy are replaced by the slaves of the service economy which deprive them of their sexuality, internal organs, and the time and emotional space to love.

Internal and External Spaces, Boundaries/ Border Crossing, and Liminal Spaces

Dirty Pretty Things (like *La Haine* and *Besieged,* see chapters 3 and 4) is concerned with the division of filmic space into the internal and external, as corresponding to the realms of foreigner or native, respectively. The film's "foreign" characters spend much of their screen-time indoors. When Okwe and Senay are seen outdoors they are on their way between places because, as Senay says at the close of the film, "Always we must hide." Guo Yi (Benedict Wong), a naturalized British-Chinese mortician, is seen only at work in the hospital basement, and the nature of Juliette's (Sophie Okonedo) work as a prostitute based at the Baltic Hotel has her moving around the interior of the hotel.[56]

The external space of the non-postcard city is presented as realistic. Shots of streets are nondescript, lighting is left to the grey, British weather, giving the city a cold, dull hue, and there is a distinct absence of great tourist landmarks. This London (like Kassovitz's *La Haine*; see chapter 4) possesses no metropolitan glamour or travel-brochure gloss. In contrast, the interior of the Baltic Hotel glows with a warm golden color that makes the hotel look "pretty" (but also bordello-like) and protective like a womb, while simultaneously hiding the subversive and forbidden things that go on inside. The announcement of Ivan (Zlato Buric), the hotel porter, that "tonight, London is colder than Moscow" confirms the city as a hostile environment. Conflict occurs when the interior and exterior come into contact. The entrance of the Immigration Enforcement Directive (a governmental and therefore "native" organization) into Senay's flat, the hotel, and then the factory creates panic. During the surprise visit to the flat, the sound track becomes fast-paced and chaotic and the camerawork jerky as internal space is disrupted by an external force. The disruption is physically manifested by the officer's disregard for property and privacy. Senay's iron is spat on, cosmetics on her bathroom shelf thrown into disarray, and a book of matches stolen. This scene of violation, of brutal penetration into Senay's private space coupled with complete disrespect for her intimate possessions, anticipates her rape by Sneaky, the rape of a virgin Muslim woman which signifies the ultimate violation of the interior of her body and soul.

The theme of crossing borders and boundaries is further accentuated by the film's use of the liminal spaces of the hotel and the airport. Hotels and airports, as many scholars have observed, are places of transit, and the space that the postcolonial subject occupies is transitory. The ultimate irony, of course, is that in Frears's film the hotel functions as a hospital. However, unlike the spa hotel of *Journey of Hope* that is turned into a healing hospital, the hotel/hospital of *Dirty Pretty Things* is a sinister hospital operated by Sneaky and designed to steal migrants' organs under the most unprofessional, unhygienic, and dangerous conditions. Even when this hospital is "upgraded" and refurbished by Okwe, it only mimics the look of a "real" hospital but operates in an illegal underground manner nevertheless.

The "hospitable space" of the hotel in *Dirty Pretty Things* is revealed to be less than hospitable for its workers, as its name "The Baltic" suggests. The name not only refers to the icy welcome "enjoyed" by the hotel's "guestworkers" but to the enlargement of the EU through the addition of the former Eastern Bloc countries, also invoked by the presence of Ivan, the Russian porter. The hotel is a Dantesque purgatory on the road to the morgue and Ivan (the Terrible?)[57] is the guardian of its gates. The hotel, as a metonym of the global city of capitalism, is built on the stratification of space, using the economy of the base-superstructure metaphor.[58] The car park in the underground, shot in a sort of sick greenish-dirty hue, is the base; this is the place where the trade of organs/kidneys takes place. The reception area above is elegant and spacious and designed in red-warm colors. This is the window for the display of hospitality, but also of surveillance (the incoming workers, most of them migrants, are under the constant controlling and watching gaze of CCTV). The "guest" workers (an ironic euphemism for uninvited foreigners) who work there are surveyed by cameras, and the armies of maids who come early in the morning to clean the mess left by the overnight guests are scrutinized by overhead cameras and later watched by the immigration officers who themselves look like a racist caricature of foreigners (the face of one of them is adorned by a Saddam Hussein-like thick black mustache) but speak British-accented English. The guest rooms are located in the upper area (the superstructure). These rooms are for the tourists, the truly desired guests—as long as they pay good money and contribute to the booming global service economy of London.

Within the hotel, Okwe and Senay's lack of status forbids them to cross certain boundaries. The hotel rooms at the upper levels of the complex are reserved only for real guests and no characters enter them until they are deemed "worthy" by Señor Juan: Okwe is invited in as a doctor and Senay as a patient. Even when characters cross boundaries at the invitation of the more socially superior party, there are underlying motives, such as when Señor Juan encourages Okwe and Senay into the guests' rooms for business. The involuntary transformations of identity that characterize life for the hotel workers are emblematic of migrant workers' passport-less existence. The passport, a symbol of identity and belonging, is also a key to freedom, as Rushdie so aptly reminds us. Without one, the official boundary of the airport and the freedom beyond become inaccessible.

But the airport is also a space of disillusionment as much as it is a space of hope. It is a space/border between hell/dystopia (London) and paradise/utopia (New York). Guo Yi, the mortician, tells Ivan the legend from Greek mythology about the ferry operated by the Charon, boatman on the river Styx, which transports souls from the land of the living to the underworld kingdom of Hades. London in *Dirty Pretty Things* is indeed an underworld where the migrants are doomed to die. It is a cannibalistic city that devours their energy, vitality, and innocence and deprives them of hope for a better life. The liminal spaces in the film are the spaces of the migrant's existence between life and death. Before flying to New York and experiencing the pain of leaving, Okwe tries to comfort Senay by repeating her former naïve description of New York as the city of lights where the police ride on white horses and people skate in Central Park: "Very soon you will see the lights of the city,"[59] to which she responds, "I know that it won't be like that." Senay has matured as a result of the "operation" performed on her by Señor Juan and has been "cured" of her naïve blindness to the real nature of the displacement experience. The airport scene is shot against the background of a pinkish sunset not unlike the poster of a chartered island in Tanya's flat in *Last Resort*. Indeed, Manhattan is an island, much like Britain is, but perhaps not a paradise island as the kitsch reproductions of mass-manufactured fantasies would have us believe.

For Okwe and Senay, the airport departure gate is a threshold that they wish to cross from their status of invisible in the internal space of London to the external freedom of America, which in the words of Frears himself "has always been the dream that people want to realize."[60] The airport which actually opens the film is a space of desire and fantasy promising them the retrieval of their lost identities (Okwe is seen offering his help to passengers who were, as he says, "dumped by the system"). For them, the airport is a physical boundary of domination; in London they would remain victimized as they are, but their new destinations hold promise for better lives. By the time they reach the airport, they have taken the first steps toward freedom by rebelling against Señor Juan's tyranny, through their operation, which in itself is representative of exterior (foreign) forces invading the victimizer. However, the film's cyclical narrative physically brings the protagonists back to the location where they began the film—Senay and Okwe escape through the airport. They may escape their troubles temporarily but there is uneasiness and uncertainty about what the future holds for them. Perhaps they will encounter more of the same treatment that they suffered in Britain or even worse.

The Invisible People

Karen Alexander questions whether it is important that the foreign presence is recognized in British cinema. Her answer is inevitably "yes." Frears's film, to cite her words about previous British films on the black diaspora, draws attention to a "section of the [national] community so often constructed as silent," or perhaps more accurately "invisible."[61] She discusses how the ignorance of the full spectrum of society means that the national face that Britain presents to the external world is inaccurate and exclusive. Alexander also insists that filmmakers should have a hand in putting the problem of immigrant identity, and the consequent exploitation of it, on the screen. "The Britain that is being disseminated on cinema screens around the world is steeped in heritage, literary culture, and conventional ideas of class relations. It is also overwhelmingly white, in sharp contrast to our workplaces, high streets and bedrooms which tell a very different story."[62] Although in *Dirty Pretty Things* the foreign presence as a whole is depicted as essential to the country and particularly the city's economy, the individual foreigners, on the other hand, are easy targets of exploitation. The foreign presence is acknowledged but only in the specific context of a workforce. In the film the most symbolic representative of white England is the person who delivers the organs from the hotel/hospital. It is not an accident, therefore, that he delivers these iconic words when Okwe and his assistants bring Señor Juan's fresh kidney to him: "How come, guys, that I've never seen you before?" "Because we are the invisible people. We're the people that drive your cars, clean your rooms and suck your cocks," Okwe replies.

At the beginning of the film, when Okwe arrives at the cab station, he takes the cross from his boss and says, "My name is now Muhammad." As in *La Haine* (see chapter 4), the coalition of the invisible oppressed is multi-ethnic and multi-religious and the solidarity between the foreigners crosses the boundaries of race, ethnicity, nationality, class, and religion. Senay is a Muslim from a small village in Turkey. Okwe is a highly educated Christian black African Nigerian and Ivan is a white Russian Slav. Juliette is a black Briton presumably from a West Indian, Caribbean, background. When Okwe prepares a dinner for Senay and himself, he jokes: we make a lot of interesting things from pork in Nigeria. But when he sees her shocked expression (she stops chewing the food), he smiles and says, "But here of course I used lamb."[63]

The solidarity built among the newcomers does not exist with the migrants from the previous "waves." It is a Pakistani sweatshop owner who sexually abuses Senay, taking advantage of her vulnerable situation. There is also a hierarchy of migrants: the EU members like Señor Juan, the legal migrant, the "certified" refugees (like Guo Yi, the Chinese who works in the morgue), the asylum seekers like Senay, and the illegal immigrants like Okwe. Guo Yi tells Okwe, "I am a certified refugee. You are illegal. You have nothing." *Dirty Pretty Things* examines London's treatment of its foreign presence as a whole (refugees and migrants, both permanent and journeying through the capital). Regardless of their permanence or legal status (or lack of it) they are all presented as marginalized, dominated, and exploited by their host country/city.

Frears's film draws attention to this point by allowing its narrative to be told, and thus viewed, from the perspective of outsiders. Until *Dirty Pretty Things*' climatic operation on Señor Juan, all the ethnic characters spend the entire film avoiding being seen, for to be seen is to be recognized as illegal, and to lose what little freedom one has. However, once they have reached the threshold of the airport, Senay and Okwe are willing to declare themselves to the airport staff behind the protection of their new identities. Only at this point, when they have—ironically—forged passports, markers of "false belonging," are they ready to reclaim their lives as their own under the gaze of others. This reclamation of identity is made salient by Okwe's closing scene. He phones his daughter in Nigeria from the departure lounge, unafraid that the sun outside is illuminating him for all to see.

In *Dirty Pretty Things,* the marginalized and the invisible are made central and visible by the narrative which allows only the perspective of the oppressed foreign presence (from the outside in), making the film a study of migrant "experiences of Englishness."[64] Okwe's repeated changes of uniform as he moves between jobs demonstrate how invisible migrants appear to the public; no one questions him as long as he wears a uniform. He does not arouse any suspicion as long as he pretends to be a cleaning person because this is what is expected of black migrants. No one, of course, would expect him to be a doctor. By the close of *Dirty Pretty Things,* however, Okwe and Senay have bought themselves new identities. Okwe's profile is raised above that of "just another African" by Señor Juan's need for a doctor.[65]

Who are the white people in this closed universe/planet of "foreign presence" in this multicultural London? They are doctors and nurses in the hospital, the buyer of the "truffles" (a code name for the illegally traded internal organs), and one of Juliette's clients who beats and injures her until Okwe comes to her rescue. The last white person whom we see is the passport controller at the airport. He lets Senay go with her new identity as an Italian from Naples (on the African/dark connotations of the Italian south, see chapter 3). But Frears subverts stereotypes of foreigner and native in addition to those of black and white. The racist stereotyped roles of native and foreigner as "good" and "evil," respectively, are inverted. Señor Juan is the "evil man," while Okwe, confounding the "ideological constructions of 'blacks' as either exotic or threatening 'Others,'"[66] is the hardworking and very moral character.[67] Senay's boss at the clothing factory, a Pakistani, is presented as greedy, a bully, and a sexual predator. His minority status and/or being an old immigrant himself do not prevent him from exploiting the new, vulnerable migrants.[68]

Heart of (Capitalist) Darkness

As the narrative progresses, the morals of the protagonists are corrupted. Okwe operates on Señor Juan, and Senay agrees to sacrifice her virginity (a real sacrifice/sin for a Muslim woman) in exchange for a forged passport. Even though Okwe and Senay find themselves corrupted by the reality of asylum and migration, their "good" characters never become "evil." Despite

Figure 2.2. Senay (Audrey Tautou), a Turkish asylum-seeker
in London, in Stephen Frears's *Dirty Pretty Things.*
COURTESY OF THE BFI

what seems to be a submission to the logic of capitalist asylum (the capitulation to the rape and the operation), this accommodation is seen as temporary,
driven by the natural urge to survive. The other foreigners also adopt a range
of survival strategies. The Russian becomes cynical, the Chinese philosophical and detached, and the Turkish woman fights, surrenders, but is ultimately
saved by the African Nigerian Okwe, who tries to maintain his dignity and
humanity at almost any cost. In the scene in which Okwe exposes his identity,
telling Senay about his wife and asking her to forget him, she questions him:
"But do you love her?" This is the first time that we see Okwe lose his temper
and shout, "Forget about all your silly dreams . . . for you and I there is only
survival." There is no place for the heart in the fight for survival in capitalist
London.

Figure 2.3. Okwe (Chiwetel Ejiofor), a Nigerian refugee in London
(defined as an "illegal immigrant" by the British authorities),
in Stephen Frears's *Dirty Pretty Things*.
Courtesy of the BFI

The heart as both a "manufacturer" and container of emotions and love
is a prominent motif in the film, which builds its thriller dimensions around
the journey of discovering how a human heart has been found flushed out
in the toilet at the beginning. At a certain point, Senay (while looking for a
"sanctuary" in the morgue) leans her head over Okwe's chest and remarks,
as she feels his heart beating, "So you have got a heart after all." The human
heart found in the toilet is the major, organizing metaphor of the film, recalling again the prominence of the heart motif in Lang's *Metropolis*. This,
the film implies, is what London and capitalism are doing: flushing human
hearts in the toilet and treating the refugees like a form of waste. The heart of
the migrants, Frears suggests, is the engine of the city. The city, as the title of
the film ironically suggests, is like a toilet that needs to be flushed, cleaned,
and purified by the migrants. If you stop migration or, rather, if you devour
migrants (as the Moloch devours the slave workers in Lang's *Metropolis*), you

block up the city like the toilet clogged by the heart in one of the hotel rooms. The greedy city of London, the capital of the global service economy, destroys and devours the beauty of the human heart. London is like Lang's Metropolis that devours its slave workers who toil in the underworld of the dead to keep the city going. The slaves of *Metropolis* and the migrant slaves of London are sacrificed to the Moloch of capitalism.

But the heart is also the "heart of darkness," the secret heart of the empire. Except that in contemporary Europe the heart of darkness is no longer located in the colonies but in the heart of whiteness, Europe. The Empire is devouring the postcolonial subject in its heart—London. The postcolonial subjects "invade" the heart of the empire, the capital, the heart of the nation. Yet, even at the heart of the old empire and even after its official demise, they continue to be devoured deep within its global bowels.

The War against the Strangers and the Devouring Moloch of Global Capitalism

It is perhaps not accidental that *Dirty Pretty Things* was written by Steven Knight and produced by Paul Smith, co-creators of "Who Wants to Be a Millionaire?" Produced within the logic of capitalist film production, *Dirty Pretty Things,* despite its liberal critique, condenses and encompasses the contradictions of this logic.[69] As Ross Forman suggests, films "dealing with the concept of Fortress Europe—even when they are sympathetic to immigrants and the hardships they endure upon arrival in a Europe nearly always prefigured as a kind of Promised Land—primarily come from the perspective of the European. As such, they often replicate a colonizer-colonized paradigm, through which the former is empowered to represent and to speak for the latter."[70]

A more favorable reading of the critique proposed by *Dirty Pretty Things* would view the film as an overarching accusation against the criminality embedded in the global capitalist system, which not only exploits "illegal immigrants" but also forces them to become "legally criminals" by creating an economical situation that pushes them to resort to strategies of survival defined as illegal and therefore criminal. The asylum seekers are paid so little money (if at all) that they are forced to work illegally and consequently become easy prey for exploitation. Hence they become double victims of the global system that is inherently corrupting and corrupt. If Senay and Okwe, the "good" and "moral" heroes of *Dirty Pretty Things,* stay in London, they will eventually become corrupted. The logic of the narrative, therefore, forces them to leave (Okwe goes back to Nigeria and Shenay leaves for New York).

Those (like Ivan) who have already been corrupted by the system, or alternatively victimized by it (Juliette), or fatalistically and philosophically accepting it (Guo Yi), stay.

It is important to mention that in Frears's film the logic of British asylum is inseparable from the logic of global capitalism. *Dirty Pretty Things* criticizes the predominant view of global capitalism, which sees migrants as commodities. Globalization's refugees, according to this view, are entitled to asylum only insofar as they can be circulated within the chain of commodities of the global free market. Their worth depends upon their value as a human commodity, and not on their inherent worth as human beings in a state of need, despair, or danger. This view fits the new ideology/philosophy of asylum politics, which is no longer based on the principle of human rights but on the logics of economic rationale. Indeed, this presentation of refugees reflects the growing dominance of late global capitalism in which the world comes increasingly to be seen in terms of an instrumental or "scientific" rationality of the free market, which views people as a resource that can be possessed, exploited, and ultimately controlled. The new approach toward asylum and migration, as Liza Schuster forcefully argues, is based on utilitarianism, focusing on the economic benefits rather than the desire to uphold human rights.[71] Migration is viewed in economic terms rather than in terms of universal rights, and celebration of ethnic diversity and multiculturalism. It is a labor-market-driven approach which, again, recalls *Metropolis*'s representation of the workers-slaves "who are treated as objects to be used, controlled and—as we see in the scenes of the Moloch machine—consumed."[72] If the global free market is open to the flow of commodities, it will be free for refugees as long as they accept being treated as commodities or human spare parts to become, in the words of Hardt and Negri, part of the "virtual panopticon of network production."[73] In the clamor for free trade, in the forms of free capital flows and free movement of goods and production, the third part of the economic stool, free movement of labor, is inevitable. If the refugees volunteer to become commodities either by exchanging their internal organs (kidneys in *Dirty Pretty Things* and *Spare Parts,* blood donation in *Last Resort,* sex and virginity in all these films) for a forged passport, a new and "legal" identity, then they can be "legalized" and tolerated.

Dirty Pretty Things uses the grisly "currency" of human organs; Okwe finally capitulates to the logic of late capitalism and agrees to the transaction of Senay's kidney and his medical knowledge for new identities. Indeed, a recurring motif in *Dirty Pretty Things* is the exchange of money. Okwe initially refuses a bribe from Señor Juan to keep quiet about what he has seen, but after learning from Ivan how to take advantage of the system (by providing unofficial room service), he realizes the power of money in his position in a capitalist society. He soon is paying Juliette for her part in the operation and bribing Ivan to carry out his instructions when he flees the hotel. Thus capitalism seems to be a more prominent factor in oppression than racism. Sarah Gibson suggests that the "xeno-racism" that is directed toward the body of the asylum seeker is located within the economic sphere, linking asylum control to the welfare state in Britain. This, according to her, represents a movement away from biological and cultural racism, to an economic racism within Britain and Europe. In Frears's film, the space of the hotel is a space where service economies and economies of racism coincide.[74] *Dirty Pretty Things* is about economic racism, racism against the poor of the world. Within the logic and logistics of global capitalism, the body, literally and metaphorically, becomes the migrants' main asset, playing a significant role in the economic dialectics displayed by global capitalism.

In *Dirty Pretty Things,* the migrants are forced to give, "donate" their internal organs to the Brits, in order to become part of the national body, the body of the nation. They mix their blood with that of the natives, or rather they involuntarily sacrifice themselves for the natives, invoking the organic (traditionally the fascist) metaphor of the nation as a living body-organism. Their sacrifice revives the nation, bringing new life to the metropolis of London, which they energize and fuel with their blood, sweat, and tears. Okwe's hyperactivity, his race against time, sleeplessness, and chronic fatigue, visually epitomize this tireless energy on the altar of the global city. The migrants supply the vital organs to the sick and aging nation which they rejuvenate.[75] They exchange their organs for a passport, their blood for a new identity. This exchange is at the core of the economical formula, the scheme of exchange at the heart of global capitalism (a similar dynamic of exploitation is evident also in *Besieged,* where freedom is traded for sexual love; see chapter 3). The immigration debate as projected into *Dirty Pretty Things,* despite its neoliberalism-inspired economic racism, is still determined by the old-fashioned traditional racism of blood and belonging, blood and nation of origin. The conflation of economic racism based on the rhetoric of global capitalism and traditional "classical" racism based on the pseudo-scientific language of racial purity is indeed central to the prominence of the body/medicine/healing discourse in many diasporic migrant films. It is not a coincidence that *Dirty Pretty Things* evolves around the hotel/hospital and its main protagonist is a medical doctor. This extended medical imagery can be found in all the diasporic and migrant films where hospitals, doctors, blood "donations," and body parts are constantly present.

The objectification and commodification of the refugees is supported by the film's own politics of representation. Frears objectifies his foreign characters through the gaze. His use of the gaze is quietly aggressive rather than openly hostile. The camera moves around and spies on its subjects, drawing attention to their presence rather than its own—characters become spectacles to be consumed. Objectification through the gaze reflects capitalist oppression itself. Okwe, having been introduced as a cab driver, is identified as a doctor and then a night porter before the spectators even learn his name. Similarly, during her first conversation with Okwe, Juliette establishes her identity as a hooker. The hotel security camera draws attention to the workers' invisibility by only acknowledging their presence as cleaners or doormen. Frears draws attention to the idea that the marginal only exist to work for their host country. Okwe's life does not belong to him but to his masters; his day is dictated by his work schedule and they deprive him of rest and sleep.[76] The film enhances these themes by simultaneously combining the realistic level, the thriller and the structure of Greek mythology. The repetition of the shot of an alarm clock on the lobby desk and watches and other clocks draw attention to time and the monotony of oppressed, working lives; it alludes to the commodification of time originating in the credo cultivated by modernity and capitalism that "time is money." Modern time, objectified by the clock, becomes the crucifix of the slaves of global capitalism, best symbolized by the iconic scene in *Metropolis* where one of the workers is seen "crucified" on a huge clock, pleading like Jesus on the cross, "Father, Father, why have you forsaken me?"

As portrayed in *Dirty Pretty Things*, global capitalism is assisted and manifested by other cultural apparatuses, among them language, which, as many scholars of nationalism (notable among them Benedict Anderson) claim, establishes identity.[77] It is also worth pointing out that Frears's characters for the most part relate to each other in a foreign language (English). English, which has become the lingua franca of global capitalism, is the tool of their oppression but also of their team spirit. Not only does English unite them as their common language, but also partly, due to their accents, masks their identities from "past" lives. Ironically, English builds solidarity among the foreigners. It is their only shared language. Yet their accents mark them as foreigners. In the last scene, when Senay calls her cousin in New York, she chooses to use English because, embarking on a new life, she wishes to leave her former ethnic identity behind.[78]

Language, which acts as a barrier to the immigrant entrance into the host society, can also become his or her entry ticket. The second generation, the daughters of the immigrants, Frears suggests, will be integrated. In a moving scene in which we see Okwe visiting the seriously wounded Somali refugee who is heavily bleeding as a consequence of being operated by Señor Juan and who cannot be taken to the hospital by his family, who fear disclosing their identity as illegal immigrants, Okwe tries to explain in English to the African family how to use the medications. But nobody in this large family seems to know English until a little girl, the youngest daughter of the refugee family, starts talking to him in perfect non-accented British English. Acting as an interpreter between Okwe and the refugee family, she becomes the agent of integration, communicating with ease in two languages, signifying both the "foreign" and the "host." Silence also plays a significant role in the film's overall economy of language and communication. Silence in *Dirty Pretty Things* frees its protagonists. Their silence hides them from the authorities while, on the other hand, they know that verbal expression of feeling would incarcerate them. For example, Senay's quiet subservience to the factory owner degrades her but keeps her free from the immigration authorities who are after her, just as her acquiescence to Señor Juan's demands brings her a little closer to a new identity.

Dirty Pretty Things portrays how the ultimate logic of global capitalism is materialized and embodied in economic cannibalism, the trade in human organs. If the access to the material resources of the Developing World becomes more difficult, as the Iraq War testifies, then there is still the human resource in the form of labor, organs, sex, and nurturing. The logic of global capitalism is such that the exploitation now takes place not only in the third world itself but in the Western metropolis as well. The migrants, the desperate people of the third and developing world, who come to the metropolis of the rich West, are forced to sacrifice their last and most precious resources, their lives, their professional expertise, their organs, their sexuality. Like the slave workers of *Metropolis* who appear robotic and zombie-like, so are the slaves of the new global city epitomized by the never-sleeping, always-working, half-alive and half-dead Okwe. "Perhaps the concept of the 'secondary barbarization' best sums up the overall impact of the present-day metropoly on the world periphery," Bauman suggests.[79] This rendering seems to perceptively capture not only the spirit and ethics of late global capitalism, lacking the "heart" and emotions that define human life, but also of Frears's cinematic critique of it. As a city of migration, Frears's London is the ultimate consuming and controlling global city, Europe's Promised Land, heavily fortified from within against its "invading others."

3

THE WHITE CONTINENT IS DARK

MIGRATION AND MISCEGENATION IN BERNARDO BERTOLUCCI'S *BESIEGED* (1998)

Slavery broke the world in half, it broke it in everyway. It broke Europe.
It made them into something else, it made them slave masters, it made
them crazy. You can't do that for hundreds of years and it not take a toll.

Toni Morrison, interviewed by Paul Gilroy

THE European capital, now a space of miscegenation and multi-culturalism, is also perceived ambivalently, as a place that pollutes the country, the "body" of the nation. The city, according to this racist and nationalistic view, poses a danger to the homogenous and "authentic" national culture. It is the other within. And indeed, the ethnoscapes of the hybrid cinematic cities in the European migrant and diasporic films are almost devoid of white "indigenous" Europeans. In *Dirty Pretty Things,* as we have seen in the previous chapter, there are almost no visible white English people, while the invisible people (the "foreigners") are everywhere.[1] Even in Bernardo Bertolucci's *Besieged,* the Italian film at the center of this chapter, the nostalgic gaze at one of Rome's most romantic and iconic historical landmarks, the Piazza di Spagna (the Spanish Steps), reveals spaces (presumably near the Termini and Piazza di Republica) where only nonwhite, dark foreigners can be seen. Yet though creolized and darkened,[2] Europe is still the heart of whiteness, the place where being "visible as white is a passport to privilege."[3] Miscegenation, which in contemporary Europe comes with migration, is perceived as a threat to this privilege. European colonizers and their settler descendants have always been terrified by the fear of miscegenation, "the sexual union of different races and ethnic groups. The fear of mixing blood stems from a desire to maintain the separation between the colonizer and the colonized, the 'civilized' and the 'savage,' yet that binary masks a profound longing, occluding the idea of the inevitable dependence of one on the existence of the other."[4]

One of the dominant themes in the migrant diasporic films that both reflects and negotiates the anxiety regarding miscegenation is the trope of "forbidden love," the cross-racial love story or union which very often is presented as the "solution" (or allegory) to the "immigration problem." Stories of "forbidden love," dealing mainly with interracial romances, are a recurring theme in Western culture. Colonialist practice was obsessed with the products of miscegenation, "particularly in those areas where black and white has also been further hierarchized as slave and free."[5]

An analysis of the underlying sexual economy of the cinematic narratives on forbidden love between blacks and whites reveals a love formula that is a further expression of the dominant white voice, namely the voice of fear.[6] In the realm of contemporary European cinema, *Ali: Fear Eats the Soul* (*Angst Essen Seele Auf*, Rainer Werner Fassbinder, Germany, 1972), a cross race-class-age-religion narrative about the relationship between Emmi (Brigitte Mira), a sixty-year-old cleaning woman, and Ali (El Hedi ben Salem), a North African migrant in his thirties working in Germany as an auto mechanic, is one of the foundational cinematic texts on "the invasion of Europe" by the African/Arab/Muslim "foreigner." The film can be viewed as a proleptic text anticipating the "exodus" of migrants to Fortress Europe, the "invasion" and "penetration" of old Europe (embodied by the old body of Emmi) by the new, dark, and vigorous European other (symbolized by Ali's body, which is proudly displayed by Emmi and Fassbinder's camera to her envious racist female colleagues). However, in Fassbinder's film this "forbidden" contact between the aging white/feminine body and the young black/brown super-masculine body of the *Gastarbeiter* (guest worker) does not culminate in procreation and cross-fertilization, due to Emmi's advanced age.[7]

Bernardo Bertolucci's *Besieged* (1998) is a more recent example of a European film about miscegenation, which like Fassbinder's earlier film is occupied with the highly charged master/slave dialectics. The film centers on the evolving relationship between Jason Kinsky (David Thewlis), an English pianist and composer who lives in an old house he inherited near the Spanish Steps in Rome, and Shandurai (Thandie Newton, who played in the film adaptation of Toni Morrison's *Beloved* [1998]), a young African woman refugee[8] who studies medicine and works as Kinsky's maid and cleaning woman. Like many other European films made about migration to Fortress Europe around the same time, *Besieged* was conceived by an "insider" from the host and/or dominant culture (Bertolucci) and not by an authentic member of the ethno-Diaspora or the immigrant community itself. As such, *Besieged* constitutes a form of social document about the ambivalence embedded in the attitude of the European host society toward migrants and outsiders and particularly toward the issue of miscegenation.

Yet in one respect *Besieged* is slightly different. As a director who himself has become a voluntary (privileged) "immigrant" in London since 1981, Bertolucci is no longer a "typical" symbolic representative of the Italian host society. His decision to come back to his roots in Italy but through the back door, trying to see his "homeland" afresh as a foreigner or a tourist might, was motivated, he has confessed in many interviews, by his growing tired of his big epic Orientalist "trilogy of the other" (or what I call "from Mama Africa and China to the Dalai Lama"): *The Last Emperor* (1987), *The Sheltering Sky* (1990), and *Little Buddha* (1993), in which he was looking for utopias outside the West.[9] Bertolucci's renewed tour of Italy began with *Stealing Beauty* (1996), which dealt with the growing community of privileged Anglo-Saxon émigrés in Tuscany (known in Britain as Chiantishire), and continued with *Besieged,* whose protagonist Kinsky is also a privileged Brit (with a Russian surname) living in the iconic space of the English Romantic poets, Shelley and Keats, near the Spanish Steps.

Perhaps more than most minority or accented films,[10] *Besieged,* made by an established European art-director, is an emblematic film that both projects and captures the current contradictions of contemporary European attitudes toward what is usually described by the media, as well as by European politicians (including the center-left parties who try to cater to popular racist sentiments), as the tidal wave of refugees and asylum seekers swamping Europe. Consequently, *Besieged* can be read as a film about a current stage of identity crisis experienced not only by Italy but by Western Europe perceiving itself as being threatened by an "invasion" of "inassimilable" and "contaminated" others.[11]

Some critics found the film's portrayal of Kinsky and Shandurai's relationship "patronizing or even racist." They believe that Shandurai's eventual love for her employer is "equivalent to a slave's capitulation to a master." Other critics, for example, argued that "it is true that Bertolucci's stance in *Besieged* is that of a liberal humanist; his depiction of Third World political turmoil and racial tension in the European Diaspora seems naïve when compared with the films of African and Latin American directors." Still, they maintain that the "protagonists' romantic *pas de deux* does nevertheless reveal how Europe, particularly Italy, is coming to awkward terms with its new multicultural status."[12] My reading of *Besieged* expands on these discussions of the film. I attempt to offer a different perspective on this potentially controversial film by showing how *Besieged* both invites and resists a postcolonial, anti-immigrant, and racist reading and permits multiple subversive interpellations. My point is not necessarily to condemn the film as xenophobic or racist but to read "across" it, to see what it says (or fails to say) about the changing color of Europe. In examining the way *Besieged* grapples with cultural identity and the dominant view of Europeaness as whiteness, this chapter considers Bertolucci's construction of a new image of Italy/Europe.

Migratory Dislocations: From Latin America to Africa

The plot of *Besieged* is based on a story by British Jewish writer James Lasdun, *The Siege*.[13] In the original story, Kinsky is a middle-aged man and the domestic worker, Marietta, is from an unnamed country in Latin America. Bertolucci decided to make Kinsky younger so that, in his words, he would not be perceived as a middle-aged man who fantasizes about young women (the kind of encounter he certainly did intend to portray in *Stealing Beauty* and *The Dreamers* [2003]).[14] In the novel, the major tension between the two protagonists is based on class as well as on a tension between the West (Britain) and the Latin American third world. The story portrays Marietta as a leftist political exile (what in contemporary European immigration discourse is described as a genuine asylum seeker, unlike "bogus asylum seekers" or "benefit asylum seekers" in the public, political, and popular discourse on immigration) who had judged Mr. Kinsky "to be an eccentric, overbred product of European capitalism"[15] who "had money invested in countries such as her own, where governments could be relied upon to keep wages negligible, and profits correspondingly enormous." The story suggests that Marietta "hoped, and believed, that his breed would one day vanish from the face of the earth."[16]

It is no wonder that Bertolucci, a highly politicized director during the 1970s and 1980s, was attracted to this story that involves a confrontation between a decadent and exploitative West, epitomized by the over-refined character of Kinsky, and an oppressed and exploited third world, represented by the character of Marietta. Yet Bertolucci chose to dislocate the plot from London to Rome (a "migratory" movement which parallels both his own personal and professional trajectory, as well as the self-reflexive narrative and production choice of the film itself) and transform Marietta into a black woman from an unnamed African country under the oppressive rule of a military regime, and Kinsky into a British expatriate living in Rome. These narrative dislocations not only made the film more topical and relevant to the contemporary Italian and European sociopolitical agenda, but also pushed further the binary oppositions of the original narrative. The romance, as portrayed in the film, becomes an interracial affair involving and invoking the complex issues of miscegenation and multiculturalism facing a contemporary Europe consumed by xenophobic fears of the other.

The Dark Continent Revisited

The film opens with its titles running on an evocative image of an aged black African musician, suggesting an epic folk singer, as he sits beneath a huge tree arching over the earth.[17] There is no translation of the song into English and it is not clear in what African language it is delivered. The powerful visual image, accompanied by the touching music with its incomprehensible lyrics, conveys an almost transcendental image of Africa as a timeless and ahistorical entity.[18] This long take into the heart of darkness creates a mute and exotic image of Africa to be contemplated and consumed by the gaze of the Western spectator. Yet, despite its apparent exoticization and fetishization of the other, it also sets forth one of the major themes of the film, the attempt at breaking through what is perceived to be the silence of Africa and establishing new channels of communication and dialogue between Europe and Africa, black and white, colonizer and the colonized.

From this ambiguous image of "Africanness," the film moves to images of handicapped and mutilated African children in the rehabilitation institute where Shandurai works. The mutilated children recall television and media images of legless and armless African children who have become the victims of minefields planted during many of Africa's turbulent civil wars. These images were particularly widespread in the Western media during the various campaigns to clear the mines. Africa, which usually does not enjoy the exposure and attention devoted to other nonwestern places, during the late 1990s received a measurable amount of publicity and exposure in the West due to the involvement of Princess Diana.[19]

The evocative shots of the aged singer and the mutilated children establish the image of Africa in the mind of the spectator. On one hand, the poetic and epic image of the elderly African musician, playing a primitive instrument and clinging (literally and symbolically) to the spiral roots of the huge African tree, invokes the impression of an ancient and timeless continent. On the other hand, the images of the injured children, the inheritors of this primeval land, are a testimony to the suffering of this continent torn by civil and ethnic conflicts, famine, and disease. The past and future of Africa, these images seem to suggest, are in danger. It is left to Shandurai and her husband, Winston, the representatives of the African mid-generation, to save Africa from disaster. Yet Winston's attempt at reeducating the young generation of Africans is brutally suppressed by the dictatorial regime (a political articulation of the motif of the *padre/padrone* so prevalent in Bertolucci's work),[20] and he is put in jail while Shandurai, his wife, has to leave her healing work with African children and flee to Europe in search of safety and education. The film implies that Winston will stay in Europe whether his wife joins him or not. The attempt to heal and cure "the sick man of the world," in the highly imploded language of one of Africa's current political leaders,[21] from within, seems doomed to fail. Africa is beyond salvation/redemption, and its potential "indigenous healers" (prime educator Winston and superb medical student Shandurai) are forced to leave it and escape to Europe.

During her final exams in medicine at the University of Rome, Shandurai lists a long and quite gruesome list of diseases, ending with Ebola, thus equating Africa with this disease. It is quite interesting that Bertolucci chooses Ebola, and not AIDS, as the signifier of Africa, perhaps because Ebola is not only an incurable disease which has reached the state of epidemic in Africa (much like AIDS), but also because in Africa it is believed to be sorcery. Furthermore, unlike AIDS, which although it is thought to have originated in Africa is also a Western disease associated in the Western public imagination mostly with the gay community and drug users, Ebola is almost exclusively an African epidemic. Thus, the image of Africa that the film establishes from the outset is not far from that prevalent in the West and cultivated and perpetuated by the Western media, which tends to portray it as a place of conflict, war, and disease.[22]

The Anxiety/Fantasy of Miscegenation

Sexuality in *Besieged* transcends the specificity of the relationship between Shandurai and Kinsky and becomes an allegory, a political parable on the encounter of the new Europe with the "Africa within," the by-product of African migration to the continent.[23] *Besieged* continues the long cultural tradition of constructing fantasies of national (or even transnational) unity via romantic love across racial and class divides. And yet, as we shall see below, a close reading of the cinematic text reveals it to be imbued with both celebration and anxiety about miscegenation. *Besieged* not only reflects on pan-European attitudes toward Africa and blackness, but also implicitly alludes to Italy's particular colonial past, its African adventure/expenditure, its unprovoked conquest of Ethiopia, and the massively murderous invasion of Abyssinia in 1935. Part of the ambivalence projected toward "Africanness" and blackness in *Besieged* can be viewed in light of Italy's own black roots and the view (still held today by the *Lega Lombarda/Lega Nord*)[24] that the Italian south (the *Mezzogiorno*) is the frontier between civilized Europe and barbarous, savage Africa.[25] Kinsky's and Shandurai's love story thus becomes (to cite Bertolucci himself on the love story of *Last Tango in Paris*, his 1972 film with which *Besieged* establishes complex intertextual relationships) "a centrally symptomatic affair for our times."[26] It becomes a love story of two continents, Europe, represented by Kinsky, and Africa, represented by Shandurai. To further complicate the race issue it is interesting to note that Lasdun's original text implicitly suggests that Kinsky is Jewish. His surname is Russian and his physical features, particularly his black and curly ("always unkempt")[27] hair, fit the stereotypical image of the European Jew (but also of the black).[28] In Bertolucci's film, however, Kinsky retains his Russian Jewish name but is played by an actor who looks and acts "typically" English.

Besieged's ambivalent attitude toward miscegenation, expressed through its portrayal of the interracial romance between Shandurai and Kinsky, both invites and resists racist and colonial reading, hence exposing the contradictions embedded in the attitude of white Europe toward race. After all, as Robert Young perceptively observes, "hybridity can simultaneously work in two ways: it can homogenize and it can heterogenize. It can whiten the blacks, or it can create forms of subversion that would work against the very culture that invented it."[29] According to Lola Young, "Many of the anxieties that white people have about black people have been of a sexual nature,"[30] and it is exactly this anxiety that is at the "heart of darkness" of *Besieged*, whose ambivalence about cross-racial sexual encounters echoes a similar theme in Bertolucci's earlier film, *The Sheltering Sky* (1990).[31] The fluctuations between miscegenation anxiety and fantasy that run throughout the film are played out in Kinsky's and Shandurai's musical duet that begins initially with two soloists, captured by the image of two fishes swimming aimlessly in the enclosed space of an aquarium appearing in the scene. This poetic visual image echoes the mental state of the two protagonists when Kinsky first confesses his love to Shandurai. From two lonely and isolated fishes they join to become a couple in a shared bed at Kinsky's inherited home. The choreographed duet image repeats symbolically in the resolution of the clash of musical cultures in the film (classical music versus African/rock/popular music) into a "blended," hybrid music.

Harmonious as it may be, it is debatable whether Kinsky's and Shandurai's musical duet, the free "dancing" scene of the cleaning lady and the piano-playing master, provides reactionary or progressive imagery of miscegenation for the spectator's gaze. The duet of the white master with the piano and the black servant with the vacuum cleaner, one of the climatic scenes of the film, constitutes a disturbing image of interracial love whereby the white man, Kinsky, is inspired by the cleaning lady, his black muse.[32] This theme repeats visually as well, in the lovers' duet of gazes. Communicating their emotions through music, movement, and gaze, they create an audio-visual courtship, a complex imagery of miscegenation.

The romanticization of the black cleaning woman, transformed into an inspiring muse, takes an additional disturbing overtone given the real and larger sociopolitical context of contemporary migration to Europe, particularly the growing number of African girls trafficked to Europe for either domestic servitude or sexual exploitation or both—a twenty-first century version of slavery. Taking the question of the film's ambiguous message a step further, does *Besieged* break the dichotomy of master/slave? Or, alternately, does it present the final degradation of African women, exploiting the last resources that the third world has left to sell—sex and nurturing, as Shandurai's love goes to the white master? Bertolucci also seems to suggest that housework is sexy, thus reinforcing the idea of women cleaning up after men that has long been a male fantasy. The body of the black cleaning woman is not only fetishized, but it also becomes an ornament, an aestheticized beautiful form which, like the other artifacts in Kinsky's mansion, adorns the white master's decadent Roman flat.[33]

The aestheticization of domestic, dirty labor is most notable in the scenes when Shandurai is descending or ascending the magnificent spiral staircase in Kinsky's home. The graceful movements of Shandurai along the stairway, reminiscent of the famous stairs in Hitchcock's *Vertigo* (1958), are a visual spectacle of a beautiful black form in a decadent European villa. Shandurai becomes a seductive ornament within the stunning visual choreography of the film, built, according to Bertolucci, like a musical work.[34] She becomes an ornamental expression of black labor (literally, symbolically, and legally). In the ideological scheme of the film, Shandurai is the ultimate beautiful and refined "primitivist" ornament in Kinsky's stunning mansion. She is, perhaps, the most beautiful object of the many artifacts with which he surrounds himself.

Figure 3.1. Shandurai (Thandie Newton), a young African refugee and a "black muse" in Bernardo Bertolucci's fantasy of miscegenation, *Besieged*.
COURTESY OF THE BFI

In the real "New Europe," it should be noted, in contrast to the benign version of black labor Bertolucci's style shows, Shandurai's work is part of the growing untaxed black labor economy based on the exploitation of illegal vulnerable immigrants. To the contrary, both Bertolucci and his interviewer in *Cineaste*, Bruce Sklarew, discuss the numerous references in the film to "whiteness" and obsessive cleaning in terms of "therapy," thus completely suppressing the interlinked dimensions of class and race which are integral not only to the particular narrative construction of *Besieged* but also to the larger contemporary European context.[35] Yet, as I shall show later, Shandurai's repetitive, almost compulsive dusting and cleaning of Kinsky's decadent flat and its artifacts can be read subversively, on the level of the film's political symbolism, as an act of re-dusting old Europe of its archaic and old-fashioned values and traditions.

The film's ambiguous message can also be evaluated in terms of the dialogics between the lovers. Their musical duet/dialogue starts as a monologue when Kinsky confesses his love to Shandurai for the first time. His confession is arrogant, insensitive, egocentric, and ultimately Eurocentric. When Kinsky tells Shandurai in a patronizing tone, "We can go anywhere. I'll go anywhere with you. We can go to Africa," Shandurai in an emotional outburst cries in response: "What do you know about Africa?" And indeed Kinsky, as most Westerners, knows nothing about Africa, the dark spot on the European conscience. Later in the film, Kinsky may have learned to conduct a more equitable dialogue between himself and Shandurai, Europe and Africa. But the question still remains whether this is indeed a dialogue between equals. Does their joint cross-cultural hybrid music composed of different tastes, preferences, and traditions constitute an example of a true dialogism? The title of the film, running on an image of an African folk singer, leaves the words of the song incomprehensible to the Western audience. Bertolucci chose not to translate the African song. His choice thus reproduces the incomprehensible silence of Africa as manufactured by the Western media and perceived by Western audiences. "What do you know about Africa?" becomes the cardinal question posed and challenged by the film but also built into its own ideology. Communication, between man and woman, white and black, master and slave, Europe and Africa, the colonizer and the colonized, thus remains within the boundaries of a phallocentric binary logic.

This binary logic is echoed also by the structure of the film and its orchestration of the gaze of desire. In the first part of the film Kinsky spies on Shandurai, his curious gaze attempting to penetrate and explore her difference.[36] In the second part of the film, Shandurai spies on Kinsky, trying to make sense of his changing behavior after he confesses his love to her and she commands him: "You get my husband out of jail" (implying, according to one reading, that if he does that, she—or rather her body—would be his).[37] In one of Shandurai's daydreaming sequences, the African singer appears dressed in a red shirt and Western suit. In this scene, Shandurai is seen removing posters of the African dictator, whose face is replaced with Kinsky's. In Shandurai's dream, the tyrannical boss (the *padrone*) turns out to be none other than Kinsky, her white master.

Shandurai's only moment of true liberation is conveyed in the scene when she dances with Agostino, her gay friend.[38] Their friendship is based on the solidarity of the outsiders and the marginal, the "others" of Italian society. Shandurai's childlike attributes (her baby face, her "naïvete" when confronted with the serious, heavy European music) fits traditional colonialist attitudes that view "primitive" people as children. Indeed, only children come to Kinsky's special concert and Shandurai becomes like one of them.[39] These children are Kinsky's students whom he tutors (like his attempt to tutor her). But as a tutor/*padre* Kinsky fails to educate Shandurai, who resists his attempts to make her his "fair lady," a black African woman who appreciates European music. Her partial capitulation, her surrender to the white master, occurs when she joins his music with the dance and "music" of the vacuum cleaner. The film leaves it open as to whether Shandurai is Kinsky's student or the reverse. Their musical duet seems to suggest that they both are tutors and students alike, teaching each other yet also learning from one another. In the remarkable concert scene, the camera privileges the face of a little blonde girl who is the only one who follows Kinsky's performance with admiring eyes, with some tight close-ups. The little blonde girl seems to be hypnotized by his playing (unlike the black "girl," Shandurai, who does not understand or appreciate Kinsky's playing), and the shots of her attentive and apprecia- tive facial expression, which suggest her admiration and understanding of European high culture as well as enhance her white beauty, are interrupted by intercuts to the semi-bored black face of Shandurai. One type of racial beauty and its associated cultural capital (or lack of it) is compared to another. It is as if Bertolucci is asking the spectators to compare and contemplate (or per- haps consume) two binary types of female beauty and their adjunct cultural associations.[40]

It is quite interesting to note that although *Besieged* constructs the black woman as an object of desire, both for the protagonist and the spectator's gaze, it constructs the white European male as an object of desire for Shan- durai only. This is most obvious in the last scene when Shandurai ascends to Kinsky's bedroom and tenderly opens the buttons of his shirt to reveal a white delicate flesh. While in most contemporary analyses of racial encounters the tendency is to discuss the other's (the nonwhite) body as the object of desire and exoticized fetishism, in Frantz Fanon's "The Woman of Color and the White Man" the discussion centers on the white man as the object of desire for the woman of color. Fanon argues that the great dream that haunts both the mulatto and black woman, to marry a white European man, is based on their belief that such a union will enable them to move up the social ladder, "from the class of slaves to that of masters."[41] And indeed, it can be argued, this desire is conveyed, visually and symbolically, in *Besieged* through Shan- durai's ascending from the basement into Kinsky's bedroom upstairs in the last scene of the film.

Europe and the Third Space

Despite the binary logic so evident in *Besieged,* the film can be read as at- tempting to challenge and deconstruct the very same logic with which it is imbued. It tries to break the binarism of man/woman, black/white, master/slave, expatriate, and voluntary privileged exile/involuntary exile-refugee. The role of music is instrumental in achieving this flight from binarism and it also shifts from contrapuntal to duet. While Kinsky, as the wealthy old-fashioned romantic English expatriate, lives near one of the landmarks of Rome, Shandurai, as the African refugee, lives in hybrid, third-world Rome. Her Rome is not only the Spanish Steps, the space inhibited by Keats and Shelly, the English Romantic poets, but the Rome of the third space inhabited by migrants and people of the third world. Shandurai is shown shopping in open crowded markets (supposedly near Rome's Stazione Termini or Piazza di Republica), where only migrants and nonwhites are to be seen. Shandurai's Rome is the other Rome, or the Rome of the others: migrants, foreigners, homosexuals (Agostino, the homosexual, is her only friend). Shandurai makes Kinsky go out into the world, outside the secluded privileges of his mansion, class, race, and culture. She forces him to confront reality, to face the Rome that is beyond the boundaries of white privilege.

Few capitals, as John Dickie observes, "have generated a field of connotations as complex as Rome, symbol at once of glory and decadence, transnational Christianity and national redemption, imperialism and civic republicanism."[42] Bertolucci's *Besieged,* however, contributes yet another dimension to the image of the eternal city: miscegenation through migration. Inherent in this new image of Rome is a radical change in the kind of Italian nation one imagines. And nowhere is the combined phenomenon of miscegenation and immigration more salient than in contemporary Western Europe's metropolitan centers, which have become hybrid spaces of class, ethnicity, nationality, and internationality, a "third world space" within the first world.[43] The contemporary Western metropolis, Rome included, has become the locus of the first world's metropolitan centers' fears and anxieties of being linguistically and culturally engulfed ("swamped" as the former British Home Office Secretary, David Blunkett, notoriously put it) by inassimilable others viewed as demographically, economically, and culturally threatening. Eurocentric and xenophobic rejection of the other engenders an apocalyptic vision of the West symbolically annihilated by uncontrollable others. The fears of the city being contaminated and polluted through miscegenation by immigrants are particularly powerful with regard to the capital, the center of national pride. Thus the Spanish Steps, one of Rome's landmarks, occupies a central symbolic role in the film's projection and negotiation of these anxieties. As Dickie points out in his discussion of *Roma, città aperta* (*Rome, Open City* [Roberto Rossellini, 1944]), the opening scene, in which singing German soldiers are seen marching across the Spanish Steps, encapsulates Rome's "dominant system of *differentiation*."[44] In Bertolucci's film, however, the center of Rome is also invaded, but this time not by the foreigners of the Nazi army but by an "army" of foreigners, poor refugees from the third world.

Kinsky's house, situated in the heart of historic Rome, can also be seen as a metaphor for Europe, specifically "Old Europe": white, privileged, dusty, cluttered, over-refined, eccentric, and decadent. This is "Fortress Europe," closed to non-European others. Yet, the film seems to suggest, the fortress of wealth and privilege should be open to others, to create a multicultural "New Europe" where miscegenation, popular culture, open-air "ethnic" markets, and nonwhite migrants exist side by side with white privilege. Within the scope of this utopian vision, Europe becomes the third space: space of miscegenation and hybridity. If Kinsky's home territory, crowded with artifacts and saturated with Western refinement, is the material embodiment of the values of decadent, white, and privileged Europe, the totality of its cultural capital, then its transformation into an empty apartment, after he sells all his possessions in order to free Shandurai's husband, is the new European habitus shared by the wealthy white Europeans and their nonwhite guests (or slaves).

Indeed, the English expatriate's mansion becomes the metaphor for Europe in more ways than one. The uncovering of the walls of Kinsky's mansion from their rich red brocade tapestry is a symbolic enactment of the unveiling of "Old Europe." Europe's decadence (a recurrent motif in Bertolucci's work) is thereby exposed and refurbished. Shandurai repeatedly tells Kinsky: "There is so much to dust," thus suggesting the need to renew and clean old, dusty, and cluttered Europe. Expanding the focus radiating outward from the house, the space of Rome is itself becoming in part a "third world space" (especially near the Stazione Termini), losing its traditional romantic appeal in favor of a new shared space for old and new Europe. As much as Kinsky's mansion needs to be emptied of its old wealth, transmitted from one generation to the next, so, the film implies, does the continent's old wealth, based on her imperial power, need to be shared with poor and impoverished Africa. A complementary reading would understand the film as suggesting that "Old Europe" and particularly Italy, which suffers from the lowest birth rate in Europe, need new blood.[45]

Interlinked with the idea of Europe as a new shared space, the third space of the rich and the poor, is the class metaphor that is built into the film's narrative and visuals. The spatial division of Kinsky's home is, in fact, a replica of the Marxist metaphor of base and superstructure. Shandurai lives downstairs in the basement, where she is under the surveillance of her master's curious gaze. Kinsky (the white upper-class patron) lives upstairs. The dumbwaiter connects the master and slave and is used as their main channel of communication, the mediator between privilege and non-privilege. At the end of the film, Shandurai ascends to Kinsky's bedroom and when miscegenation takes place the stratification of space by class division seems to disappear. The classical Marxist metaphor is invested with the symbolism of racial and global divisions of whiteness versus blackness, first world versus third world, as well as the south/north divide. An additional layer of meaning is thus added to the stripping of Kinsky's house of its excessive accessories (the ultimate signifiers of western culture), namely the attempt to break down the global structure of racial and class privilege.

Kinsky's home is not only a space of luxury and decadence but also a tomb, a Roman catacomb where the inheritor of white privilege leads an isolated and secluded life. Kinsky lives semi-dead and semi-deaf in his enclosure, with its oft-closed shutters. Shandurai brings her vitality to Kinsky's sepulcher. Her stormy intrusion into his sealed-off life is a European director's fantasy of a symbolic message sent by the third world to the first world that it is about time to negotiate shared space. The European masters have now to share their space with the slaves. This is a call for negotiation before it is too late. Hence Kinsky's act of stripping himself from material things recalls another film by Bertolucci, *The Last Emperor,* where Pu Yi is stripped of his luxurious possessions and like Voltaire's Candide is left to cultivate his garden.

The Heart of Whiteness

Does *Besieged* convey romantic racism or a racist romanticism? Does it offer a universal and ahistorical "message" on the power of love which disavows the historical situation of global market forces and the exploitation of semi-slave migrant workers? Does it offer a celebratory reception of hybridization and miscegenation, or does it reveal a latent fear of it? (Bertolucci himself in many interviews referred to this hybridization as a positive "cultural 'contamination,'" hence using a racist discourse in order to subvert it.)[46] *Besieged* is a film not only made by a director commonly referred to as a European art cinema filmmaker, but also heavily imbued in style and content with what has come to be regarded as traditional European sensibilities: the cult of high art, visual density, nostalgia for old Europe, and so on. Yet, as my analysis attempts to show, *Besieged* not only indulges in traditional "Europeanness," but also challenges and criticizes it, thus exposing European ambivalence toward its others. This ambivalence, in turn, opens the space not only for the expansion and collapse of the category of Europeanness into blackness and/or African-ness but also for contradictory, yet complementary, readings of *Besieged*.

A favorable reading of *Besieged* views it as a progressive film celebrating hybridity. It is not a colonialist film but rather an emancipatory film that tries to close the gap between two worlds. In this view, it is a film about a positive cross-fertilization of Europe and Africa, a creolization and hybridization of cultures and colors, of two civilizations, continents, and colors. Shandurai's music is gradually absorbed by Kinsky, who learns to love and respect her difference. Consequently, his music becomes less and less Western, taking on the sound of what is now known as "world music." A less favorable reading of the film would regard the absorption of African music by Kinsky as another postcolonial strategy of appropriating or rather stealing the native/indigenous culture while turning it into yet another exoticized Western commodity.

A positive reading of the film would argue that *Besieged* presents wealthy and decadent Europe through the metaphor of Kinsky's flat, stripping and baring itself of its ornaments, artifacts, and cultural fetishes (including its classical music) in order to conduct a dialogue of equality with poor Africa. The competing interpretation would question the significance of buying Winston's freedom with money and through bribery. Adding ambiguity to this reading is the fact that Kinsky appeals to Shandurai not when he is rich but, paradoxically or not, only when he becomes poor. He manages to "possess" her when he becomes dispossessed. A critical reading of the film, however, would argue that Kinsky's behavior is only exploitation and racism masquerading as altruism. Indeed, he lost the artifacts that adorned his mansion and decorated his refined lifestyle, but at the same time he won the most beautiful object of all: the black woman from Africa. This reading resonates also with a critical reading of the religious aspect of *Besieged,* which depicts an Evangelical Christianity imported by African migrants into the Eternal City. The good black priest who helps Kinsky to release Winston from jail tells him, "He who tries to save his life will lose it and he who gives it away will be saved." Kinsky emerges in the film as a Christ (and also as a Buddha) figure. The film posits the icon of the dispossessed and altruist Kinsky, the white master and not the black slave, as the ultimate victim.

Besieged can also be read as an economic transaction. Kinsky, the white man, buys the release (freedom) of Shandurai's husband and in so doing achieves the status of liberator of black slaves. But is it possible to buy freedom? And what is the significance of Winston being in Europe? Will he necessarily succeed (because he is well educated and potentially maintains the desired status of a "genuine asylum seeker"), or might he become one of the millions of poor black migrants in Europe, referred by European anti-immigration discourse as "economic migrants"? Read as an economic equation, the transaction is hardly liberating. According to the implied contract between them, Kinsky will release Shandurai's husband and she will become his. He will own her. If Shandurai will open the door to Winston (which is the question left open by the film's ending), they both will be Kinsky's slaves. Kinsky thus will have two black slaves. The image of Winston, a black African in a foreign city, banging at the door of Kinsky's mansion becomes (like the image of the refugees banging at the glass wall of the heated pool spa in *Journey of Hope*) an iconic image of the desperate others banging at the wall of Fortress Europe.

A more favorable interpretation of *Besieged* would argue that Kinsky learns how to conduct a dialogue of equality, or a dialogue between equals, by dispossessing himself/Europe. But can there ever be a dialogue of equals in such a context? Bertolucci's *Last Tango in Paris* opens with a "naked" flat in Paris as a setting that brings out the real "essence" of love and its sexual material base. Although opening with a cluttered, packed house, *Besieged* also ends with an empty, bare one, presumably exposing the essence of pure love based on selfless sacrifice. But is it really selfless and is it really a sacrifice? The white and refined European thinks that he can possess Shandurai just as the white master in the past owned his black female slaves. Is not their new contract (I'll be yours if you release my husband) a postcolonial replica of slavery? Does *Besieged* really critique the power relationship of the liberal version of the master/slave formula, or does it, implicitly or explicitly, subscribe to it?[47]

The black continent in this film is an abstraction, a continent of the mind, an imagined dark continent. Shandurai comes from an unnamed African state. Unlike in the "trilogy of the other," Bertolucci no longer goes to the other (China, Africa, India/Nepal/Tibet) to shoot this film because the other comes to Europe instead. This is the other within. It is no longer possible to ignore Africa because it no longer exists only in the periphery of the globe but at the heart of whiteness, Europe. The heart of darkness is thus inverted. The heart of darkness, rather than residing outside the European body, is transplanted into it. In *Besieged,* as in *Stealing Beauty,* Bertolucci goes back to Italy. But this is not Chiantishire populated by middle-class Brits and Germans in search of Europe's sunny romantic south; this is Rome, Italy's capital, "invaded" by poor migrants from Africa and Asia.

Much like *Last Tango in Paris, Besieged* is a love story between two continents, two cultures. Here, however, Europe is not confronted with America but with Africa, and more precisely with the Africa within (unlike *The*

Sheltering Sky, for example, which depicts a traumatic encounter between a white American couple and black Africa).[48] Bertolucci himself has said that the film could be "considered a kind of postmodern variation on the *Tango* theme."[49] A quarter of a century after *Last Tango in Paris,* Bertolucci's revolutionary thesis on sex and politics, the Italian director returns to the same territory and tells the same story, about a man and woman from two different backgrounds and cultures who meet in a flat. As in *Tango,* the man and woman meet only inside the space (womb) of the flat, secluded from the outside world. And, as in *Tango,* they know nothing about each other. But whereas in *Tango* the scandalous effect derived from the presentation of the relationships as purely sexual, *Besieged* is a story about a selfless and sacrificial love. Whereas in *Tango* the flat was completely empty (except for a mattress on the bare floor), in *Besieged* the flat is crowded with furniture, sculptures, and tapestries. Gradually, however, it is stripped of its content, and toward the end we see Kinsky lying on a red mattress in an empty flat in a position that recalls Brando's position in *Tango* before the famous (and notorious) sodomy scene, in which Brando (wearing a red sweater) compares his rape to the symbolic rape enacted by the whole social system, represented in his "red" sermonizing rhetoric by the bourgeois family and the church. A television set now stands in the place where once the piano (the ultimate signifier of European refinement) stood and in the background a sound track of a car race replaces the romantic music of the piano, signifying, perhaps, the death of old Europe.[50] *Besieged*'s ambivalence exposes Europe's longstanding ambivalence about Africa, the "dark continent," which is also the "white man's burden" and the "dark spot on the European conscience," in Tony Blair's famous dictum.[51]

4

INTIFADA OF THE
BANLIEUES
LA HAINE REVISITED

*They [the Jews] have allowed themselves to be positioned by the
stereotype that others have of them, and they live in fear that
their acts will correspond to this stereotype. . . . We may say that
their conduct is perpetually overdetermined from the inside.*

Jean-Paul Sartre, Anti-Semite and Jew

*All the same, the Jew can be unknown in his Jewishness. He is not
wholly what he is. One hopes, one waits. His actions, his behavior,
are the final determinant. He is a white man, and apart from some
debatable characteristics, he can sometimes go unnoticed.*

Frantz Fanon, *Black Skin, White Masks* (in response to Sartre)

Mathieu Kassovitz's *La Haine*, which came out in 1995 and regained
new life and "surplus value" during the 2005 and 2007 riots in France,
chronicles, in mock-documentary fashion, one day in the life of three
male youths from a *banlieue* (a rough, housing estate/housing project near
Paris): the black Hubert (Hubert Koundé), the white Jew Vinz (Vincent Cassel), and the *beur* (second-generation North African) Saïd (Saïd Taghmaoui).
The renewed interest in the film, concurrent with the eruption of the autumn
2005 riots in France, is a further testimony to the ongoing symbolic political
power associated with this film and its potential to explain, explore, and an-
ticipate complex phenomena related to youth culture and consequent social
unrest. During the 2005 riots (but even before), Kassovitz achieved "expert"
status on a controversial and complex social phenomenon—purely by virtue
of having directed a fictional film about youth in the *banlieue*.[1]

Figure 4.1. The "black/blanc/beur" trio of *beur*/*banlieue* cinema:
The black Hubert (Hubert Koundé), the white Jew Vinz (Vincent Cassel),
and the *beur* (second-generation North African) Saïd (Saïd
Taghmaoui) in Mathieu Kassovitz's *La Haine*.
COURTESY OF THE BFI

Most of the discussions of *La Haine,* winner of the Cannes Film Festival
in 1995, the French Cesars in 1996, and one of the major films to appear in
postcolonial, increasingly multi-ethnic France, focused on the film as representative of the three "b's" of *beur*/*banlieue* cinema, or, in the words of
Mireille Rosello, on the "black/blanc/beur" trio.[2] Although *La Haine* is not
the first film associated with the French genre of the *banlieue* film, it has
already been canonized as its prime example due, perhaps, to the fact that it
was the first film representative of this genre that enjoyed international success. The film's critique of urban alienation and racism against migrants and
ethnic minorities challenges dominant assumptions about French national
identity, and its success in globalizing images of oppression suggests that
there is a wide interest in the popularization of social critique through film.

Many critics have suggested that *La Haine* conducts transatlantic dialogue with American urban subculture and American popular culture as a

way of examining, articulating, and forging French and European identity through cinema. They also have suggested that *La Haine* managed to transcend its particular local French context and become part of an emerging Western, or even global, genre of film about the revolts of migrant and ethnic diasporas in the ghettos and urban margins of the big metropolitan centers of the West. Critics have also argued that *La Haine* seeks to connect the urban rebellion depicted in the film not only to a global ghetto culture but to wider postcolonial struggles.[3]

Missing from among these many insightful and important interpretations is a significant reference to the fact that the first *banlieue/beur* film (or, in the words of Sharma and Sharma, "the most celebrated and most commercial of the so-called 'banlieue films' to emerge out of France in recent years")[4] was made not by an "authentic" member of the *beur* community but rather by a French Jew. The only meaningful exceptions are some of the independent low-budget Maghrebi filmmakers in France who produced *banlieue/beur* films around the same time as *La Haine*.[5] These filmmakers accused Kassovitz of "being an outsider and producing an inauthentic account of the *banlieue* in France."[6]

This chapter expands on previous discussions of *La Haine* by concentrating specifically on the construction of the image of the Jew within the film's representation of a multi-ethnic, multiracial, and multi-religious trio. Through this exploration, I hope not only to raise questions regarding self-representation of "the Jew" in *La Haine*, but also to reflect on the justified ethical questions raised by the *beur* filmmakers, who criticized Kassovitz on issues pertaining to "authenticity," the legitimacy of representing "other" communities, and commercial exploitation of oppressed minorities in cinema. By shifting the boundaries of the debate on *La Haine* from the *banlieue* genre to the relationship between what I call the "post-Holocaust" French Jew and the postcolonial context which characterizes the condition of contemporary France, I attempt to offer a different perspective on this highly controversial film.

The reason I attribute so much historical importance to one film, overloading it with meaning, is my understanding of *La Haine* as an emblematic film on and of the new Europe. As a film about the experience of migration from the colonial periphery to the postcolonial metropolis, *La Haine* not only signifies the emergence of Europe's new strangers and others, but also the shift from the "Jew" as the classical other of old Europe to the principal others of the new Europe: the postcolonial Arabs, the South Asian Muslims, and the African blacks.

The image of the Jew in *La Haine* presents the complexity of the idea of the Jew and of the Jewish response to his projection of difference in Western culture in general and in European cinema in particular. My concern in this chapter is not only the image of the Jew in *La Haine,* but the forces that shape this image of difference. My assumption is inspired by the observation made by Sander Gilman that "the Jew in the Western Diaspora does respond, must respond, to the image of the Jews in such cultures."[7] Kassovitz's response is to construct a new image of the diasporic Jew, which responds not only to traditional images of the Jew in Western culture but also to the weakness and vulnerability associated with the Jew as a victim of the Holocaust. Through the figure of Vinz, the post-Holocaust Jew, the film resists the traditional stereotype of the Jew.

Following Kassovitz himself, I focus on the representation of the Jewish male, which, as Gilman suggests, "lies at the very heart of Western Jew-hatred."[8] In the post-Holocaust Jewish imagination, it is the male who is assigned to revenge Jewish victimization epitomized by the Holocaust.[9] Vinz's ambivalent relationships to power, manifested through his obsessive fascination with and fetishization of the pistol—the phallocentric signifier of male power—versus his inability to actually shoot and kill, as evidenced in the scene with the skinheads, therefore represent the larger post-Holocaust Jewish condition.

Through the figure of Vinz, *La Haine* constructs a Jewish identity, which, like all Jewish identities constructed across Western cultures after the Second World War, cannot be dissociated from the memories of the Holocaust. As Jonathan Webber perceptively observes, "In Jewish perspective, it was the Holocaust that constituted the unmaking of Europe; it is this, and virtually only this, that has to be seen as providing the basic script of today's Europe."[10] The Holocaust is also the "script" that provides Kassovitz's screenplay with the figure of Vinz, the new post-Holocaust Jew in the new postcolonial Europe.

For obvious reasons, to represent a Jew after the Holocaust, particularly in European cinema, is a problematic and delicate endeavor. The absence of the Jew, and particularly contemporary living Jews, from postwar European cinema is, paradoxically, more "visible," especially given antisemitic representations that proliferated in European cinema before and during the Second World War. This absence is almost total when it comes to French films made by non-Jewish directors. Yet, according to René Prédal, the Jew made a comeback to French cinema in the 1970s with *Les Aventures de Rabbi Jacob* (1973), directed by Gérard Oury.[11] This revival, however, was generated mainly by Jewish filmmakers whose films have constructed mixed documents of real and imaginary Jewish self-representations. These films do not represent how the national subject (those whose belonging to the dominant group is seldom, if ever, called into question) views Jews and Jewishness. But they correspond to the way those inscribed as others or insiders-outsiders see themselves or want to present themselves to the dominant French culture for which the Jew and Jewishness continue, as Rosello suggests, to remain "an elusive signifier."[12]

Who is this "imaginary" Jew constructed by *La Haine*? Why do I call him imaginary? How is he contextualized within the framework of postcolonial and post-World War II France as manifested in the *banlieue* genre? And what role does he play in the "new" or "post-Europe"? These and similar questions gain an even greater significance in light of Elizabeth Ezra's observation that the history of French antisemitism cannot be conflated or confused with France's colonial legacy. However, these two exclusionary discourses, according to Ezra, often go hand in hand and both are "at least to some extent, born of the same desire on the part of France to stake out a place for itself in the phantasmatic hierarchy of cultures."[13]

The "comeback" of the Jew in French cinema is, to a certain extent, part of the return of the Jew, Jewishness, and Judaism as an exotic "ethnic" commodity in the French, and to a large extent the European, cultural scene.[14] Kassovitz's films *Métisse* (1993) and *La Haine* are particularly interesting in this context because they not only create the "black/blanc/beur trio" but they also construct the Jew within this trio as an invisible ethnic: a "white" member of a multicultural trio who is eventually exposed as a poor, working-class, and therefore non-stereotypical contemporary West European Jew.[15]

The Young Angry Jewish Man: The Ambivalence of Jewish Power in the Post-Holocaust Age

In the post-Holocaust Jewish context, the task of redeeming Jewish weakness, epitomized by the Holocaust, was assigned to the "new Jews" (i.e., the Israelis and particularly the mythological Sabra). Beginning in the late 1970s, with the growing confidence of the Jewish communities in the Diaspora, both in the United States and Europe (predominantly residing in France, the second largest Jewish community in Europe after the post-Soviet community), this "task" was also adopted by some marginal yet militant ultra-nationalist Jewish groups and organizations.[16] *La Haine* both exemplifies and problematizes the dialectics associated with Jewish power in the post-Holocaust age in two key scenes: the encounter of the trio in a public lavatory with the elderly

Jew who tells them a story about another Jew, Grunwalski, and the trio's encounter with the skinheads. These scenes are central to understanding not only the image of the Jew constructed by Kassovitz, but also to the idealized multi-ethnic trio to which his Jewish protagonist belongs.

The first scene introduces the audience to the Holocaust Jew, the survivor played by Tadek Lokcinski, the Jewish grandfather in Kassovitz's *Métisse,* who like many Eastern European Jews and Polish Jews of the Holocaust generation is very short and has a distinctive Yiddish accent. To the French audience, he looks like Popeck, a Jewish actor who in the late 1970s initiated French culture into Eastern European Jewish culture and made it popular and chic for the French intelligentsia.[17] In this scene, the little old Jew tells the trio about a man named Grunwalski who missed the cattle train en route to a labor camp in Siberia because he goes to relieve himself in the woods. When the train is about to leave, his trousers are not on and he is too embarrassed to run after the train while his private parts are exposed. Grunwalski eventually died of cold after the train left.[18] This thought-provoking narrative digression confronts the spectator with Jewish weakness associated with the Holocaust, of the predicament of being literally "caught with one's pants down." It gives the trio and the spectators alike some food for thought and leaves them wondering about the meaning of the story. What is ostensibly a digression in fact emerges as a narrative locus providing the historical and ideological pretext for Vinz's behavior.

The location of the scene is significant. It takes place in a men's public toilet, an all-male public (yet semi-private/secret) space invested with associations of prostitution, AIDS, and casual homosexual relations, including anal sex. The story about Grunwalski, as told by the elderly Jew, also deals with anal themes, and its thematic core is centered on the consequences of the desire to defecate in privacy. The choice to use the men's public toilet as the background mise-en-scène for invoking the Holocaust is indeed unusual, although only one of many puzzling stories, unresolved anecdotes, bizarre jokes, and digressions from the main narrative that characterize the plot structure of *La Haine.* But the connotations of "being caught with one's pants down" is not restricted only to the anal connotations of being in a men's room (alluding to its phallic connotations, this is also a place where men compare each other's penises). The subtext of not wanting one's pants to fall down is the fear of exposing one's circumcised penis, a fear explored in many representations and stories about World War II and the Holocaust, best exemplified by Agnieszka Holland's *Europa, Europa* (1991).[19] Yet of all the narrative digressions in this film, the most disturbing and enigmatic is this bathroom encounter with the elderly Jew and his story about Grunwalski. Saïd speaks for the spectators in repeatedly asking, "pourquoi il nous raconte ça?" (Why is he telling us this?), and Hubert's vague explanations only accentuate the ambiguity.

The similarities between the story about Grunwalski and the state of the postcolonial trio, an "anal" story told in a public lavatory, Grunwalski missing the train and the trio missing the metro, the Jewishness common to the "little Jew" and "big Vinz," the history of racial oppression and the attempt to maintain human dignity even in the face of racial persecution, beg for an allegorical reading. What is the relationship, then, between this episode that introduces the Holocaust through the back door, or, to put it crudely, through the lavatory door, and the major plot of *La Haine*? Does the story told by the little Jew bear any significance for the life of the three? Can it help them in any way to resolve their own problems? Are there any similarities between the story of Grunwalski and that of the trio and the little Jew? And does this little story, as told by the little Jew (an almost insignificant story in itself within the framework of the "grand narrative of the Holocaust"), imply that the Holocaust has any "lesson" for the postcolonial trio? Does the Jew's story contain the potential answer to the conflict between Vinz and Hubert over how to respond to Abdel's death, an expression of racist oppression? (Vinz's wish is to avenge the death by murdering a French policeman, whereas Hubert's objection is based on the arguments that hatred breeds hatred and violence begets violence.)

The careful attention given by Kassovitz to the mise-en-scène of this narrative digression shows that he attributes enormous significance to what seems on the surface to be a narrative slippage and pushes the spectators even further toward an allegorical reading of the scene. In the frame, we see only Saïd's and Hubert's reflections appearing on the bathroom mirrors while their backs are facing each other. Saïd talks over the phone and does not take part in the discussion between Vinz and Hubert. The little elderly Jew surprises the three when he emerges from the toilet. He does not look at all frightened (something that we would expect from an involuntary witness to a discussion over whether or not to murder a policeman, a little "white" guy confronted by three big, aggressive-looking youngsters), and without pausing for a moment he starts telling his story in heavily accented French. In contrast to the three, whom we see only as reflections, the little Jew is seen not as a reflection in the mirror but as a direct image. His figure thus attains a certain quality of reality (he is "real" and not a reflection of the real, to paraphrase Godard's famous aphorism) but, conversely, he gains a certain quality of phantom surrealism because in a room full of mirrors he is not reflected at all.

Figure 4.2. Introducing the Holocaust through the lavatory door. Vinz (Vincent Cassel) and Hubert (Hubert Koundé) in Mathieu Kassovitz's *La Haine*.
<small>COURTESY OF THE BFI</small>

Does the Jew intend his story as a pedagogical parable for the three because he heard their discussion and wants to teach them a moral lesson through his story, or is he just queer (literally and metaphorically)? And even if he did not intend to deliver a didactic message, does his story still contain a moral lesson? Perhaps even a post-Holocaust lesson? These questions seem to perplex the trio as well. However, their attempt to make sense out of this bizarre story fails and Grunwalski's story remains an unresolved riddle, an empty story devoid of meaning, a story about a meaningless and grotesque death.

The failure of the young men to make sense out of this encounter with the little Jew and his story generates yet another allegory: an allegory on the blindness of postcolonial Europe to read its present in light of its recent past. Europe's failure to understand the consequences of racism and to treat its postcolonial and other minorities justly, even in light of the aftermath of the Holocaust, is the tragic point where the Holocaust and the postcolonial meet. The inability of the three to read their own life narratives against the backdrop of Grunwalski's story (which can be seen as a commentary on the meaninglessness of racism and genocide) signifies the artificial rupture between the post-Holocaust state of the so-called post-Europe and its ongoing racializing practices in the age of postcolonialism.

Kassovitz introduces this theme most prominently in Vinz's idea of avenging Abdel's death by murdering a policeman, which provokes Hubert, who is more pragmatic and self-controlled, to denounce Vinz's desire. A verbal conflict ensues and Saïd and Hubert separate from the hateful and vindictive Vinz. Vinz's loneliness, his feeling of being deserted even by his closest friends at this painful moment, is conveyed through a Godardian composition which shows him isolated in the frame on the backdrop of a huge stone or concrete sculpture of an open palm holding a head. The huge sculpture dwarfs Vinz and exposes his fragility and sense of helplessness and isolation. The visual choreography of the shot creates an ironic gap between the grandeur of Vinz's revenge fantasy and the limits of his power. "I know who I am and where I come from," Vinz cries out to his friends who have deserted him. In this scene, as in many others in the film, Kassovitz enables the spectator to read the film's heroes "against the grain" by enjoying and sharing the ironic perspective of the omniscient narrator who, despite Vinz's challenging and provocative cry, does not know who he is and certainly not where he comes from. Positioned at the threshold of committing murder, Vinz's words recall a famous mishnaic precept: "Akavia Ben Mahallel said: Ponder three things and you will avoid falling into the grip of sin: Know whence you come, whither you go, and before whom you will be required to give an accounting."[20] Vinz alludes, however, not to the earth from which we come and to which we return but to his moral commitment, his expression of solidarity and sense of shared destiny with the wretched of the earth, the oppressed minorities of the *banlieue*. But in retrospect, after the spectator is made a witness to Vinz's death, his words obtain a full and fatal tragic meaning. If the words of the rabbinic Jewish text are meant to steer believers away from crime, then Vinz's cry for revenge reverses the original meaning of the Jewish text.

The logic of the narrative provides Vinz with an opportunity to avenge the unjust death of Abdel, his Arab friend, not through the murder of a police officer but rather through the murder of a skinhead who, along with his friends, attacks Hubert and Saïd. Vinz faces the skinhead, his pistol aimed at his bleeding head, but is unable to shoot him. Vinz's epiphany, his moment of enlightenment and truth, which is also the moment of reconciliation with his friends, occurs when he acknowledges his "weakness," his basic respect for human life and his fear of killing. Vinz confronts his Jewish weakness exactly at the moment when revenge and power can finally be obtained and even morally justified (as Hubert whispers to Vinz, "there are bad cops and good cops but the only good skinhead is a dead skinhead").[21] Kassovitz amplifies this moment of revelation in a self-reflexive manner.

The young skinhead is played by none other than Kassovitz himself, a Jewish director who within the diegetic world of *La Haine* acts like the creator, a sort of cinematic god in charge of the fictional space in which his creations are at the mercy of his powerful hand (much like the cinematic image of the sculpture of a huge open palm holding a head). This weird moment when Vinz, the child of Kassovitz's imagination, holds a pistol to the bleeding face of his director/creator, who made him suffer in the labyrinths of a narrative hell, is a moment of poetic justice which empowers Vinz. Vinz discovers that the meaning of real power is the acknowledgment of the limits of power (an acknowledgment which, by the end of the film, is revealed to be problematic, if not tragic). This scene also epitomizes the dialectics inherent in the state of the post-Holocaust Jew. The fictional Jew (Vinz) looks like a skinhead. Indeed, before the confrontation with the skinheads, Vinz says, "I see skinheads," to which Hubert reacts by saying, "You are a skinhead." Yet Vinz cannot shoot the fictional skinhead played by a real Jew who is also the source of enunciation and narrative authority of this film. The scene thus creates a situation of reflective duality of the self and its double/other. It is the moment when the Jew confronts his other/double in the mirror.

Vinz's fascination with phallic power and guns is ultimately revealed to be tragic. He cannot materialize his fantasy of absolute power by using it against the right "target" (the skinhead) and he renounces it exactly at the moment when its materialization could have saved his life. Thus does Vinz (who many times throughout the film declares that he will kill a cop so that they [the police] "know we don't turn the other cheek") accept his symbolic role as the Jewish Jesus who renounces hatred, revenge, and violence. In a symbolic gesture, Vinz gives his gun to Hubert who, contrary to stereotypical portrayals of blacks in American cinema (particularly in the blaxploitation cycle), is the most educated, restrained violence hater of the three.[22] A few moments later, the unarmed Vinz is killed by an armed police detective. The Jew who renounces violence, Kassovitz implies, brings about his own liquidation.

Why, in the words of Sharma and Sharma, are "hatred and the desire for violent revenge against figures of authority and an oppressive social formation . . . most evident in the character of Vinz"?[23] Sharma and Sharma explain

Vinz's fascination with guns and fetishes of power as the reaction of "marginalized masculinity,"[24] but they do not answer why of all the "marginalized ethnics" the Jew is the most violent and frustrated male.[25] Why in this film is the Jew's masculinity the most fragile and vulnerable? In terms of stereotypes, particularly those of contemporary violent American cinema to which *La Haine* constantly alludes and refers, we would normally expect the black to be the most violent and vengeful, and certainly not the Jew, traditionally portrayed as the victim of violence rather than its perpetrator.

The skinhead episode, therefore, is a key scene that provides us with a clue to understanding Kassovitz's portrayal of the not-so-typical Diaspora Jew. Vinz's "non-Jewish," "skinhead-ish" look is a subversive appropriation of the stereotype of the "Aryan" skinhead, and his unused gun is a manifestation of frustrated Jewish masculinity. In the perceptive words of Sharma and Sharma, Vinz is "on the brink of psychosis," and for him "violence is ultimately cathartic."[26] Vinz's morbid fascination with power is a travesty, a delayed revenge fantasy against the *goy*. Revenge, it should be noted, whether delayed or unsatisfied, has become a dominant (though not always open and/ or conscious and acknowledged) theme in post-Holocaust Jewish life and especially in the imaginative space of desire that the State of Israel occupies for many Diaspora Jews who perceive it as a tool of revenge against the *goy* (conveniently displaced onto the Arab and particularly the Palestinian).[27]

The image of the character of Vinz projects ambivalence. Although he is vengeful and obsessed with violence, at the moment of "truth" he is discovered as "weak." Despite his fantasies of violence, real violence makes Vinz sick. The diasporic post-Holocaust Jew is unable to redeem the shame inflicted on the Holocaust Jew by the possessors of absolute power. It is not surprising, therefore, that in the final scene the Jew returns to his "normal," "natural" place: that of the victim. Sharma and Sharma argue that the violence in *La Haine* should be understood in the context of the "boredom, indifference and alienation"[28] that characterize life in the *banlieue*. As far as modern reality is concerned, I agree. However, in the case of Vinz, I would argue that his relationships to violence and his almost primordial anger should be understood in a particular context related to the symbolic space that he occupies as the post-Holocaust imaginary Jew who has to negotiate Jewish ultimate subjection to organized violence in the form of the Holocaust.

The scene in Asterix's flat (Asterix is the name of a French popular comic series)[29] is used as a cinematic metonymy for this political process, a symbolic stage of confrontation between "ethnics" and migrants against "Frenchness" and particularly between the Jew and the "pure French." The difficulty of the three young "ethnics" to enter into Asterix's fancy flat (located in one of

Figure 4.3. A Jewish fantasy of absolute power: Vinz (Vincent Cassel),
the young angry Jewish man in Mathieu Kassovitz's *La Haine*.
Courtesy of the BFI

Paris's chic neighborhoods) symbolizes the difficulty for them to enter the center of the French national body. It seems that the young men possess neither the real nor the symbolic password to enter into this luxurious residence. Asterix's name shows that his is a "real" and "authentic" Frenchman, a Gaul who lives, in the words of Saïd, in a flat the size of a castle. Yet this "rooted" Frenchman is a drug dealer, a heavy user of cocaine who does not actually own the luxury flat. His excessive, extravagant, and exhibitionist sexuality (he dresses like Tarzan, moves in a sort of dancing gait, has long hair, and his behavior is seductive-aggressive) also problematizes his "straight Frenchness" as well as his sexual identity. Asterix challenges Vinz to a phallic battle over masculinity, made apparent when the two compare pistols hidden deep in their pants. This competition is not only over the size of their pistols but also for mastery over their "tools"; it turns into a comparison of "symbolic ethnicity" whereby the size of the circumcised penis of the Jew is compared to that of the non-Jew, the "real" Gaul. The competition turns into a performance, a staging of symbolic penis envy of the French Jew toward the French non-Jew, who demonstrates unquestionable superiority over the male Jew in mastering his pistol/penis.

This performance of competitive masculinity, tainted with racial overtones, develops into a power game of Russian roulette which can be seen as an act of symbolic suicide by Vinz and recalls his imitation of Travis Bickle from Martin Scorsese's *Taxi Driver* (1976) in front of the mirror at his home. Then, too, Vinz aimed a pistol at his own reflection in the mirror, in a sort of proleptic symbolic gesture of death wish or self-destruction. It could also be viewed as an unconscious prophecy of his imminent death, and as an expression of split identity. When the three men find that they are no longer welcome in Asterix's kingdom, they leave his apartment and he shows them how he secretly neutralized Vinz's pistol. Vinz's inferiority is thus publicly exposed and his feeling of humiliation and defeat is reinforced by the policemen who are waiting for them outside in the street. The attempt to break into the center through the hybridity of Asterix, the Gaul, fails. Asterix, despite his queerness, is still more powerful than the "ethnics"; it is he who makes the rules and breaks them at the same time. The violence portrayed in *La Haine,* despite its racial-ethnic dimensions, is also part of the heritage of May '68 and its radical cinema (it is therefore not surprising that many critics referred to Kassovitz as the child of Godard).[30] As Jewish French sociologist Shmuel Trigano observes, the May '68 events marked the end of "the hypercentralization of French society and political culture so characteristic of the Napoleonic model and opened the way to the recognition of secondary identities for French citizens."[31]

The Wandering Jew, Social Mobility, and Symbolic Spaces

The *banlieue,* as Berenice Reynaud argues, is a genre that uses the metaphor of space as an allegory for the unfair distribution of social justice.[32] The exclusion of the *banlieue* and its inhabitants from the metropolis and its loci of socioeconomic and cultural power is also generated, reproduced, and perpetuated by its geographical distance from the city center. As much as the migrants are culturally and symbolically excluded from the traditional symbols of Frenchness (the Eiffel Tower, Edith Piaf's *chansons*), so are they physically and mentally segregated in the outskirts of the city, at its periphery. In this respect, *La Haine* is also an attempt to re-imagine the city, an attempt at conquest by those who live at the margins and for whom the city, and everything it stands for (culture, money, assimilation), is distant and almost inaccessible.[33] Myrto Konstantarakos observes that the motif of mobility dominates both the verbal and the visual discourse generated by the black/blanc/beur trio of this hyperactive, nervous film.[34] The rootless trio wanders endlessly in the urban spaces of the *banlieue* (shot in Chanteloup-les-Vignes, the renewed Cité des Muguets) and central Paris as if their physical mobility is a compensation for their lack of social mobility. And because they do not own cars, and cannot even drive,[35] their physical movements, and consequently the potential for their social mobility from the *banlieue* to Paris, become difficult and problematic. The trio depends completely on public transportation (the metro)[36] in order to get to and from Paris. And because the policemen who tortured Saïd and Hubert at the police station detain them (deliberately) until very late at night, they miss the last train to the *banlieue* and get stuck in Paris in front of the Eiffel Tower, the tourist icon of Paris.

Within the framework of this spatial dialectic of oscillation between physical movement and social immobility, Vinz occupies an interesting position. In contrast to the stereotype of the diasporic Jew as ambitious, competitive, and socially mobile, Vinz is stuck at the bottom of the social ladder, forever doomed to live in the postcolonial ghetto of the *banlieue*. Unlike the image of the modern and postmodern diasporic Jew whose energy is cerebral and channeled toward social mobility, Vinz's energy is focused on physical aggression. Confined to the cement-covered, greenless wasteland of the *banlieue* ghetto and suffering from urban claustrophobia, the hyperactive, restless Vinz is always on the move in search of trouble. His aggressive body language, tense facial expression, and almost psychotic behavior turn him into a disturbing ahistorical image of the restless wandering Jew in search of revenge.

The overall pattern of movement in the film also demonstrates the allocation of space according to class. In the first part of the film, the heroes move within the space of the *banlieue*. In the second part, they venture out of the *banlieue* to Paris and move inside the city. The heroes' movement, as well as that of the camera and the plot, are almost endless. This nervous movement not only conveys a sense of restlessness and lack of peace of mind, but it also expresses a state in which fixity and belonging are impossible because the latter demands possessing a place or belonging to a place, something that is beyond the experience of the three young males. The trio's odyssey in Paris can thus be interpreted as a ritual return visit in reaction to the brutal invasion of the agents of the center (the cops, the media) into the *banlieue* after the riots. In reaction to the agents' intrusion into their community, the migrants' last resort of resistance, the trio embarks on a tour of revenge, penetrating into the space of the center city forbidden to ethnics and migrants like themselves.

Jewish Passing: Between Black and White

Many critics of La Haine have observed that the color scheme of the film goes from the white Jew to the dark brown Arab to the black African. The use of a black-white continuum also contributes to a new aesthetic of the nonwhite. It neutralizes the color pigment and creates an idealized trio with a new aesthetics of the second generation of migrants. They are young, healthy, and beautiful and have the potential to vitalize and invigorate old Europe rather than to destroy it from within as the racist discourse claims.[37] The paradox intrinsic to this color scheme represented by the male trio (designed perhaps in the spirit of "the united colors of Benetton") is that the symbolic space that the Jewish Vinz is supposed to occupy is that of the "white," and therefore a blond, blue-eyed (Jewish) actor was cast.

Yet the association of the Jew with whiteness, particularly in the European context and even more specifically in the French context, is problematic for a number of reasons. First, as many scholars have noted, in the European mind, traditionally, the Jew has not been perceived as white but as Oriental and even black.[38] Second, the fact that a major part of the Jewish community in France (about half a million) came in a massive influx into the country in the 1960s from North Africa following its decolonization visually contradicts the "whiteness" of the Jew.[39] Furthermore, as the history of blacks and Jews and the view of the Holocaust have been discussed in the general context of the modern history of racism in the West, the status of Vinz as a signifier of whiteness becomes all the more complex and intriguing. The view that the Holocaust of European Jews can be seen in relation to the modern history of racial slavery in the Western Hemisphere, not necessarily as a provocation but as a resource from which, as Paul Gilroy suggests, "we might learn something valuable about the way that modernity operates," is shared by many black intellectuals.[40]

Why, then, did Kassovitz have to construct this idealized trio that mixes ethnic and religious differences? Sharma and Sharma suggest that "Kassovitz seeks to present a humanized representation of racial minorities in La Haine," and therefore each of the protagonists "embodies a particular disposition and response to their hostile social conditions."[41] Although I agree with their reading, the question remains as to why Kassovitz chose to include a Jew within this trio (as opposed to another ethnic minority)[42] and why he turned him into the representative of the "white." A more comprehensive answer to this question is that the alliance that Kassovitz creates can be seen as an expression of his position regarding the debate within the Jewish community in France about growing racism against migrants (particularly Muslims).

In *La Haine,* Kassovitz remaps the symbolic space that the Diaspora Jews occupy today. He realigns the Jew with other oppressed minorities, suggesting that the new others in contemporary Europe are migrants and refugees from the poor countries who replace the "classical others" of Europe: the Jews and the Romanies (Gypsies). Moreover, the trio of *La Haine* represents the three largest monotheistic religions: Judaism, Christianity, and Islam, all originating in the Jewish faith. The film suggests not only that these three religions have a common origin, but that European civilization is and should be respectful of the Judeo-Christian-Muslim tradition on which it is based (despite the expulsion of the Muslim component from European self-perceptions and self-definitions).[43]

The color-blending theme is complemented by other types of remarkable coexistence exemplified by the trio. In addition to the ethnic and religious differences among the young males, there are also differences of class, education, and ownership of cultural capital. The articulate Hubert (whose upper-class name signifies a strong desire for social mobility) speaks articulate French, whereas Saïd does not. Hubert does not curse as much as Saïd and his diction is more standard. Hubert's manners and behavior are also less nervous and hyperactive than those of his friends, Vinz in particular. There is more evidence of ambition, a striving toward success and social mobility in Hubert's family than in the others. For instance, his industrious sister asks him to help her with mathematics classes and Hubert himself persistently talks about his wish to get out of the *banlieue.* Yet Hubert's family, like the families of his two friends, is without any male presence. Hubert's mother, who presumably raises her children on her own, indirectly encourages her son to be a petit criminal. She asks him to bring lettuce for salad but does not give him money to buy it, thus encouraging him to shoplift in the supermarket. The film implicitly suggests that the three young males choose criminal lives due to parental and familial neglect. The young males are the products of female-dominated families which, according to the film, are weak and dysfunctional; their rebellion against societal oppression can therefore be understood as the result of a lack of a male model in their families.

Vinz's domestic space is also dominated by a female figure, a grandmother with a salient Yiddish accent, thus marking her as a Jewish immigrant from Eastern Europe.[44] The grandmother is concerned more with Vinz's Jewish identity (which she associates with observing religious practices) than with his "social deviation." When Vinz's sister says she can't go to school, because it has been burnt, Grandma says: "Burning the school! Savages! You start like this and you end up no longer going to the synagogue." Vinz responds: "I'm not the one who burnt the school!" Grandma, however, continues to reproach Vinz: "But you're not going to the synagogue either," hence inferring that it is worse to lose one's religious-cultural identity than to burn schools. The presence of the Jewish grandmother signifies on one hand the unexplained absence of the father, but on the other hand demonstrates Jewish generational continuity.

It is quite significant that the two Jews (besides Vinz) who appear in the film as Jews—the grandmother and the man the trio meets in the public toilet—are elderly, Eastern European Jews, survivors of the lost generation whose culture was annihilated as a result of the Holocaust. The appearance of these two Jewish representatives of a lost civilization enhances the identity crisis of Vinz, the post-Holocaust Jew. As a young male, Vinz's crisis of ethnic-religious identity is echoed by a crisis of masculinity manifested through his ambivalence toward phallic power. To emphasize this search for identity in many of the film's scenes, the young males, and Vinz in particular, are seen closely scrutinizing their faces and bodies in the mirror, exploring and investigating their young manhood and comparing it to icons and role models of masculinity represented in American popular cinema. Vinz's troubled masculinity reflects also on his struggle with his Jewish male identity.

Vinz's attempt to revolt against the femininity associated in the European mind with the Jewish male[45] is doomed to fail. The scene in which he watches a boxing match both reflects and projects his deep ambivalence and confusion between sex and violence, love and hate, desire and destructiveness. The two boxers are men, one black and the other *beur,* thus constituting a super-virile-macho replica of his friends Hubert and Saïd. The struggle between them turns into an embrace that is both erotic and suffocating. The scene is shot in slow pace (unlike the very fast pace of the film in general) and is a bit blurry, adding a sensual dimension to the physical touch between the two males, the objects of Vinz's fascinated gaze at the spectacle of the black and brown bodies. The trio (and Vinz in particular) occupies a feminine submissive space (particularly in their relationship with the cops) and their experience of exclusion and humiliation feminize and emasculate them. Vinz's fascination and attraction to violence does not empower him but, to the contrary, makes him weak and vulnerable.[46] It relocates him in the traditional feminine space reserved for the Jew in the European imagination.

The darker sides of the trio—the Arab Saïd and the black Hubert—represent in the racial economy of the film France's still bleeding colonial wound.

In the midst of this postcolonial color scheme is the white Vinz. The black-and-white photography not only echoes the dialectics of black/white skin pigmentation but also enhances the contradictions inherent in the choice of black-and-white photography ("arty," over-stylized, and nostalgic versus "realistic," documentary-like, low-quality/poor cinematography associated with news production, the third world, and "poor cinema"). These aesthetic and artistic contradictions also reproduce the inner tensions intrinsic to the postcolonial state of contemporary France and its struggle as a nation-state based on the tradition of the Republican model with the new ideas of multiculturalism and communitarianism as it rapidly becomes an immigrant society.

These dichotomies are reproduced by the film's sound track as well.[47] Reggae and rap music dissolve (or conflict) with Edith Piaf's famous chanson "Non, je ne regrette rien" (I Have no Regrets). This mixed and hybrid sound track, as Sharma and Sharma suggest, can be read as articulating an agency to potentially imagine a utopia of truly nonracist multicultural France. Yet it can also be read as a manifestation of dystopia, of conflict over cultural hegemony. Piaf's song, associated in the popular imagination with iconic Frenchness, is challenged by the new sounds of the rap and Reggae that originate in the postcolonial subject. Can these two sound tracks coexist (multiculturalism)? Can they create a synthesis (a melting pot which serves the Republican model), or do they create a contrapuntal situation (cultural conflict)? Yes, Kassovitz seems to say, in the urban margins of Paris of all places, in the no-Paris zone, in the non-French space of migration and otherness, there are transnational dimensions. It is a space full of Reggae music, black rap, Americanized French, and constant references to New York as the capital of urban resistance. The *banlieue* thus is represented as a transnational, multi-ethnic space that threatens the French nation-state and its claim for hegemony and homogeneity. It is the Bosnia within, which contains the threat of either Balkanizing France or turning Paris into a city resembling Sarajevo ("a city-martyr," in the powerful words of Balkan cinema scholar Dina Iordanova).[48]

Post-Holocaust, Post-Colonialism, and the Apocalyptic Imagination

"What is more typical of today's new Europe—Maastricht or Sarajevo?" social-anthropologist Jonathan Webber asks.[49] As in *Beautiful People* and *Northern Skirts*, Bosnia plays a major (though less visible) role in the overall ideological economy of *La Haine*. The news about Abdel's death arrives in conjunction with news about Bosnia. The words in neon, "Bosnie: Guerre Ci-vile" (Bosnia: Civil War), are accompanied by "Mort d'Abdel Ichana" (Death of Abdel Ichana). The trio's private grief thus becomes symbolically public through the two seemingly unrelated cases in which Muslims are the victims of European racial and ethnic hatred. The association made in this episode between the genocide of the Muslims in Bosnia and the murder of Abdel by a French policeman reminds the spectators that the Balkans is within. The threat of ethnic hatred is not confined only to the "other" in the "barbaric" Balkans but is right here in Paris, one of the glorious capitals in the heart of "civilized" Western Europe. Thus, the film suggests, European colonialism is not dead. But unlike classical colonialism, it prospers and thrives not outside Europe but inside, in the heart of the center of the old empire. Similarly, the film suggests, the Holocaust is not the last chapter in European history as long as there is a genocidal war raging in Bosnia and as long as established, institutionalized racism against ethnic minorities in Western Europe is still thriving.[50]

La Haine opens with a galactic explosion that looks like a meteor blow-ing up the earth but is actually the image of an exploding Molotov cocktail or a petrol bomb invoking the radical iconography of the revolutionary May '68 cinema, particularly that of Godard.[51] Through this apocalyptic image, Kassovitz introduces a powerful visual metaphor of global catastrophe. Ul-timately, *La Haine* suggests, the internal forces (the anger and frustration of the poor migrants and the ethnic minorities concentrated in the giant post-modern metropoles and subjected to different manifestations of racism and persecution) will destroy the planet. The Bosnia within, namely, the ethnic tensions created by racial intolerance, will eventually liquidate the globe. The planet will annihilate itself rather than be destroyed by external cosmic forces. Racial tension is presented in *La Haine* as a social time bomb ready to explode at any minute. The exclusion and repression of ethnic-racial minori-ties will lead, Kassovitz suggests, to the destruction of the social fabric not only of French society but of the whole Western world.

What is the role played by the post-Holocaust Jew in this apocalyptic vision of the West? And why did Kassovitz choose to align his Jew with rep-resentatives of ethnic minorities who are immigrants? This question reso-nates in debates within the French Jewish community as to its self-perception or definition. Are the Jews of France immigrants or are they French Jews? Identity politics assume a great significance in terms of the relationships between the French national body and the Jewish minority, as the term "im-migrant" connotes strangeness, foreignness, being outside the center, and therefore occupying a less privileged national and civil space. What is the significance of "ranking . . . Jews alongside other groups in the new category (in this case immigrant communities) with which the Jews feel they do not share a common destiny or identity?" asks Jonathan Webber.[52] According to Trigano, putting the Jewish community on a par with the general immigrant community and the Muslim community and equating the interests of these immigrants with those of the Jews "had the effect of delegitimizing it. More precisely, it made the Jewish community a phenomenon foreign to France."[53]

The debate as to whether the Jew should or can align with the "immigrant community" is alluded to in *La Haine* through a brilliant cinematic demonstration of the ambiguities inherent in the politics of "passing." After the trio leaves Asterix's flat, Saïd and Hubert are violently apprehended by policemen who ask them to show their identity cards. Because of their dark skin, Saïd and Hubert are immediately marked as immigrants, foreign to the bourgeois chic French *arrondissement*. Vinz, however, wears his "white mask" and is initially not perceived as an "outsider" by the policemen, who enable him to pass unnoticed. But when the policemen begin to suspect that Vinz is related to the other two, they begin questioning him too. Vinz denies any relation to his friends, claiming that he came to visit his aunt who lives in this bourgeois neighborhood. When the policemen, doubting his story, begin pressing him harder, Vinz escapes. His denial of any relation to his two friends, as well as his escape, saves him from the humiliating interrogation and torture at the police station—recalling the famous torture scene from Gillo Pontecorvo's *The Battle of Algiers* (1966), now an icon of France's colonial trauma—but ultimately fails to save his life. This scene, which also exemplifies the notion of moral engagement in the tradition of Jean-Paul Sartre, reifies the political and ethical dilemma confronting Vinz as well as the French Jewish community: Where does Jewish alliance and moral responsibility lie? With the weak and underprivileged or with the powerful and privileged? Should Jews "pass" as white Frenchmen or should they stick with the oppressed minorities? Should the Jews escape in order to save their skin only or should they demonstrate their solidarity with the persecuted even at the price of being harassed and humiliated by the establishment?

Kassovitz's film suggests that the moral alliance of the Jews (despite their social mobility and shifting toward the center of French society) should be with the underprivileged ethnic minorities, with France's and Europe's new others who challenge its hegemonic symbols of traditional national identity. As such, *La Haine* raises fundamental questions regarding how Jews wish to reconstruct their identities in the new Europe. Do they want to assimilate into the established culture of the majority society or do they wish to identify with the minority or ethnic groups of the nation-state who, particularly in the French case, challenge its republican or civic model? As Trigano observes, "Everything in modern French political culture is hostile to the label 'community': the supreme value, embodying the very identity of the nation, is the state."[54]

The emergence of "the Jewish community" in France is often explained as a post-traumatic reaction of the "post-Holocaust Jew" to the wartime experience under the Vichy regime.[55] Kassovitz's lesson from the Holocaust, as my reading of *La Haine* suggests, seems to be different. *La Haine* is, in the words of Sharma and Sharma, both "ostensibly a dystopian text of despair and anger"[56] but also a utopian text whose fictional black/blanc/beur trio implies that in postcolonial France a multiracial, multi-ethnic, and multi-religious coalition of the oppressed can perhaps transcend not only the existing social order and its racist culture but also the danger that the victims of past racism (the post-Holocaust Jews) may become indifferent to the plight of Europe's new victims.[57] *La Haine*'s utopian suggestion was, ten years after its release, taken on board by Kassovitz himself, who during the 2005 riots took a very principled and uncompromising position vis-à-vis the confrontation between the authorities and the protesters (see below). The riots began in early November 2005 when two teenagers of African origin were accidentally electrocuted while hiding from police in Clichy-sous-Bois, north of Paris. The violence was fueled partly by resentment at France's discriminatory treatment of its north and black African communities, a far cry from the "liberty, equality, and fraternity" of the country that likes to call itself the birthplace of human rights. Nicolas Sarkozy, then France's interior minister, notoriously referred to the rioters as yobs, louts, and rabble (*racaille*), threatened to "clean them off the streets," and imposed emergency measures, including curfews, to try to bring an end to the riots. Visiting the notorious *banlieue* north of Paris, he vowed, "The louts will disappear—we will clean this estate with a Karcher [high-pressure hose used to clean buildings]."[58] Yet Sarkozy's harsh measures contributed even further to exacerbating the urban riots.

In his blog published on Tuesday, November 8, 2005, Kassovitz wrote: "Working Class France . . . For some days now, radio and television stations from around the world have been contacting me requesting interviews regarding the events that have been shaking up the suburbs of France. . . . As much as I would like to distance myself from politics, it is difficult to remain distant in the face of the depravations of politicians. And when these depravations draw the hate of all youth, I have to restrain myself from encouraging the rioters. . . . This time, Nicolas Sarkozy has gone against everything the French Republic stands for. The Liberty, the Equality and the Fraternity of a people."[59] In *La Haine,* it should be recalled, while the trio smokes marijuana on a Parisian roof overlooking the Eiffel Tower, they discuss France's *grands mots—liberté, égalité, fraternité,* dismissing them laughingly. After all, their own lived experience has been nothing but a testimony to the application of this lofty, universalist rhetoric to the life of France's migrants and ethnic minorities. Yet despite their cynical attitude toward the French Republic's official color-blind discourse, their own trio, with its cross-racial, religious, and ethnic divisions, is, ironically, a true manifestation of these principles.

The state of emergency introduced in November 2005 during the worst violent protests against racism and unemployment in nearly forty years was lifted only on January 4, 2006. President Jacques Chirac ended the emergency measures but gave regional officials power to impose curfews and carry out searches without a judge's order. Shortly afterward, however, a new youth rebellion in the suburbs (where France's poor and immigrant populations have been traditionally confined) broke out. The youth of the *banlieues* was joined by a student uprising. The 2006 uprising, when the *banlieues* came together with the city centers and two-thirds of France's universities, including the Sorbonne, were occupied, on strike, blockaded, or closed, was sparked "by opposition to an 'easy-hire, easy-fire' contract designed to ease France's crippling youth unemployment." It was supposed to allow employers to fire workers under twenty-six after two years and without giving a reason. But the festering anger went deeper than the new employment contract. It was a fury at what the rioters saw "as the lie of the Republican ideal of *liberté, fraternité, égalité* that underpins French society. This is a country where, because everyone is supposed to be equal, and equally French, ethnic minorities are not counted. But also where no matter how many degrees you have, most young people believe your chances of a decent job are non-existent if you have a non-French name or an address in an immigrant suburb."[60]

This circular movement between life and representation, the paradox of art imitating life and vice versa, as exemplified by the sociopolitical dynamics associated with *La Haine,* sharpens the relationship between cinema, politics, and ethics. Kassovitz's political stance in real life, as well as the ultimate choice made by the Jewish protagonist of *La Haine,* recalls Hannah Arendt's advocacy (inspired by the ideas of the Jewish intellectual Bernard Lazare, who lived in France during the Dreyfus Affair) of the Jew as a conscious pariah rather than a *parvenu.* Lazare's idea, Arendt wrote in April 1944, was "that the Jew should come openly as the representative of the pariah, 'since it is the duty of every human being to resist oppression.'"[61] Although in *La Haine* the Jewish Vinz is ultimately the one murdered by the French police, a murder which re-creates the Jew as history's victim once again, the fact is, as Rana Kabbani forcefully reminds us, "that Jews are not the foremost victims in the carnival of hatred. That dubious honour goes to Muslims, Europe's largest religious minority, numbering over 20 million. They are the continent's poorest and most badly housed citizens . . . the result of neglect . . . of injustice among the young in Muslim ghettos."[62] It seems that Kassovitz, despite turning his young angry Jewish male into the victim (or perhaps martyr) of the new Europe, is well aware of the shifting status of the Jew in post-Europe. He is therefore calling upon the Jews to become conscious pariahs and to warn the new Europe that the war against the postcolonial has become a war against the third world, and its diasporas in the first world.

5

THE CAMP TRILOGY

MICHAEL WINTERBOTTOM'S
IN THIS WORLD, CODE 46, AND
THE ROAD TO GUANTANAMO

Today it is not the city but rather the camp that is the fundamental biopolitical paradigm of the West.

Giorgio Agamben

Haine (1995) envisioned the time bomb buried in the *banlieue*. This time bomb was demonstrated in a typically French manner through mass demonstrations and riots. Eventually, however, the *banlieue*'s arch-enemy, Nicolas Sarkozy, was elected as France's president in May 2007.[1] In Britain, the metaphorical ticking time bomb broke the shield of metaphor and turned into a real bomb planted on July 7, 2005, on a London bus and on an underground route by what the media like to call homegrown terrorists, British-born-and-bred Muslims perceived as the "enemy within."[2] The London events of 7/7 triggered an ongoing public debate in Britain about traditional thinking on race and the need to redefine the project of multicultural society, the status of Muslims and Islam in British society, the emergence of faith and religious identity, and the commitment to a new equality and human rights project, thereby putting into crisis Britishness itself. Moral panic campaigns generated by media and policy makers, bloated with inflammatory rhetoric against "invading" asylum seekers, Romanies (Gypsies) corrupting the English countryside, and Muslim terrorists, have created a climate of fear in which the erosion and suspension of civil liberties and the enforcement of growing surveillance culture have been tolerated by a shocked public. London, the most cosmopolitan city in the world, has experienced a shift from the reign of metropolitan multiculturalism to that of the Metropolitan Police. "London under Attack," the tabloid headlines screamed. The threat of "Balkanization" hinted at in *Beautiful People* has materialized, according to the critics of multiculturalism. The fragmentation, destruction, and collapse of the greatest historical "experiment" in metropolitan multiculturalism (from Sarajevo to London) have turned into the dubious "victory" of the Metropolitan Police, tragically symbolized by the savage murder on July 22, 2005, of Jean Charles De Mendez, a Brazilian migrant who lived in London. Police first claimed that the killing was part of an anti-terrorist operation following failed attempts to detonate explosives in London's transportation system a day earlier. It is within this climate of fear that Winterbottom's recent films, including what I term his "camp trilogy," have been initiated, produced, and received.

Many film critics have both praised and criticized Winterbottom for his "chameleon talent for adapting to new genres" and "insistence on the collaborative nature of film-making."[3] Yet despite the prolific nature of his work, the same topoi and motifs run throughout his oeuvre, obsessed as it is with themes of war, migration, border crossing, class identity, desire, sexuality, and nationhood, and the role of news and entertainment in a media-saturated globalized world. Most recently, these themes have been explored through Winterbottom's focus on the crisis zone of the Afghanistan/Pakistan border in *In This World* (UK, 2002), *Code 46* (UK, 2003), *The Road to Guantanamo* (UK, 2006), and *A Mighty Heart* (USA/UK 2007), the director's most recent film at the time of this writing. *A Mighty Heart* is about the Jewish American *Wall Street Journal* reporter Daniel Pearl, who was kidnapped and beheaded in Pakistan while researching a story about Al-Qaeda's links with the Pakistani military. The film has already been described by critics as completing "what might be called a loose Pakistan trilogy that began with *In This World* (2002) and *The Road to Guantanamo* (2006)."[4] It seems that these two films have turned Winterbottom, in the eyes of Hollywood at least, into an expert on the Afghanistan-Pakistan region, currently a highly sensitive area for the American empire and its crusade against Islam in the form of the "War on Terror." Furthermore, in an attempt to "balance" the picture conveyed by what Hollywood presumably saw as a biased view of the region (i.e., critical of America) provided by Winterbottom's incomplete trilogy, he was invited by Paramount to make a film on the "other side," the brutal murder of Pearl in Pakistan. Whether Winterbottom's mighty heart, solicited and financed by American money, indeed readdresses and redeems the "biased" view represented in his other two films is a complex issue which I will not address in this book.[5] Rather, in this chapter I attempt to offer an analysis and discussion of *In This World, Code 46,* and *The Road to Guantanamo,* Winterbottom's camp trilogy.

In an age when "the camp" is proliferating prominently in popular culture, as on entertainment shows such as *Survivor* and *Big Brother,* centered on the "survival" of the fittest in confined spaces where "inmates," voluntary prisoners, are subject to a rigid set of rules, potential punishment, and public, televisual rituals of humiliation and degradation, Winterbottom's trilogy retrieves the more sinister connotations of "the camp" associated with the Nazi concentration camps, slave labor camps, and ultimately the death camps. In his trilogy, Winterbottom represents the camp as a space of exclusion, punishment, and torture to which people are exiled, not in Western-style entertainment shows promoting and celebrating free market competitiveness and neo-capitalism's survival of the fittest (i.e., the most aggressive), but camps they are forced to inhabit.[6] Each of the films in this trilogy introduces a different representation of the idea of the camp and the real and symbolic space it occupies in what Naomi Klein perceptively describes as disaster capitalism based on the shock doctrine. In what follows, I analyze each film individually, focusing on the evolution of the idea of the camp in Winterbottom's trilogy and its relationships to "this world."

From the Global Village to the Global City: *In This World*

Whereas Stephen Frears's acclaimed film *Dirty Pretty Things* (2002) "shows the lives of illegal immigrants once they reach Britain"—in the words of Fiachra Gibbons—Winterbottom "wanted to show why they made the journey."[7] In my opinion, he also wanted to show how they made the journey and its economic and emotional costs. *In This World* begins in February 2002 in the Shamshatoo refugee camp near Peshawar, Pakistan, where 53,000 Afghan refugees are housed in primitive conditions. Some of them have been there since 1979, when they fled the Soviet invasion of Afghanistan. Others came to escape the 2001 U.S. bombing. Some, like 16-year-old Jamal (Jamal Udin Torabi), the protagonist of the film, were born there. Jamal, an orphan, earns less than one dollar a day working in a brick factory. When he learns that his uncle Wakeel is thinking of sending his older cousin Enayat (Enayatullah) to London, this enterprising boy, who speaks English, volunteers to accompany him. "You're better off in your own country," one of the men in the community warns them, but Jamal and Enayat are eager to embark on their overland journey from Asia to Europe. They travel in the back of pick-up trucks across the desert into Iran, where they are held up for ten days before boarding a bus to Tehran. But a checkpoint official removes them from the bus and they are escorted back into Pakistan. They ultimately reach Tehran by an illicit route and, concealed in a fruit truck, are driven toward the mountainous border. They cross a snowy Kurdish-controlled pass on foot and enter Turkey. At Istanbul, they and other refugees are locked in a freight container on a ship bound for Italy. En route, most suffocate and die, including Enayat, but Jamal survives. In Trieste, he steals to procure a train ticket to Paris and reaches the Sangatte refugee center. He is befriended by Yusuf, a North African migrant, and at Calais the two stow away under a lorry bound for Britain. Captions state that Jamal was refused asylum but granted exceptional leave to stay in Britain until his eighteenth birthday. *In This World* was the winner of the Golden Bear, the prize of the Ecumenical Jury, and the Peace Film Prize at the 2003 Berlin International Film Festival.

Docudrama and the Brechtian Effect

Made as a digital docudrama video, *In This World* was intended to make a forceful intervention into the heated global debate about human trafficking, economic migration, and the war in Afghanistan, and indeed it is a powerful testimony to the trials that refugees face in their escape from their troubled homes to Fortress Europe. The film begins and ends in two refugee camps, Shamshatoo in northwest Pakistan and Sangatte in northern France, while "Winterbottom's small camera traverses the distance between the two, and makes these infamous sites part of a vivid screen story."[8] The dynamic style used by Winterbottom's digital camera recalls the sense of immediacy and liveliness created by Italian Neorealism and the French New Wave. His appropriation of the documentary style (customarily used by Western media to provide information about the "rest of the world") conveys the feeling that his film in not just about the plight of a fictional character, but bears a testimony to a broader political phenomenon. Thus, for example, the nightmarish, claustrophobic scene in the freight container in which the "passengers" are entombed for a forty-hour ferry journey to Trieste shows the horror of the refugees inside the suffocating darkness of the container, screaming and banging hopelessly on locked metal doors, and invokes the real-life tragedy of the fifty-eight Chinese found dead in similar circumstances at Dover in June 2000.[9] The brief evocation of the since-demolished Sangatte camp also provides an extraordinary degree of access to a world rarely seen on television screens.[10]

Although Winterbottom professes to dislike the term "docudrama,"[11] his cross-border film seems to fall into the boundaries of this genre. The film's

Figure 5.1. Jamal (Jamal Udin Torabi) and Enayat
(Enayatullah) on their overland journey from Asia to
Europe in Michael Winterbottom's *In This World*.
COURTESY OF THE BFI

screenplay by Tony Grisoni is based on interviews with refugees and observations of their journeys, and its lifelike, documentary appeal derives mostly from Winterbottom's use of small digital cameras and his casting of a pair of nonprofessionals, Jamal Udin Torabi and Enayatullah, in the leads. Yet, although the film blurs the boundaries between fiction and reality (recalling Godard's famous phrase regarding the fiction of reality and the reality of fiction), we never lose sight that these are not actors but real people participating in a staged journey that follows the route taken by many seeking to travel to Western Europe.

In a Godardian fashion, the film combines a didactic, highly politicized voiceover, reciting the horrifying statistics behind the unfolding human drama enacted for the spectator's gaze. Some critics have indeed described the film as "guerrilla filmmaking,"[12] alluding to its debt to a militant cinema

verité tradition. The film's oscillation between an intimate yet epic docudrama creates complex relationships between reality and fiction, recalling
both Godard's[13] and Fassbinder's work. The reality-fiction dialectics embedded in this film have acquired heightened significance as a result of the
spectators' knowledge and awareness that the fictional ending of the film is
not the real closure of the film's drama. This blurred distinction is further
enhanced by the fact that Jamal used the film itself as a way to smuggle himself into Britain.[14] A few days after he returned to Pakistan when the shooting
ended, his mother decided that the $7,000 he earned as an actor should be
used to get him back to Britain, where he would one day be able to succeed
and support his four siblings. Eventually the Eurostar, a symbol of connection between the continent and the UK, a country torn between Europe and
the United States, becomes Jamal's transport into the Promised Land of this
Western world. Unlike the mythic Orient Express which connected Europe
to Asia, the Eurostar is confined to Europe alone. The Eurostar, which in this
film is the means for escape to the "freedom" of the West (which means doing
dirty work for westerners), was also used by the actor himself as an escape
route to Europe.

The use of docudrama to explore an issue that dominates British news
carries with it a moral and political significance. The trick of the docudrama
is that the spectator cannot disavow the horrible reality and escape to a more
tantalizing fiction, nor can he or she be deluded that "this is only a movie"
when it, too, becomes unsettling to the comfort zone of the suspension of disbelief. Rather, she is forced not to feel but to think or to revert to Fassbinder's
famous synthesis of the tradition of the Hollywood melodrama with that of
the Brechtian epic theater, introduced by his famous dictum "to think with
the heart."[15] Consequently, the spectator is caught (literally) between the two
genres, which play against each other as well as against the spectator's hori-
zon of expectations. Thus, for example, when Jamal finds out that his cousin
is dead, there is no emotional exploitation of the scene (as, for example, in
Journey of Hope). Winterbottom's epic docudrama, like Godard's Brechtian
revolutionary style (evident also in Kassovitz's *La Haine*), uses titles, captions,
and subheadings to create a reflective distanciation effect.

The Brechtian reworking of mythic elements is carried over into the
journey along the Silk Road. In fact, during production, the film was known
as *The Silk Road*. This was used primarily as a cover, since officials in many
countries were told the film was a documentary about that historical subject.
Later, it was known as *M1187511*, which was the UK Home Office's file number for the real-life Jamal's application for refugee status. Before its release,

however, the title was changed to *In This World*. As Winterbottom explains on the cover of the DVD release, there was a subtitle in the film in which Jamal was translated as saying that Enayat was dead. Upon seeing this translation in the film, Jamal informed Winterbottom that it was inaccurate. What he had actually said was that the man was "no longer in this world."[16]

Border Crossing

The film exposes the paradox embedded in the geographical/physical border crossing that is part of the migrants' journey to the Promised Land. In order to become legal refugees, Enayat and Jamal have to cross the border between Iran and Turkey illegally. This paradox is also exposed in *Journey of Hope*, where the refugees are warned by the traffickers that they can be legal only if they hand themselves in to the authorities and ask for political asylum.[17] The border crossing is shot in black and white, as if Jamal and Enayat are viewed from a patrolling border policeman's point of view. They are seen through the infrared of the camera's eye as if they are moving targets. To the border police, they are not human beings in flight from deprivation and misery but moving duck targets. Once in Turkey, they are smuggled in a lorry with a young Turkish couple with a baby and an Iranian man to Trieste. We see the Turkish trafficker playing with the baby, and a shot of the Ali Mehmet's Mosque in Istanbul fills the frame (recalling a similar shot in *Journey of Hope*). This shot signifies the symbolic transitory moment, the movement from Asia to Europe embodied by the Turkish city and its hybridization of east and west. Jamal and Enayat are seen walking on the waterfront in Istanbul and the following title says: "40 Hours Later." The images that accompany the title show inside space of the stuffy, airless lorry (the womb that turns into tomb) and the suffering refugees within.

When they arrive at a desolated parking lot in Trieste (a nonplace), all the people inside the lorry except for Jamal and the baby are dead. The Italian traffickers take the baby and Jamal escapes from the lorry. "Two weeks later" we see Jamal as a street peddler, speaking Italian to well-heeled Italians in elegant bars and cafés. Jamal steals the purse of an Italian woman and with the money buys a train ticket to France, where he ends up in yet another refugee camp, the infamous Sangatte. Jamal is first seen in a tent in the camp telling jokes to the other refugees, and next crossing the Channel to Britain with Yusuf, his new friend (who boasts that he was in London before and worked as an assistant manager in a restaurant) under the bottom of a big lorry. The film's last shot shows Jamal praying in a London mosque. The prayer is not translated into English, as if in respect to the privacy of his prayer, to the loneliness that he probably feels in London, uprooted from his family and his transit home the refugee camp, or alternatively as an expression of his "difference" and of the growing new cultural world within this European world. The mosque thus becomes the only available spiritual and physical home for Jamal, the refugee who has never had a real home in this world.

The geographical border crossing is accompanied and mirrored by linguistic border crossings. Pashto, Farsi, Arabic, English, Turkish, Kurdish, Italian, and French are not only the languages used in the film but also the languages that Jamal manages at one level or another to master.[18] Jamal, like Mehmet, the child in *Journey of Hope*, is linguistically more eloquent than the grown-ups. His linguistic competence is part of the survival kit of the migrant. In Italy, Jamal works as a peddler and speaks Italian. In Sangatte in France, he tells the other refugees jokes in English. Throughout the whole journey (particularly in Turkey), Jamal asks people whose language he does not know if they speak English. Despite his tender age, he already understands the linguistic power of globalization and the role of English as the global lingua franca, the language of domination as well as the language that spreads domination. But at the same time, Jamal's question (addressed mainly to peasants in remote rural areas) exposes the contradictions of globalization and the tension between the local and the global. These people, obviously, do not know English, yet he expects peasants who live on the periphery of the globe to communicate with each other in English, the language of the globe's hegemonic powers that exercise their superior military force on the world's peripheries. One of the paradoxes of globalization, the film implicitly suggests, is precisely the fact that its victims (economic victims as well as war victims) want to migrate linguistically and geographically to its centers of power. The Afghani people, bombed by America, are shown at the beginning of the film chatting in groups in the camps and expressing their desire to immigrate to America and to master its language of domination.

Global Human Waste and the West

The refugees seen in Winterbottom's *In This World* are one of the by-products of globalization. They are not only stateless but also part of a transnational, global community of refugees, constituting an exile within exile, a world within a world. The permanence of the transit camps where they live is part of the globalization of the refugees themselves. They are not global citizens but rather global refugees who inhabit no place, no space, and no identity.

The refugees like Jamal who were born in a refugee camp in Pakistan are deported back to Afghanistan even though they have never lived there. The refugee camp embodies the paradox of the permanence of transience, boasting, according to Zygmunt Bauman, "a new quality: a 'frozen transience,' an ongoing, lasting state of temporariness, a duration patched together of moments none of which is lived through as an element of, and a contribution to, perpetuity."[19] Winterbottom's film, however, demonstrates that the refugee camp, the space of human waste, is not confined to Asia alone, but can be found in the heart of Western civilization itself, in the border zone between France and Britain. Jamal's last station before reaching the Promised Land in Kilburn, North London, is the notorious Sangatte camp in Calais, France.

Refugee children play a significant role in the migrant's drama both in the real world and in its fictional manifestation. In the diasporic migrant film, as is evident, for example, in *Journey of Hope,* the children or the young are often chosen by their families to go to the receiving country, presumably because they have a better chance of reaching their destination. Jamal, for example, knows that in order to evade imprisonment by the Pakistani police/ border guards he has to bribe the border patrol and he does it in a very sophisticated way. When the border guard finds a Walkman while searching their travel bags, he asks them what it is; Jamal immediately responds, "This is for you." Enayat, in his naïveté, is furious at Jamal's having given away what was presumably their only valuable possession, and Jamal has to explain to him the basics of survival (bribery is the only way to avoid prison).

In *Journey of Hope,* despite the hope of the father and the grandfather that the child will be their savior, he does not survive. In *In This World,* however, the child survives. Jamal, the refuge child, who is constantly being harassed and exploited by the adult world, enjoys maternal care on one occasion only. A Kurdish peasant woman takes pity on the two young refugees and especially on the young Jamal. She caresses his head gently, then feeds and nurtures him. In a following scene, Jamal and Enayat are seen playing football with other children from the small village on the border between Iran and Turkey. This is one of the few moments of grace which they enjoy on their journey, a rare instance of pleasure where they act and play like normal children, and not as premature refugees struggling to survive. In Trieste, before Jamal steals the purse of the Italian woman, a petty theft that enables him to buy a train ticket to France on his way to London, the children of the "normal" Italian family are shown pleasurably licking ice cream. This image of Western "normalcy" (recalling the moment of tourist pleasure enjoyed by the child in *Journey of Hope;* see chapter 1) is also a reification of privilege that is denied to the refugee children. The ice cream as an icon of simple basic pleasure denied to the child refugee appears earlier. When Jamal and Enayat arrive in Teheran, they buy ice cream in an "irresponsible," impulsive moment of self-indulgence. Enayat reproaches Jamal for buying the biggest scoop of ice cream and Jamal explains to him that he had to, he just could not control himself. What is a taken-for-granted indulgence for a European child is shown to be a potential source of risk for the Afghani refugee child. There are two species of children in this world, the film implies: the haves and the have-nots.

Yet the real protagonist and hero of the film is the journey itself. Staged along the historic route of the Silk Road, this journey gains epic and mythic proportions that transcend the here and now, implicitly suggesting that migration is not a new phenomenon of human history but has always been part of a global movement of people (and not only of goods, commodities, and the Western extraterritorial elite as the global free market ideology would like us to believe). Ironically, the evocative mythical dimension invoked by the Silk Road has a very contemporary resonance and relevance. For thousands of years, the Silk Road was a complex and sophisticated network of communication, an interactive geopolitical zone for the exchange of new ideas, inventions, and exotic commodities. The route has survived different conquests, wars, and changes, passing through dozens of empires and civilizations that have emerged and then disappeared. Winterbottom's choice of using part of the Silk Road as the geographical and physical setting of the film implicitly suggests that nothing can stop the movement of people. And indeed, the strength of the film, as Chris Darke observes, "resides entirely in its understanding of migration as movement."[20]

Furthermore, Winterbottom makes a political statement by using the setting of Marco Polo's *Travels,* a revolutionary piece of writing which "radically altered European understanding of Asia by forcing the West to recognize a superior culture in the East"[21] and furnished it, as Zhang Longxi observes, with "a better reservoir for its dreams, fantasies, and utopias."[22] Polo's book was one of the founding texts of "Orientalism," imprinting the idea of an exotic East as a symbol of difference and as the ultimate Other/double of the West. Polo's travels, as Paul Smethurst suggests, changed the Western view of the world, shifting its geopolitical center (according to the European medieval, Christian-biblical view of the time) from Jerusalem to the great civilizations in the East. This "recasting of the world into a more dynamic and multi-centered geographical space" was, according to Smethurst, "the first step toward what we now call globalization."[23] *Travels,* Smethurst concludes, "had a moral for Medieval Europe: let diversity and tolerance replace division and xenophobia—a moral no less relevant today than in Marco Polo's time."[24] It can be argued that Winterbottom's moral is not very different.

As Chris Darke observes, *In This World* takes us into "the underside of globalization in which people are trafficked like goods for currency. . . . In setting themselves the task of accompanying Jamal and Enayat on their journey, the film-makers have sought to show the human qualities, the courage and stamina, of those described as 'economic migrants,' a term which, when set against that of 'refugee,' Winterbottom describes as leading to an 'insidious distinction.'"[25] This point is made even more interesting if we accept William Dalrymple's provocative thesis that Marco Polo was not an adventurer, as is often thought, but "a hard-nosed businessman who went East not as tourist but economic migrant."[26] Winterbottom's film not only humanizes the immigration debate, transforming it from a crime drama or even a terrorism drama (as it is often played in the tabloid media) into a "mythic human drama," but also reveals, in the powerful words of Darke, "the world inside the world,"[27] the world of stateless, homeless refugees excluded from this world. And, indeed, the film's opening voiceover provides dry facts about globalization's refugees: there are about fourteen million refugees "in this world," eight million in Asia and one million in Peshawar.[28] This world within a world is a motif which Winterbottom further developed in his subsequent science-fiction thriller *Code 46*.

The Global *Banlieue* and Fortress Communities: *Code 46*

Branded as a love story, *Code 46* is set in the near future, where the institutionalized prevalence of cloning means that the law prevents any possibility of enacting incest between unsuspecting genetic relatives. William (Tim Robbins), a detective who investigates identity fraud, falls in love with Maria Gonzales (Samantha Morton), who is a suspect in one of his cases. Maria is a clone of William's dead mother, and therefore when she is discovered to be pregnant with his child she is in violation of Code 46, the law established by the Sphinx Company which controls the city where she lives. Maria undergoes a forced abortion, her memory is selectively wiped clean to obliterate her relationship with William, and she is infected with a virus that triggers a negative response when he attempts to touch her. William finds her and takes her to the "al fuera," the outside, where they believe that they are safe. While Maria is eventually able to overcome her frightened response to William's touch, she cannot overcome the compulsion to confess as a result of the virus that was implanted in her body. Escaping from the special forces sent by the Sphinx Company to catch them, they have a road accident as a result of which William's memory is erased. He goes back to his wife and son in Seattle and Maria is banished permanently to the "al fuera" in the desert.

The initial reaction to Winterbottom's *Code 46* may be one of surprise. After all, what is the relationship between *Code 46*, a science-fiction film featuring American and British actors and highly stylized and futuristic setting, and Winterbottom's previous, socially conscious, and semi-documentary film *In This World*? Yet a more careful look at the film reveals not only affinities between *Code 46* and *In This World* but even a strong ideological link. To a certain extent, *In This World* can be viewed as a prelude to *Code 46* or, alternatively, the two films can be seen as mirroring each other in a myriad of interesting ways. This point has not been lost on Winterbottom himself, who in response to Geraldine Bedell's question regarding her feeling of discomfort at "moving from the intense political commitment of *In This World*" to what is, "on the face of it, a much more commercial proposition in *Code 46*," responded that "quite a lot of elements of *In This World* crept into *Code 46*." "There's the same idea of some people living in protected zones and others as outsiders,"[29] he explained.

A significant background influence on *Code 46* was Winterbottom's experience while making *In This World*: "One important thing was the frustration of passports, visas and all the bureaucracy that goes with traveling through a lot of different countries—the problem of not having the right paperwork. That became part of the back story, the need for papelles, the road-blocks and security, and the difficulties of cross-border travel in general."[30] The papelles, the futuristic replacement of the passport, thus come to symbolize the transition from a world governed by the nation-state (for which the passport is a signifier of inclusion/exclusion) to the transnational, global world (for which the papelle is the signifier of belonging/non-belonging).[31] The papelles/passports also connect *Code 46* to *Dirty Pretty Things,* which revolves around the fight to obtain passports as part of the "illegal immigrants'" survival struggle (see chapter 2). Living without a passport in this world is like living without a papelle in Winterbottom's allegorical future world. Yet *Code 46*'s message is that it is not the future which is so frightening, but the present. The film creates an eerie, uncanny feeling by blurring the distinctions between the imagined world of the future and the world we inhabit now. This imminent future, the film implies, is closer than we may think—a future dominated by a "climate of fear" and characterized by overcrowded mega-cities guarded by high-security checkpoints and surrounded by "outside" desert areas, peopled by non-citizens excluded from the privileges enjoyed by those "inside"—"al fuera" in the film's hybrid lingo.

Much like Jean-Luc Godard's *Alphaville* (1965), a science-fiction film shot in the grey, wintry streets of Paris, depicting the "City of Dreadful Night" where Lemmy Caution (Eddie Constantine) leads Natasha von Braun (Anna Karina) from the dark city in emulation of the mythic route of Orpheus leading Eurydice out from the underworld,[32] so in *Code 46* William leads Maria from the underworld of the mega-city of Shanghai (the inside world of the included ones) to Jabel Ali and the desert (the outside world of the excluded, the "al fuera"). The film thus combines recognizable features of the science-fiction film, a love story, a film noir thriller, Greek mythology, biblical motifs, and biopolitics to comment and reflect on the construction and ideology of both ghettoized and gated-fortress communities in this world.

Ghetto versus Gated Communities

Code 46 demonstrates how "this world" has become more gated and ghettoized. Indeed, both *In This World* and *Code 46* are about who is granted the privilege of the Western lifestyle and who is excluded. Those who are included live in the mega-city of Shanghai, a "biopolitical space," to borrow this highly charged notion from Giorgio Agamben's resonating theory,[33] a Babylon of a transient population composed of different ethno-racial groups that inhabit temporary spaces and speak a "global-hybridized language." Winterbottom's use of a near-future setting, in a world that "is meant to be more of a parallel to the world of today"[34] and his hybridization of different genres, creates an uncanny feeling. We are both familiar and unfamiliar with this world and, in an almost formalist fashion, we are invited to recontemplate the recognizable, to reexamine and reinvestigate "this world," our seemingly familiar world.

The world constructed by Winterbottom is built around the principle of binary oppositions that, according to David Desser, are typical of the ideology and ecology of the science-fiction genre.[35] These binary oppositions are of inside/outside, desert/city, male/female, night/light (the people in Shanghai work in the dark, night underworld; the people of the desert and Jabel Ali live under a blazing, burning sun), civilization/wilderness, and gated/ghetto communities. Ultimately, the binarism culminates in the dialectics of "self" and "other," which further constitutes the ideological kernel of this fortress world. Within the framework of this binarism, Shanghai represents the postmodern global city which, despite its lack of national boundaries and characteristics, its multi-ethnic population, and generic urban landscape, is a gated community, fortified against undesirable migrants from the outside who lack the desired papelles to gain access to the inside. Winterbottom's Shanghai is populated by what Zygmunt Bauman calls the global extraterritoral elite, while the surrounding desert and Jabel Ali represent what he terms the other pole of extraterritoriality: the global refugee, inhabiting the ghetto of/for the poor.[36]

Desert versus City

In order to represent the slums of Jabel Ali, Winterbottom filmed in the desert surrounding Dubai. Winterbottom's choices of Shanghai and Dubai as locations, as Virginia Crisp suggests, "lead to the extension of the inside/outside opposition into an opposition between the city and the desert,"[37] an opposition that was deliberately constructed by the director, who commented that he was "using places for their culture," and that he chose Shanghai and Dubai in order to create the visual opposition of "city versus desert."[38] Jabel Ali, the film's major location and the real geographical area surrounding Dubai, looks "very much like the images of Shamshatoo, the Afghan refugee camp at the beginning of *In This World.*"[39] In Michael Winterbottom's explanation of why he chose Jabel Ali as the location for the "al fuera," he explains that in many ways he sees people as no longer citizens of the nation but citizens of the city:

> In Dubai the local population is much smaller than the immigrant population, so it's very multi-cultural. There's the idea of a city being not so much part of a nation, you're not from India or China or America, you live in the city or outside the city, you're in the system or outside the system. . . . You get that sense of a population being used for very functional reasons: people having to leave where they are from in order to make a living.[40]

This situation in Dubai, as Crisp observes, makes it the perfect setting for *Code 46* because it represents the global workforce of people who are members of the transient population of the supra-city.[41] Yet this transient, cosmopolitan rootlessness does not represent any emancipation or liberation from oppressive national belonging. Shanghai, the mega-city of the near future, constitutes a gated community inaccessible to the undesirable others from the "outside" but also inhospitable to its own inhabitants, who live under the constant scrutinizing gaze of the panopticon world city turned into a ghetto of insecure transience.

The desert of Jabel Ali, though presented as the space inhabited by the undesirables, society's outsiders and outcasts, is also, historically, the birthplace of civilization. Ur, in Mesopotamia (Iraq), is the most ancient city in the history of civilization and Ur Kasdim (Khaldea) is, according to the Hebrew Bible, the birthplace of Abraham. The Hebrew Bible itself is full of stories about quarrels, fights, and struggles between the settlers (the city dwellers) and the nomads of the desert. The desert, associated with the Orient, is also a metaphor for the collective menacing id of Western civilization, which causes the physical and psychical disintegration of the white race despite the fact that, or perhaps because, it is the birthplace of the first monotheistic religion, Judaism, as well as of the third, Islam.[42] It is not an accident, therefore, that the film ends with the banishment of Code 46's Maria to the "Oriental" desert and the return of her illicit lover William to his family in Seattle, the rainy city.[43]

The film establishes two images of the "Orient" and the "Oriental." One is that of Shanghai, located in the Far East, and the other, Jabel Ali, in the Near East.[44] Thus, Shanghai, the mega-city of the near future (which invokes the image of the "Oriental" futuristic city in Ridley Scott's Blade Runner [1982]), can be read as representing the rising East, the fast-developing Orient, and the emergence of the new Oriental empire, whereas Jabel Ali may represent the underdeveloped world, the Arab world, associated in the Western popular imagination with the desert, the nomad, the refugee, and Islam. Thus, the world depicted by Code 46 is the world inhabited by the global elite on one side and the global refugee on the other. Shanghai, the Asian city, is both gated against and surrounded by a "planet of slums."[45] The film thus propagates two images/icons of Orientalism: the South Asian (most of the residents of Shanghai look either Chinese or Indian) versus the Arab/Muslim. And indeed, these are the two dominant images of the East as it is perceived today in both public and popular Western discourse: the image of the emerging giants in the so-called Far East incarnated by the dragon China and the elephant India, and the chaotic underdeveloped Near East embodied by the "medieval" Arab/Muslim world incarnated by Afghanistan and Al-Qaeda. Ultimately, however, Shanghai and Dubai in Code 46, as well as in reality, embody the shift of power to the Far and Near East. Both are the emerging new financial centers of the globe.

Hagar: The Mother of All Refugees

At the end of Code 46, when Maria has been banished to the desert, the clothes and headscarf that she wears are reminiscent of the archetypal image of the refugee woman,[46] thus turning her into an icon of the modern global refugee woman. From a postmodern replica of the human and robot Maria in Lang's *Metropolis,* from a Godardian-like heroine with a Mao-style hat invoking Juliet Berto in *La Chinoise* (1967), and from a chic modern Western woman, she is transformed into the archetype of the premodern, ancient woman expelled to the wilderness beyond the boundaries of civilization. In this archaic image, Maria incarnates the biblical Hagar, the mother of Abraham's first son, Ishmael.

The biblical story has established the image of Hagar as the pariah, the outcast who becomes a heroine, a mother of the Arab nation. At the end of the film, as in the biblical story, Maria/Hagar is in the outside, expelled to the desert to live in a state of exile. Maria is dressed in hybrid clothes that resonate with both Muslim and biblical women, signified mainly by the headscarf/veil that she wears. Yet her colorful robes accentuate her whiteness, her blond hair, and her (non-Oriental) blue eyes. The unavoidable question as to why Winterbottom chose a white woman to become the icon of the ultimate global refugee[47] seems to be embedded in the film's ideology, which challenges and questions the boundaries erected between the inside developed world and the outside undeveloped world. The iconic image of Hagar, the mother of all refugees, is transformed into the postmodern image of the Muslim/Arab/refugee woman and a conversion from Maria to Hagar occurs. It should be noted, however, that the shift from one religious image of femininity to the other is not necessarily arbitrary. After all, the Qur'an confirms Jesus' virgin birth, and one of its special chapters is entitled "Mary," after the mother of Jesus.[48]

As the ejected, rejected female slave, a woman of color, a migrant, and a foreigner (she is Mitzrit-Egyptian)[49] living in a foreign country, Hagar epitomizes the experience of marginalization, exploitation (both for labor and sex, whereby her fertility is used as a tool, a womb submitted to the task of giving birth to the nation),[50] and migration. It is not surprising, therefore, that Hagar has become a feminist and postcolonial icon.[51] Like Abraham,[52] tested by God to sacrifice his son Isaac, Hagar receives a promise of a child, but must undergo the ordeal of almost losing that child (paralleling Maria's experience in *Code 46*).

According to the biblical account, God appeared to Hagar in the desert and promised that Ishmael would grow and be a "wild ass of a man," one who would be neither dominated nor domesticated, nor would he be a slave like Hagar; rather, he would be free in the desert: "His hand would be against all, and all would be against him," but he would succeed in erecting his tent before all his siblings. The ambiguity of the closure of *Code 46* (Maria and William had sexual relations during their escape to Jabel Ali, in a repeated act of violation of the cloning incest taboo) leaves us with the possibility that

Figures 5.2 (ABOVE LEFT) and 5.3.
(ABOVE) From a Godardian-like
heroine with a Mao-style hat invoking
Juliet Berto in *La Chinoise* (1967), and
from a chic modern Western woman,
Maria Gonzales (Samantha Morton) is
transformed in Michael Winterbottom's
Code 46 into the archetype of the woman
refugee: the biblical Hagar, the mother
of Abraham's first son, Ishmael.
COURTESY OF THE BFI

Figure 5.4. (LEFT) The image of Maria
in the future desert where "freedom is
just a memory" recalls the final image
of Kit (Debra Winger) in Bernardo
Bertolucci's *The Sheltering Sky* (1990),
described by the Italian director as a sort
of existentialist/ecological allegory about
a "desert world to become tomorrow's
reality" and "the only place in the world
where even memory disappears."
FROM THE AUTHOR'S PRIVATE COLLECTION,
COURTESY OF BERNARDO BERTOLUCCI

Maria is pregnant again with William's child and thus to the rebirth of a new Ishmael. As the post-human Hagar, the disquieting image of Maria at the end of the film suggests the return of the repressed, the revolt of the outcasts and the refugees against their expulsion and exclusion. Winterbottom emphasized this many times in interviews, saying that he sees the problem of refugees being locked out of Britain as part of a much larger global issue:

> You have millions of people in Pakistan working for a pittance. They see on someone's TV people with mobile phones, the technology that connects everyone. . . . They live in a world dominated by ours, but they have no access to it because they do not have any money. As long as that situation continues, there are going to be people who would like their fair share. . . . It's the nature of society that some people are outside it. It's true at all times that there are people who will be victimized, that there are people who will be excluded. And these will continue yearning to breathe free, claiming a right to survive day-to-day as much as to enjoy the civil liberties that everyone, especially Brits and Americans, take (or should be able to take) for granted.[53]

The fictive world constructed by *Code 46* is closely entangled with the "security state," the climate of fear since 9/11, and the idea of global insiders and outsiders. These are people defined only in terms of legality and "illegality" and consequently of falling outside humanity itself, or, to put it more bluntly, living "life unworthy of being lived . . . as the German expression *lebensunswerten Leben* also quite literally suggests."[54] Guantanamo and the black sites of America's gulag (the CIA's "extraordinary rendition" network), as well as those incarcerated in detention centers around the world for no legal reasons other than their ascribed "refugee" identity, characterize this world.[55]

Cloning and biopolitics, we should remember, are the ultimate projects of capitalism, manifesting the fantasy of absolute power and complete domination over nature, the triumph of corporate capitalism. This form of capitalism, in Agamben's words, possesses the "disciplinary control achieved by the new bio-power, which, through a series of appropriate technologies . . . created the 'docile bodies' that it needed."[56] If the global city of *Dirty Pretty Things* is about the cannibalistic dimension of capitalism and its devouring, all-consuming nature, then the mega-global, near-future city of *Code 46*, controlled by the Sphinx Corporation, is not only the nightmarish dystopia of total control but the contemporary biopolitical space where the decision on bare life "becomes a decision on death, and biopolitics can turn into thanatopolitics."[57] In this biopolitical space, as the motto of *Code 46* suggests, "freedom is just a memory" (the full motto is "In the future, freedom is just a memory"). This frightening motto has inspired Winterbottom's subsequent film, perhaps his most politicized work until now, *The Road to Guantanamo,* a film about the ultimate deprivation of freedom, about bare life in the American camp.

Ideological Journeys: *The Road to Guantanamo*

Whereas *In This World* and *Code 46* demonstrate how the inequalities of globalization give rise to the figure of the global outsider projected onto the eternal refugee, forced to permanently inhabit temporary camps of exclusion—"the camp as permanent state of exception," according to Agamben[58]—*The Road to Guantanamo* goes one step further. This film shows the bare life of the ultimate outsiders, those who, under the aegis of "the war on terror" and the threat of "medieval, anti-democratic and anti-modern barbarism" (supposedly Islamic fundamentalism), which has triggered the emergence of the discourse on "the clash of civilizations,"[59] have been incarcerated in the black holes of the neoliberal West, the extrajudicial secret spaces of torture, punishment, and humiliation. Guantanamo, in reality as well as in Winterbottom's film, represents the neo-capitalist camp, where the shock doctrine is practiced against the symbolic refugees of disaster capitalism.

Whereas *In This World* traces the journey of globalization's refugees from Pakistan to the mega-city of London in search of a better life, *The Road to Guantanamo* traces the reverse journey: from London to Pakistan. Unlike the economics-driven trip of Jamal and Enayat in *In This World,* the voyage of the four British-Asian men—Asif Iqbal, Ruhel Ahmed, Monir Ali, and Shafiq Rasul—is an ideological passage of second-generation, born-and-bred Brits to the culture and homeland of their migrant parents.[60] Their reverse journey, however, takes them by surprise into a place they did not plan to visit or see, the Guantanamo Bay prison in Cuba.

The Road to Guantanamo begins with the four friends' tour of Pakistan in September 2001, where one of them is due to be married. They decide to cross the border to Afghanistan, where the American bombing begins shortly after they arrive in Kandahar in the south. The four find themselves stranded in Kabul, unable to get back to Pakistan. By mistake, due to their difficulty with the language, they take a minibus north to Konduz province, which is on the frontline between the Taliban forces and the anti-Taliban Northern Alliance. One of the four is separated from the others (and is presumed to have been killed) during the evacuation of Konduz, and the remaining three are captured by the Northern Alliance after their truck convoy is bombed by U.S. aircraft. They are imprisoned in Sheberghan before being handed over to

U.S. marines, who, with officers of the SAS (a special unit of the British armed forces) detain and interrogate them at the Kandahar airbase. From there, in early 2002, they are transferred to Camp X-Ray (and later to the Camp Delta prison built for this purpose) at the Guantanamo Bay naval base in Cuba, where they are imprisoned, interrogated, beaten, tortured, and held in isolation cells for months before being released to the United Kingdom (without charges) over two years later. The film ends with the three friends (rather than the actors that play them), dubbed the "Tipton Three" by the British press, returning to Pakistan for Asif's wedding.[61] Described by Winterbottom as "part-road movie, part-war film, part-prison movie," *The Road to Guantanamo* is a hybrid film that splices together interviews with the three men, dramatized reconstructions of their experiences, documentary material, and archival news footage.[62]

Much like *In This World,* where the fiction of reality and the reality of fiction are part of the thrill and power of the film, so too in *The Road to Guantanamo* the boundaries between fact and fiction are blurred. On February 21, 2006, arriving at Luton Airport (UK) from the film's premiere at the Berlin Film Festival where the film won the Golden Bear Prize, Shafiq Rasul and Ruhel Ahmed were held by police for questioning under the 2000 Terrorism Act, along with the actors who played them in the film. Riz Ahmed, who plays Rasul, reported that he was asked about his views on the Iraq war, whether he became an actor to further the cause of Islam, whether he intended to make any more "political" films, and whether he was prepared to become a police informant.

The paradox of Winterbottom's film is that it is trying to make the invisible visible, the secretive open, and the horrifying into banal evil by exposing the most hidden place in the security state of the United States, "the gulag of our times," as the human rights group Amnesty International called the camp in its report in May 2005.[63] Located at a naval base in Cuba, the camp was established to hold suspected terrorists captured in Afghanistan as part of the U.S. "war on terror." The U.S. detention camp at Guantanamo Bay, commonly addressed as a "black hole" by the media and human rights organizations, has come under intense scrutiny since it began to receive foreign detainees in early 2002; critics have questioned its legality, but without much impact on the Bush administration.[64] Despite allegations of torture and abuse, supported by UN declarations of evidence, only the International Red Cross has been granted access to detainees. *The Road to Guantanamo,* as Bruce Bennett argues, is also a film "about visibility and publics in a different sense, since it is a film about the way in which these three British men were excluded from public spaces through their imprisonment, excluded from

Figures 5.5 and 5.6. "Prisoners of the infinite" in the American "black hole," the neo-capitalist camp at Guantanamo Bay, in Michael Winterbottom's *The Road to Guantanamo*.
COURTESY OF THE BFI

British citizenship, their national identities suspended or challenged, and excluded from due legal treatment."[65]

The issues of visibility and unacknowledged torture are highly relevant to my analysis of Winterbottom's film. Because I find myself unable to watch any form of torture or abuse, even in the form of an image, I was not able to observe the film properly, instead closing my eyes throughout the scenes depicting violence and suffering. It is the first time in my academic career that I have decided to include a film in my book despite not having seen most of it. Ironically, my voluntary symbolic blinding resonates, perhaps, with the policy makers and the public at large, which turned a blind eye to the crimes committed at this camp. Yet, horrifying as it is, Naomi Klein tells us, human rights groups point out that Guantanamo is actually "the best of the U.S.-run offshore interrogation operations, since it is open to limited monitoring by the Red Cross and lawyers. Unknown numbers of prisoners have disappeared into the network of so-called black sites around the world or been shipped by U.S. agents to foreign-run jails through extraordinary rendition."[66] In an attempt to partially ameliorate the invisibility of American-run extrajudicial black holes, Winterbottom's guerrilla style of global distribution and exhibition made sure that 1.6 million people watched the film on its first day of release.[67]

Due to my blindness to the blind-folded detainees of Guantanamo, my analysis of the film does not focus on a close reading but rather on an attempt to conceptualize the evolution of the camp in Winterbottom's Oriental trilogy. For obvious reasons, Guantanamo represents the most horrific camp in the trilogy, the ultimate black hole where the detainees become invisible to the world and dispensable to their captors. "Guantanamo Bay is a symbol of injustice and abuse. It must be closed down," Amnesty International declared on the camp's fifth anniversary.[68] But the camp is not only an example of an extreme deprivation of human rights; it is also a law-free zone, "the legal equivalent of outer space," as one of the lawyers in the Bush administration put it,[69] hence recalling the post-Holocaust discourse on the Nazi camps, which viewed them as the "other planet," one beyond the rules and laws of decent society. The notion of the other planet can be read as implicitly suggesting that the Holocaust took place in some metaphysical sphere outside and beyond human understanding and comprehension. However, I prefer to interpret Guantanamo's outer space and the other planet of the Nazi camps in the spirit of Agamben, who argues that the "correct question to pose concerning the horrors committed in the camps is, therefore, not the hypocritical one of how crimes of such atrocity could be committed against human beings" but what were "the juridical procedures and deployments of power by which human beings could be so completely deprived of their rights and prerogatives that no act committed against them could appear any longer as a crime."[70]

Beyond the Camp Experience: Planet Post-9/11

Unlike post-9/11 discourse that criminalizes migration and links it to terrorism, Winterbottom's films explore the economic and global roots of migration, terrorism, and transgression. Although *In This World* was originally conceived as a response to the United Kingdom's ongoing asylum debate, the events of September 11 (which occurred while the film was still in pre-production) gave it additional resonance: "More than a response to the asylum issue, it's also a staggeringly persuasive reminder that the West's duty to the people of Afghanistan is far from over. As Winterbottom points out, we spent $7.9 billion bombing the Taliban regime. The question remains—how much do we owe those whose lives were ruined as a result?"[71] Whereas *In This World* depicts the refugee's journey, *Code 46* is a futuristic fable on the world of the excluded, epitomizing Bauman's ideas about a world full of disposable human trash, Mike Davis's apocalyptic vision of the excess humanity inhabiting the planet slum, and Agamben's idea about zones of indistinction/exclusion where the state of exception prevails. *The Road to Guantanamo* is the material culmination of the climate of fear produced, reproduced, and sustained by the "security bubble"[72] and the ultimate brutalization and dehumanization of the rest by the West, its reduction into bare life. *In This World* shows the transition from forced migration (caused by military and economic war inflicted on the third world by the West) to the metropolitan center. *Code 46* shows the new planet of the undesired refugees, the global *banlieue*, and *The Road to Guantanamo* introduces the return ideological journey, the journey back to the parents' birthplace and the sons' reclaimed spiritual homeland and its tragic consequences. *Code 46* conceptually visualizes the global gated community, the global fortress resurrected against the inhabitants of the global *banlieue*.[73] The fictional supra-city of *Code 46* is surrounded by a "planet of slums" where the "urban edge is a zone of exile, a new Babylon"[74] controlled by corporatist capitalism in the form of the Sphinx Company, the Big Brother corporation. Guantanamo is "the other planet" where torture is practiced both as the biopolitics of bare life (recalling Agamben's theorization) and as a metaphor for what Klein calls "disaster capitalism."

Since the World Trade Center and the Pentagon attacks in September 2001, Agamben has challenged the extensive use of emergency measures (activated and "legalized" under the guise of the "war on terror") and aimed at a tighter control of people.[75] In *State of Exception*,[76] he points to the suspension of law (including the suspension of the Geneva Convention on the conduct of war) under the guise of "the war on terror" with respect to those defined by America as "enemy combatants" and interned at Guantanamo Bay in Cuba. In these black holes, the inmates have no legal identity, recalling the stateless people between the wars referred to by Hannah Arendt.[77] For Agamben, the arbitrary policies involved with the suspension of the law used to deal with asylum seekers, whose claims are assessed outside the boundaries of any state, much like the detention of prisoners in Guantanamo, constitute part of the global (American-controlled) matrix of black sites. In these sites, inmates have no legal status and therefore cannot appeal to any authority if their human rights are violated because "legally" they are non-persons: "human waste" in Bauman's imploded language, "surplus humanity" in Mike Davis's no less critical discourse.[78] Agamben, therefore, argues that the condition of the asylum seeker becomes paradigmatic as increasingly larger numbers of people find that conditions have become impossible in their state of origin. The force of law thus produces sovereign violence which creates a zone of indistinction between law and nature, outside and inside. Agamben observes that "the realm of bare life—which is originally situated at the margins of the political order—gradually begins to coincide with the political realm, and exclusion and inclusion, outside and inside, *bios* and *zoe,* right and fact, enter into a zone of irreducible indistinction."[79] This zone of indistinction is the zone in which Jamal and Enayat, the asylum seekers of *In This World,* the archaic refugees of *Code 46* incarnated by Maria/Hagar, and the prisoners of *The Road to Guantanamo* find themselves. The camp, which according to Agamben is "the most absolute biopolitical space ever to have been realized," embodies this zone of indistinction. It is the literal and symbolic space of this world, "the hidden paradigm of the political space of modernity."[80]

Like Kassovitz in *La Haine,* Winterbottom introduces an apocalyptic vision of the present and the near present. Yet there is a significant difference between the two. Winterbottom presents a cataclysm of disaster capitalism where America's "war on terror" can be more accurately described as America's war on the world, a war that, as Mike Davis powerfully demonstrates, is specifically targeted against "the 'feral, failed cities' of the Third World—especially their slum outskirts," where "the distinctive battlespace of the twenty-first century"[81] (according to the Pentagon doctrine) will be. On the other hand, Kassovitz's iconic film, like many other European migrant and diasporic films, introduces Europe's war on the enemy within, the ghetto, *banlieue* communities of the migrants and the poor, particularly the Euro-Muslims in what the xenophobic media likes to call the new Euro-Arabia.

Bruno Beschizza, of the Synergie police union in Paris, aptly described the November/December 2007 Paris riots as urban warfare: "We're dealing with an urban guerrilla tactic, with the use of conventional arms and hunting rifles."[82] Winterbottom's trilogy goes one step further to suggest that the problem is not peculiar to Fortress Europe, but applies to the current and future fortress globe, produced, perpetrated, and perpetuated by the security sector. The primary targets of the surveillance and fortress technologies of this sector, as Klein suggests, "are not terrorists but migrants"[83] who have been displaced by the forces of globalization either in the form of war, economical deprivation, or extreme weather events. Thus, Winterbottom's Oriental(ist?) trilogy introduces the true face of the "clash of civilizations," the battle of the civilized West and its fortress cities against the dark and barbarian forces incarnated according to the moral discourse of the "free world" by asylum seekers, refugees, and the poor, the "criminals" and the "terrorists" in the post-9/11 planet.

AFTERWORD
BEYOND STRANGERS AND POST-EUROPE

*Some are unhappy, about unfamiliar cultures. . . . They all need
to be reassured that there is so much to be gained by reaching out
to others; that diversity is indeed a strength and not a threat.*
Queen Elizabeth II

In Praise of Babelondon

IN January 2005, I had a spine operation. About two months later, on a bright sunny, afternoon, while I was still recovering from the surgery and visibly disabled (I was walking very slowly and limping), I took a walk near my house in Crouch End in North London. Behind me I could hear two female teenagers (ladettes) walking fast and shouting. As they approached me from behind, I felt a bit vulnerable and wanted to protect my back and my left leg, which is partially numb and painful. The teenagers caught up with me and started abusing me verbally. One of them came threateningly close and was about to punch me. I turned my head back and asked them, "Aren't you ashamed? Can't you see that I'm disabled?" (I was naïve enough back then to think that my visible vulnerability would shield me from being abused and mistreated. I had not come yet to the realization that in contemporary Britain, the most visibly vulnerable people are the prime targets for youth violence.) My comment was obviously a mistake. Once I opened my mouth, my heavily accented English disclosed that I was a "bloody foreigner" and not "proper English" (with my fair complexion and blue eyes, I can easily pass as a "native" Crouch Ender if I refrain from speaking). "Are you German? Are you bloody German?" the two blonde, blue-eyed girls shouted even more aggressively. Although I was shocked, I could not avoid reflecting on the irony of being called "German." Only two months before, my mother, a Holocaust survivor, who boycotted all things German, had passed away. She died the day after I was discharged from the hospital following my operation. Due to my condition, I could not fly to Israel for her funeral, nor could I observe the *shivah,* the Jewish mourning ritual. Furthermore, my severe back injury occurred while I was on a very short visit to Israel to see her. The pain started while I was sitting with my husband in her tiny and tidy living room in a Tel Aviv suburb, listening (for the millionth time) to her Holocaust stories. This time, however, there was a more contemporary tale of woe, of how she had been abused by a young woman, a Philippine foreign worker who had been her caretaker for a few months, about a year before her death. It seemed as if this unsettling story—about a poor young woman from the third world who stole not only the very few valuables that my mother, who lived very spartanly, possessed, but also her medicines and food—broke my heart and spine. How could anyone do that to a frail old Holocaust survivor who was not poor in the third-world sense but definitely far from being rich? And yet how could I judge the Philippine foreign worker, a young woman who was imprisoned in a small flat with an old ailing woman with whom she did not even have a common language in which to communicate? What did I know about her life?

Realizing that I was not German, but a "bloody foreigner" all the same, the two ladettes yelled: "Where are you from? Where are you bloody from?" Eventually I was rescued by a kind English lady (the other passersby and the construction workers who witnessed the incident were all indifferent to my plight). Like Blanche Dubois in *A Streetcar Named Desire,* "I have always relied on the kindness of strangers." What was even more disturbing to me than the actual incident (which unfortunately was not the last that I suffered) was what I learned about contemporary British culture from the reactions I received afterward from ordinary English people when I told them about the event. My physiotherapist, to give one example, hugged me warmly and said: "This should not stop you from going out. We do not tell disabled and frail old people to stay at home all the time just because they are potential victims." Her message (which I found out later was the "popular wisdom" in Britain) was that old and disabled people are the prime target of youngsters' violence precisely because they are easy targets. Their vulnerability makes them likely victims rather than acting as a protective shield (as is usually the case in "primitive" countries in the third world, where the old and weak still command some respect and consideration). It took me a while to absorb and digest this message, which was so alien to the way I was brought up. To add yet an even more disturbing layer of irony to this story, during the time of the incident I was organizing a conference on Fortress Europe,[1] on which I had started working prior to my injury. Due to my health condition at the time, I could not attend the conference in person and had to manage it from my sick bed. Fortress Europe thus has become for me a loaded metaphor, laden with personal, political, and professional losses and struggles, of which these examples are only the upper layers.

My initial interest in Fortress Europe began prior to my own migration from Israel to the continent where my parents were born and from which, after the Holocaust, they clandestinely immigrated to British Mandatory Palestine, determined never again to touch the soil of their cursed motherland, Poland, where their families were murdered. My husband and I left Israel in 2002, about two years after the outbreak of the Al-Aqsa Intifada, as an act of political protest. We both felt that there was nothing else we could do from there to stop Israel from ever increasing its oppression of the Palestinians. My mother, a devout Zionist, did not approve of my voluntary exile. Despite our political disagreements, her war experience has been central to my strong identification with refugees everywhere. Her survival "journey," which had a profound impact on my whole life, started in Sokolow Podlaski, the town where she was born, and from which she escaped to Siberia after the Germans invaded Poland. From Siberia she escaped to Bukhara in Uzbekistan, where she stayed until the end of the war. She then returned to Poland, via the Silk Road, to find out that all her family had been exterminated in Treblinka. From Poland, the land of the dead Jews, she went to the Fohrenwald Camp for Displaced Persons in Germany,[2] from which she was smuggled by the Zionist Underground (*Aliyah Bet*) via Marseilles in France to Mandatory Palestine.

All those "exotic" journeys (which I sketch but in outline) were about survival, accompanied by anxieties, fears, and mourning for all the losses she suffered. My childhood was overburdened with endless stories of survival of both my parents (my father, who was also born in Sokolow Podlaski, escaped with his father and sister to the Soviet Union, where they were put into a labor camp in Siberia). The "lessons" they learned from the Holocaust, however, have not necessarily been identical to mine. In all this endless recounting of their survival stories, I never heard one word about the beauty or "exoticism" of any of the places they visited.

As a voluntary and privileged exile, one of the delights/pleasures of living in London for me is its amazing multiracial, multicultural, and multi-religious fabric. My wandering eyes are in a state of permanent wonder at the diversity of humanity on display in this strange city that I am still struggling to call home. In my mind I have built a cognitive map of the area where I live which I imagine as a hexagon. On days when I work at home, based on my mood and my shopping list, I choose which axis of the hexagon I am going to journey and explore. The closest axis runs through Crouch End, a recently gentrified area popular with young families, mostly English professionals from the so-called creative industries, and crowded with trendy yummy mummies and young white women adorned with London's hottest and most fashionable accessory, a black baby (London is apparently the world's capital of miscegenation). The area's relatively stylish and quasi-posh stores and restaurants attract mostly a trendy young white crowd despite (and maybe because of) the fact that the borough has many pockets and enclaves of council estates, and shabby houses inhabited by refugees, asylum seekers, and—one may safely assume—undocumented migrants. The languages usually listed in the council booklets are Shaqip, Arabic, Urdu, French, Greek, Kurdish, Polish, Portuguese, Somali, Turkish, Albanian, and Hindi, and information can be requested in any of these languages.

If, however, I choose to turn along another leg of the hexagon, I am already in "foreign" territory. The area of Turnpike Lane is a rich mix of Little Pakistan, India, Turkey, Kurdistan, and others. There are shops with bright-colored saris, and glittering, cheap-looking gold jewelry, Halal stores, Kurdish green groceries, Indian and Pakistani food halls, a variety of South Asian restaurants, and Halal fast food. In the midst of all this, the old-fashioned shop of a Greek Orthodox tailor proudly displays a certificate from Cyprus. On Friday, the street is full of devout bearded Muslims on their way to and from the nearby Mosque. Turnpike Lane (much more "authentic" than the famous and currently highly commercialized Brick Lane) connects to High Road Wood Green, a broad commercial road, full of stores selling low-brow brands, cheap clothing, and electronic gadgets. This sleazy street is the migrant's parallel planet to Oxford Street. You will never spot a tourist or even an ordinary middle-class white English person in these highly popular spaces of consumerism. White people are to be seen, but they are either second- or third-class Europeans, newcomers to the European club from Ukraine, Poland, Bulgaria, Romania, and other such peripheral places.

If I head north from my house and begin to climb, I reach Muswell Hill, an affluent, white, middle-class, mostly English neighborhood, more expensive and respectable than the trendy Crouch End. Muswell Hill borders on Alexandra Palace and overlooks London's major architectural attractions. On a beautiful crisp day, you can see the new London skyline from there, with the famous cucumber-shaped Gherkin and the tall phallic buildings of the City and Canary Wharf, representing financial London. The park and the surrounding pond attract the most hybrid crowds I have seen anywhere, from African and Middle Eastern families dressed in traditional clothes and picnicking on authentic ethnic food to mixed groups of young people from every corner of the globe, high on wine, beer, good laughter, and more. Unlike the more bourgeois Hampstead Heath, which attracts high-heeled, well-dressed, educated, white, upper-middle-class elites (you also need a car in order to get there), Alexandra Palace is a popular and democratic space where people from all (or most) walks of life meet to socialize and have fun. Many kinds of fun are on offer there, including ice skating in winter, antique and garden exhibitions, pleasant walking paths, wild berry picking, spaces for cycling, lying on the grass and smoking grass in the summer, feeding fallow deer, watching people, observing London's skyline, navel and people gazing, and so on.

From the center of Crouch End, I can go down to Finsbury Park, which according to the MI5 and other reliable and less reliable sources—namely the fabricated files on the weapons of mass destruction possessed by Saddam Hussein's Iraq—is the recruiting center of Al-Qaeda in Europe (the head-quarters supposedly are at the Finsbury Park Mosque, where the infamous Abu Hamsa preached to the Fidel). Stroud Green, the southwestern axis of my imaginary hexagon, is full of Caribbean shops with "exotic" (for whom?) fruits and vegetables, tropical fish and sea food, big pubs and big cosmetic and (mostly hair) accessories stores for Caribbean blacks. The crowd is a mixture of freaky white young Britons, Goths, Caribbean blacks, white working-class Brits, and many others. The more Muslim (black African, Maghrebi, Arab, and Berber) part is concentrated around the mosque. Every Saturday, the area near the Finsbury Park Station, which is full of retail stores catering to the lower classes and migrants with a tight budget, becomes the weekly Mecca for cheap and affordable fashion. The migrants of the world, and the second-generation children of the different London diasporas, shop there for clothes until they drop.

My most favorite mode of travel in London is bus number 91, whose first stop is in Crouch End/Hornsey, ending in Trafalgar Square. This long (and by London standards, cheap) bus journey, which passes from London's periphery (though the notions of center and periphery in London are quite complex) to its post-Imperial center, goes through some of the most charmless urban wastelands that I have seen in my life. But for me, this graceless urban no-place is a source of visual delight, feeding my long-time fascination with the banality of urban life, its non-spectacular, non-pretty/prettified busy chaos. Combined with the unbelievable diversity of "human and racial" types and archetypes and various fashion statements (from traditional Muslim attire to English Gothic and London stylized black chic), the display is a fantastic parade of the representatives of almost, if not all, the members of our shrinking global village, keeping my amateurish ethnographic curiosity in a state of constant stimulation. The bus journey produces pleasurable aural sensations, because each seat on the upper deck of the bus, as it makes its way through this postmodern Babel (Babelondon),[3] is occupied by a different sample of humanity. Nobody speaks English on the bus but innumerable foreign languages can be heard. Some of the sounds are so foreign to my ear that I cannot even recognize the language. Bus 91 has become for me the metaphor of the new post-Imperial London, perceptively captured by *Beautiful People* (discussed in chapter 2).

But Babelondon reaches its apogee of strangeness for me not near home but at work. The University of East London (UEL), where I work, is the migrants' and diasporas' university par excellence, except that the university management will never admit to it because it is bad for business (i.e., recruiting students): in terms of image branding/marketing, it does not send a message of white privilege and prestige. It is certainly the blackest university in London and perhaps the entire world. Unlike black universities in Africa (which I have never visited), however, in a single university one finds Christian and Muslim blacks (both first and second generation) from all over Africa and the Caribbean. There is also a large black (mostly Pakistani and Bangladeshi) student population from East London (Britain's historical first home for newcomers) and even a few white English students. Post-graduate students are whiter because many of them are from European countries. Teaching in the global classroom[4] is a new and exciting experience for me. The post-graduate students in my 2008 class were from India, Pakistan, Saudi Arabia, Korea, Japan, Greece, Italy, Nigeria, the Czech Republic, Spain, and three Brits (two white and one black Caribbean).

The class and color stratification of the university is clearly marked. All the white, blonde women are administrators and secretaries (some are even on the academic staff), all the busy-looking white guys wearing suits are the managers and/or the security people, the similarly busy-looking but suit-less whites are members of the academic staff, and all the rest—the black, brown, and young pink—are students. All those who do not speak English are migrant workers (many of them from Latin America) who clean and dust this new university after hours.

I have never seen so many variations on Muslim attire, from the black *niqab* which leaves only a thin aperture for the dark eyes to imaginative and stunning combinations of bright tops with matching, color-coordinated *hijab*. The men's fashion features the latest hip-hop of Islamist paraphernalia, from Bin Laden–style turbans to Afghani headscarves, and from wild Mujahideen-style unkempt beards to fashionable Borat-like mustaches. The secular-looking students (especially the undergraduates) do not look like the typical British student. The clothes are more glitzy and "sexy" (or sexualized), the body language is more pronounced, and the conversations are louder. Sometimes I feel that I am a participant-observer in a strange masked ball taking place in the most unbelievable movie set. The surreal mise-en-scène is enhanced by the unique location and architecture of the place. Situated in the docklands, the bizarre pastel postmodern buildings of the campus built near the River Thames face the runways of the City Airport. Every four minutes or so, a plane takes off or lands. The noise is incredible and so is the sight. The strange scene is at its strangest when the air is cold and clear at dusk. As the sun sets over the river and the wedding cake–like buildings become even pinker than they were intended to be, in the din of incessant roar of the plane engines I ask myself, "Where am I?" The Docklands Campus of UEL is, undoubtedly, an extraterritorial space of difference, a diasporic entity within a city that has become a large diaspora within a continent that itself is in a constant state of flux.

Changing the Terms of the Debate

I have chosen to expose some aspects of my personal exile narrative in "Little Britain" not only in order to explain from where my interest in Fortress Europe and its "strangers" derives, but also to create a conceptual bridge to what I call a "new framing" of the immigration debate. Obviously, because I am a migrant myself (although a privileged one), some of the issues raised in this debate, both in the UK where I reside and in Europe, are not only baffling to me but also frustrating, if not infuriating. For example, fears of strangers threatening the British way of life (some of whose more salient manifestations in the public space include binge drinking, youth violence, and football hooliganism), thinly veiled as an appeal for "social cohesion" or masked as a call for "integration" into British society (despite the rigorous critique to which it has been subjected by numerous social and cultural critics, many of whom are cited in this volume), are incomprehensible to me. Everything that I find interesting and exciting in London, its unique mix of ethnicities, races, religions, and cultures, its cosmopolitan and vibrant energy, is exactly what others find intimidating and revolting. Whereas I feel enriched by being exposed to this whole world concentrated into one city, others feel that their city (and even their country) has been stolen from them. They feel dispossessed because their once "dominant" culture (so they think) has been pushed to the margins and is in danger of disappearing all together.

Indeed, the public and media debates about migration in the age of elective and mandatory multiculturalism are characterized by contradictions and ambivalences. While the tabloids are bloated with inflammatory rhetoric against migrants and asylum seekers who supposedly abuse the system and European hospitality, television shows and films encourage Europeans and particularly Britons, currently still enjoying a very strong currency, to look for and settle in the best places under the sun, preferably in Spain's Andalusia, Italy's Tuscany, or rural southern France. According to the Yougov polling company, when asked what prompted their interest in buying property abroad, 2,000 people cited ten films and television series.[5] These fictional film and television shows tempt their spectators to start a new life, or buy a second home, abroad. They never question the entitlement of Europeans to settle wherever they desire. But the right of non-Europeans or even "lesser Europeans" (mostly from Central and Eastern Europe) to settle even temporarily in Europe, either to escape persecution, torture, or death or "just" to better their life (to buy "their own slice of Paradise," to use the language of the television shows seducing Britons to buy property and live abroad) is constantly challenged, questioned, and ultimately delegitimized. The irony is evident to the outsider but goes completely unnoticed by many Europeans. The ethical gap between European expansionism (in the form of trade, tourism, property purchase, and even military conquests and invasions such as in Iraq and Afghanistan) and the denial of the right of access of the poorest people in the globe to the basic necessities of life, which in many cases they have lost due to wars and economic difficulties inflicted on them by the West, is only growing.

This conscious and unconscious obliviousness to global injustices, joined by fascination with the other's property/properties, is also manifested in other realms of popular and public culture, from world music to ethnicized fashion and cuisine. The famous ambivalence of "colonial discourse," about which Hommi Bhabha wrote so eloquently,[6] is evident not only in European cinema, the subject of this book, but also in other domains of European culture and life. Thus, for example, the Bollywood wave that has swept the West in recent years goes hand in hand with open racism, most notably unmasked in the 2007 controversy regarding the notorious *Celebrity Big Brother* (UK) television show.[7] The craze for the Gypsy/Carmen look, to give another example, joined growing persecution of the Romany people all over Europe, and Parisian catwalks displayed central Asian and Mongolian Orientalist extravaganza in John Galliano's "exotic" collection, inspired by Coleridge's poem *Kubla Khan* (from which the mansion Xanadu derives its name in Orson Welles's *Citizen Kane*), while migrants who smuggled and trafficked via the Silk Road were raided in Europe. Perhaps the most complex of these "streetcat-walk" manifestations of postcolonial ambivalence, recently paraded all over London, has been the transformation of the traditional Arab *kafiyah* into a High Street fashion accessory "re-branded" by Topshop as "the Table-cloth Scarf" and marketed in commercial catalogues (along with Che

Guevara Canvas) as a "desert scarf." "This year we spotted city kids and party animals in these," the Joe Browns Summer 2008 Catalogue boasts. In the age of Islamophobia and Arabophobia, when the media, politicians, and public intellectuals openly use racist phrases such as "Islamo-Fascism," "Euro-Arabia," "Islam's medievalism," "heartless faith," "paranoia of the Muslim mind," and the like, the *kafiyah*, the traditional outfit of the Arabs living in the birthplace of Islam, has been appropriated by western corporations as a hot fashion-fetish for chic and apolitical European youth.[8]

Europe and Beyond/Beyond Europe: Future Floods and Waves of Migration

Since World War II, what is now the European Union has absorbed different waves of migrants: from the Cold War refugees fleeing the communist bloc to the postcolonial and guest workers who in the fifties and sixties were "invited" to reconstruct the wreckage of postwar Europe, generating the economic miracle of Western Europe and particularly Germany; to the hundreds of thousands of refugees of the Balkan wars of the nineties; and since then the millions of economic migrants seeking "a slice of Paradise" in Fortress Europe. A new report, prepared for the March 2008 EU summit in Brussels by Javier Solana, the EU's chief foreign policy coordinator, and Benita Ferrero-Waldner, the European commissioner for external relations, warned Europe of "a new type of refugee, the 'environmental migrant.'"[9] The report pictures an apocalyptic future of Europe flooded by waves of migrants escaping the "ravages already being inflicted on parts of the developing world by climate change."[10] It also points out that "some countries already badly hit by global warming are demanding that the new phenomenon be recognized internationally as a valid reason for migration."[11] Climate change, the report claims, will "fuel the politics of resentment between those responsible for climate change and those most affected by it . . . and drive political tension nationally and internationally."[12] The apocalyptic future as predicted by this report changes the terms of the debate. The floods and waves of migrants will be "generated" by real environmental waves and floods, the by-products of global climate change for which the rich West is to blame. The fear of migration, articulated in the anti-migration discourse as the threat of the flood, is to be materialized in the form of an environmental, ecological catastrophe in which migration may well get "out of control."[13]

A similar apocalyptic vision is suggested by Winterbottom's *Code 46*, in which the desert has the upper hand in the long-standing struggle between wilderness and civilization. The image of Maria in the future desert where "freedom is just a memory" recalls the final image of Kit (Debra Winger) in Bernardo Bertolucci's *The Sheltering Sky* (1990). Bertolucci described his film as a sort of existentialist/ecological allegory about a "desert world to become tomorrow's reality. A symptom of the greenhouse effect."[14] The victory of the desert, "the only place in the world where even memory disappears,"[15] signifies the catastrophe to come. *Code 46* provides not so different a prophecy. Winterbottom suggested,

> Let's imagine that climate change means that areas that were once fertile are now desert, so the area around Shanghai is a desert. Let's imagine that the ozone layer is depleted and people are afraid to go out in the daytime, so they work at night. Also, let's imagine that because of these changes, living outside of a controlled urban environment is very hard, so everyone wants to live inside the city. Which means that the cities are even more densely populated than now, and in order to control that urban space you have to have some kind of privatised visa system, which gives permission for some people to live in the city. But only those who have the official papelles, which are printed in the office where Maria works. Meanwhile, the disenfranchised people who have no papelles live in the desert area, al fuera, beyond the city limits.[16]

In Winterbottom's next film, *The Road to Guantanamo*, the opposite migratory direction is taken by its protagonists in their epic journey from Fortress Europe to the war zone of Afghanistan and Pakistan, the "al fuera" of the West. In fact, Winterbottom returns in *The Road to Guantanamo* to the same landscapes and themes of *In This World,* but in reverse. Ironically, the journey of *In This World* ends with death in the "free world," whereas the journey of *The Road to Guantanamo* ends with a celebration of life. The latter film, ultimately, despite the horrors of the camp, rejoices in the victory of life over death, torture, and destruction. Toward the end of the film, Iqbal Shafik says: "You need to move on with your life and not look back at the past." The triumph of life over death and devastation is symbolized by the wedding in Pakistan, the return of the tortured groom to his promised bride.[17] The wedding ceremony acts as a mythic signifier of resistance through the affirmation of life. The Tipton Three, the British-born-and-bred Pakistani trio, also known as "the enemy within," unlike Kassovitz's French "black/blanc/beur" trio, ultimately emerges from the torture camp of Guantanamo, attempting to heal their damaged lives. Yet this happy ending for some of the "prisoners of the infinite," to use Jacques Rancière's imploded language,[18] cannot disguise the continuing appeal of the idea of the camp in our post-9/11 planet, in this real world. Only a day after Silvio Berlusconi's "comeback" to win a third term as Italy's prime minister, he announced that one "of the first things to do is to close the frontiers and set up more camps to identify foreign citizens who don't have jobs and are forced into a life of crime." He added that more local police are needed to function as "an army of good in the squares and streets to come between Italian people and the army of evil," thus reconstituting the dominant discourse of evil in the post-9/11 world.[19]

Michael Haneke's much-discussed film *Caché* (*Hidden,* France/Austria/Germany/Italy 2004)[20] introduces Fortress Europe through the home/habitat of the French bourgeois family. Seemingly protected by his bookshelves (the real ones at his Parisian flat, and the *trompe-l'œil* shelves in the TV studio where he is a host of a television literary discussion show reminiscent of the famous *Apostrophe*), the fortified walls of bourgeois European culture, Georges (Daniel Auteuil) lives in a state of permanent denial and repression. His hidden secret, which comes to terrorize him and his family decades later, is his shameful behavior as a six-year-old child toward his adopted brother Majid, the Algerian orphan whose parents were murdered, along with 200 other Algerians, by the French police in a 1961 Paris demonstration against French policy in Algeria.[21] As in *La Haine,* the still-bleeding colonial wound comes to haunt France, decades later. The refusal of France, and even its educated elite, to take responsibility for the continuation of past and present atrocities committed against colonial and postcolonial subjects (many of them living today in France's *banlieues;* see chapter 4) extends in *Caché* (much like in Winterbottom's didactic trilogy) to the rest of the West, which not only continues to hide its past crimes against the third world but continues to enact them in the present. As the television images of violence in Iraq, Palestine, and Kashmir are relegated to the background, the two parents, Georges and Anne (Juliette Binoche), become increasingly consumed by anxiety about their "kidnapped" son, completely oblivious (despite—and perhaps because of—their membership in the intellectual elite of French and European society) that there might be some connection between their family being "terrorized" and the crimes committed by the West against its imagined and imaginary "others" and "strangers."[22]

NOTES

Introduction

The epigraph is from Anni Carlsson and Volker Michels, eds., *The Hesse/Mann Letters: The Correspondence of Hermann Hesse and Thomas Mann 1910–1955,* trans. Ralph Manheim (New York: Jorge Pinto Books, 2005 [1968]), 104.

1. Thomas Mann, *Doctor Faustus,* trans. H. T. Lowe-Porter (Harmondsworth, Middlesex, England: Penguin Books, 1974 [1947]), 167.

2. John Reid, the UK Home Office Secretary on August 9, 2006. The migration literature is multidisciplinary and diverse in nature and therefore immense in volume. In this chapter it has been possible to do more than list examples to illustrate the major concepts and features which have influenced my work. The phenomenon and pattern of migration flows can be tackled from various theoretical approaches. Thus, for example, economic theory views migration as a reaction to labor market while cultural theory explores migration as a center-periphery phenomenon. Social network analysis, on the other hand, argues that migration follows established migration networks (diasporas). For an interesting article that explores this issue from these three combined approaches see Marc Hooghe, Ann Trappers, Bart Meuleman, and Tim Reeskens, "Migration to European Countries: A Structural Explanation of Patterns, 1980–2004," *International Migration Review* 42, no. 2 (Summer 2008): 476–504.

3. Jürgen Habermas, "Why Europe Needs a Constitution," *New Left Review* (September/October 2001).

4. Andrew Geddes, The Politics of Migration and Immigrants in Europe (London: Sage, 2003), 4.

5. Liza Schuster, *The Use and Abuse of Political Asylum in Britain and Germany* (Portland, Ore.: Frank Cass, 2003), 265.

6. Zygmunt Bauman, "Refugees in a Full World," in *Society under Siege* (Cambridge: Polity Press, 2003), 111.

7. The following example represents another "innovative" recycling idea that has floated around in the British public sphere. Harry Letwin (the former Jewish Shadow Home Office Minister of the Conservative party) proposed to send refugees to remote islands ("island" is, of course, another imperial metaphor for recycling human waste). The irony embedded in his suggestion is multifaceted. Not only is Britain itself an island—a small island, as the ironic title of Andrea Levy's acclaimed novel (2004) suggests—and he himself comes from a Jewish immigrant background, but the most notorious island, perhaps, associated with migration is Ellis Island, the island of tears, mainly of Jewish refugees fleeing from Eastern Europe to the promised land of America.

8. See Alan Travis, "New Asylum Centres Open by the End of Year," *Guardian* (May 9, 2003), 6.

9. Considering a range of options for health screening of potential immigrants is a recurrent theme in the political, public, and media discourse on immigration.

10. See Ashwani Sharma and Sanjay Sharma, "White Paranoia: Orientalism in the Age of Empire," *Fashion Theory Journal* 7, nos. 3/4 (2003): 301–18.

11. Don Flynn, "'Tough as Old Boots'? Asylum, Immigration and the Paradox of New Labour Policy," A Discussion Paper, JCWI (Joint Council for the Welfare of Immigrants), IRP (Immigration Rights Project), 1. Discussed in the Symposium on "New Labour New Migration Policies?" (December 4, 2003), London Metropolitan University.

12. Saskia Sassen, a leading world expert on globalization and migration, writes: "European nations—from Germany to France in their radically contrasting policies—have been incorporating 'foreign' men and women for at least two centuries. It is essential that Europe shed its image and representation as a continent whose migration history is confined to the mass migrations of the past. . . . Immigrations from near and far have been an integral part of Europe's history." Saskia Sassen, *Guests and Aliens* (New York: New Press, 1999), 157. See also Saskia Sassen, "Europe's Migrations: The Numbers and the Passions Are Not New," *Third Text* 20, no. 6 (November 2006): 635–46 (special issue, "Fortress Europe: Migration, Culture and Representation," guest editor Yosefa Loshitzky).

13. Since the early nineties there has seen a remarkable resurgence in the political fortunes of the far right in Europe. In France, Austria, Italy, Denmark, Holland, and Belgium, populist nationalism has become a significant electoral force, basing its appeal on fears about immigration, crime, and the decline of the nation-state through European unification.

14. See Jonathan Boyarin, "The Other Within and the Other Without," in *Storm from Paradise: The Politics of Jewish Memory* (Minneapolis: University of Minnesota Press, 1992), 77–98.

15. David Morley, "Postmodernism, Post-Structuralism and the Politics of Difference: At Home in Europe?" in *Home Territories: Media, Mobility and Identity* (London: Routledge, 2000), 246–65.

16. Vron Ware and Les Beck argue that until recently the term "European" has functioned "as a geopolitical category that incorporates a large number and variety of northern people who enjoy diverse ethnicities, but who generally regard themselves as 'white' in relation to other non-European groups. Although twentieth-century European history testifies to the instability and volatility of that consensus, the term 'European' has retained its associations with whiteness" despite the fact that "the concept of 'Europe' itself rests on an endlessly complicated and contested historical process whereby people from different ethnic groups become European or were repelled at its shifting borders." See Vron Ware and Les Beck, *Out of Whiteness: Color, Politics and Cultures* (Chicago: University of Chicago Press, 2002), 206.

17. Don Flynn, "'Tough as Old Boots'?" 1.

18. Teresa Hayter, *Open Borders: The Case Against Immigration Controls* (London: Pluto Press, 2004), 95.

19. Quoted in Bauman, *Society under Siege*, 112.

20. It should be noted that comparing Jews to pests and rats was a major component of Nazi ideology. The film *The Eternal Jew* is a prime example of this racist

analogy. It is also interesting to note that American Cold War fears of communist infiltration were also visualized as the invasion of pure and uncontaminated America by alien mutants in the genre of the science fiction of the fifties. Friend-of-a-friend tales about pets are also very often laced with xenophobia. "Dead pets and dastardly foreigners have furnished one urban legend that has endured for decades," that "'the immigrants are eating our pets.'" See "Stories with Legs," *Guardian Weekend* (January 10, 2004), 55.

21. Arjun Appadurai, "Disjuncture and Difference in the Global Cultural Economy," in *The Phantom Public Sphere,* ed. Bruce Robbins (Minneapolis: University of Minnesota Press, 1993), 269–95.

22. Malkki Lisa, "Citizens of Humanity: Internationalism and the Imagined Communities of Nations," *Diaspora* 3, no. 1 (1994).

23. Stephen Castles and Mark J. Miller, *The Age of Migration,* 3rd ed. (New York: Palgrave Macmillan, 2003), 281.

24. Arif Dirlik, "The Postcolonial Aura: Third World Criticism in the Age of Global Capitalism," *Critical Inquiry* 20, no. 2 (Winter 1994): 355.

25. Dirlik, "The Postcolonial Aura," 330.

26. Ibid., 336.

27. Benedict Anderson, "Exodus," *Critical Inquiry* 20, no. 2 (Winter 1994): 322.

28. Ibid., 325.

29. Philip Schlesinger, "Europeanness—A New Cultural Battlefield?" *Innovation* 5, no. 1 (1992): 13.

30. Anderson, "Exodus," 326.

31. Michael Peter Smith, "Transnational Migration and the Globalization of Grassroots Politics," *Social Text* 39 (1994): 15–16.

32. Hamid Naficy, *The Making of Exile Cultures: Iranian Television in Los Angeles* (Minneapolis: University of Minnesota Press, 1993), 2.

33. Saskia Sassen, "Rebuilding the Global City: Economy, Ethnicity and Space," *Social Justice* 20, nos. 3–4 (1993): 32.

34. Dirlik, "The Postcolonial Aura," 352–53.

35. See, for example, Chantal Mouffe, "For a Politics of Nomadic Identity," in *Travellers' Tales: Narratives of Home and Displacement,* ed. George Robertson et al. (London: Routledge, 1994), 105–13.

36. Liza Schuster, "The Origins of Fortress Europe," international conference on "Fortress Europe and Its 'Others': Cultural Representations in Film, Media and the Arts," the Institute of Germanic and Romance Studies, School of Advanced Study, University of London, April 4–6, 2005.

37. For a further discussion of the murder of Theo van Gogh in the context of the large migrant Muslim population in the Netherlands, see Ian Buruma, *Murder in Amsterdam* (New York: Penguin, 2006). The murder, among other developments, has been accompanied by a "fierce criticism of Islam and, what many people believe to be, the Muslim way of life." See Nancy Forer and Richard Alba, "Immigrant Religion in the U.S. and Western Europe: Bridge or Barrier to Inclusion," *International Migration Review* 42, no. 2 (Summer 2008): 385.

38. Trin Minh-ha observes, "It is often said that writers of colour, including Anglophone and Francophone Third World writers of the diaspora, are condemned to write only autobiographical works." Trin T. Minh-ha, "Other than Myself/My Other Self," in Robertson et al., *Travellers' Tales,* 10. Recent developments in postcolonial

film theory have focused on the notion of hybrid cinema "in which autobiography mediates a mixture of documentary, fiction, and experimental genres, characterizes the film production of people in transition and cultures in the process of creating identities." Laura Marks, "A Deluzian Politics of Hybrid Cinema," *Screen* 35, no. 3 (1994): 245.

39. Siegfried Kracauer, *From Caligari to Hitler: A Psychological History of the German Film* (Princeton, N.J.: Princeton University Press, 1947); Lotte H. Eisner, *The Haunted Screen* (London: Secker & Warburg, 1972 [1952]).

40. In Britain these films include, among others, *Ghosts* (Nick Broomfield, UK, 2007), which tells of the 2004 tragedy of Morecambe Bay, when twenty-three "illegal" Chinese migrants drowned while picking cockles on the sands; *Brick Lane* (Sarah Gavron, UK, 2007), adapted from the novel by Monica Ali; and *It's a Free World* (Ken Loach, UK, 2007), which criticizes the treatment of migrants in a free market–obsessed Britain where, in the words of Paul Laverty, who wrote the screenplay, "The joys of our economic boom are lost on the migrant workers" (see Paul Laverty, "The Flip Side of a Miracle," *Guardian* [September 22, 2007], 34).

41. Naomi Klein, *The Shock Doctrine: The Rise of Disaster Capitalism* (London: Allen Lane, 2007). According to Klein, disaster capitalism is constituted of orchestrated raids on the public sphere in the wake of manufactured and natural catastrophic events, combined with the treatment of disasters as exciting market opportunities by contemporary corporate capitalism. Klein traces affinities between the policies of shock therapy (a combined "inspiration" of Milton Friedman's free-market Chicago School movement and 1950s psychiatric methods of treatment which resemble torture more than therapy) imposed in the course of neoliberal market reform and the techniques of torture that have been routinely used by the United States in the course of "the war on terror."

1. Journeys of Hope to Fortress Europe

The epigraph is from Kate Connolly, "End of Passport Control as East Meets West in EU without Borders," *Guardian* (December 21, 2007), 25.

1. Laura Rascaroli, "New Voyages to Italy: Postmodern Travellers and the Italian Road Film," *Screen* 44, no. 1 (Spring 2003): 74.

2. Hamid Naficy, "Phobic Spaces and Liminal Panics: Independent Transnational Film Genre," *East/West Film Journal* 8, no. 2 (1994): 1. For further discussion of transnational cinema see Hamid Naficy, *An Accented Cinema: Exilic and Diasporic Filmmaking* (Princeton, N.J.: Princeton University Press, 2001); Laura V. Marks, *The Skin of the Film: Intercultural Cinema, Embodiment and the Senses* (Durham, N.C.: Duke University Press, 2000); and Elizabeth Ezra and Terry Rowden, eds., *Transnational Cinema: The Film Reader* (London: Routledge, 2006). It is interesting to mention in this context that according to Thomas Elsaesser, European cinema is in fact Third Cinema, a hybrid of Hollywood and Art Cinema. See Thomas Elsaesser, *European Cinema Face to Face with Hollywood* (Amsterdam: Amsterdam University Press, 2005). For a discussion of transnational cinema in the context of European cinema see Rosalind Galt, *The New European Cinema: Redrawing the Map* (New York: Columbia University Press, 2006); Mary Wood, *Contemporary European Cinema* (London:

Arnold, 2007); and Luisa Rivi, *European Cinema After 1989: Cultural Identity and Transnational Migration* (New York: Palgrave Macmillan, 2008).

3. For further discussion of the journey motif see Naficy, "Journeying, Border Crossing, and Identity Crossing," in *An Accented Cinema,* 222–87. Carrie Tarr suggests three categories of films about immigration in France: pre-border-crossing films, border-crossing films, and post-border-crossing Films. See Carrie Tarr, "The Porosity of the Hexagon: Border Crossing in Contemporary French Cinema," *Studies in European Cinema* 4, no. 1 (2007): 7–20. The journey film, despite sharing some affinities with the road movie, a distinctively American genre, is different in its conception of space, time, and experience. The road film is a product of American natural/manmade geography composed of vast spaces and endless highways. Its ideological core is centered on the attempt to escape the established order toward "freedom." The protagonists are usually marginal figures and very often they are involved in violence, crime, sexual libertinism, and other taboo-breaking activities. For further reading on the American road film see Steven Cohan and Ina Rae Hark, eds., *The Road Movie Book* (London: Routledge, 1997), and David Laderman, *Driving Visions: Exploring the Road Movies* (Austin: University of Texas Press, 2002). For a fascinating article on narratives of travel writing in Europe see Mohammed A. Bamyeh, "Frames of Belonging: Four Contemporary European Travels," *Social Text* 39 (1994): 36–55. For an excellent discussion of contemporary refugees see Philip Marfleet, *Refugees in a Global Era* (New York: Palgrave Macmillan, 2006). For a major theoretical and "real life"-based discussion of the refugee "problem" that questions traditional definitions, see Nevzat Soguk, *States and Strangers: Refugees and Displacements of Statecraft* (Minneapolis: University of Minnesota Press, 1999).

4. For further reading see John Hill, "'Race' and Cultural Hybridity: *My Beautiful Laundrette* and *Sammy and Rosie Get Laid,*" in his *British Cinema in the 1980s* (Oxford: Clarendon Press, 1999), 205–18, and Karen Alexander, "Black British Cinema in the 90s: Going Going Gone," in *British Cinema of the 90s,* ed. Robert Murphy (London: BFI, 2000), 109–14. It is important to mention that in the British context "black" refers to black Africans, West Indian blacks, and Asians mostly from Bangladesh, Pakistan, and India.

5. The relationship of Switzerland with the EU is complex. Switzerland has been a member of the European Free Trade Association (EFTA) since 1959. However, its application for full EU membership in 1992 was lost in the referendum that would have allowed it to join the EU. Whereas most French speakers were in favor of joining the EU, German speakers rejected the initiative. The government subsequently signed a bilateral agreement with the EU, designed to gradually open up free movement of people, transport access, and other matters.

6. For obvious reasons, organic images and metaphors of rooting and uprooting are very predominant in the discourse about exile and displacement. In the second volume of Anaïs Nin's novel *Cities of the Interior* (London: Quartet Books, 1979 [1959]), for example, Jay says to Sabina (443): "When people get transplanted, it's exactly like plants; at first there's a wilting, a withering; some die of it. We're all at the critical stage, suffering from a change of soil."

7. To enhance the Exodus motif, the Turkish trafficker tells Haydar when he pays the money to be smuggled to Europe, "Everyone is going abroad; the government will have no one to govern soon."

8. Naficy, *An Accented Cinema,* 257.

9. The notion of the "non-place" was articulated by the anthropologist Marc Auges as "the opposite of utopia: it exists, and it does not contain any organic society." See Marc Auges, *Non-Places: Introduction to the Anthropology of Supermodernity* (London: Verso), 111–12.

10. It is of some interest to note that in recent years Switzerland has become a site of "suicide tourism." Dozens of patients have traveled to Zurich to die with the help of Dignitas and Exit, two organizations that assist in suicide (assisted suicide is legal in Switzerland, though euthanasia is not). It is also interesting to note at this point that the snow-covered Alps have since the nineteen century constituted a space of death fantasy in European literature and film. Hans Castorp, the protagonist of Thomas Mann's novel *The Magic Mountain,* develops death fantasies in the snow-covered Alps. In *Trilogy* by Lucas Belvaux (France, 2003), a triptych composed of three features made in entirely different cinematic styles, the former Red Brigade terrorist finds his death in the Alps on the border between Switzerland and Italy.

11. Naficy, *An Accented Cinema,* 261.

12. Within the framework of Holocaust iconography, the suitcase has become, particularly over the past decade, the signifier of Jewish refugees and deportees and the main object on display in many exhibitions devoted to the Holocaust.

13. It should also be noted that Koller made a film called *Gripsholm* (Switzerland, 2000) that takes place during the summer holiday in Sweden, about a Jewish essayist and journalist with a clear vision about Germany's future and his German girlfriend the summer before the National Socialist Party comes to power. The film was based on a semi-autobiographical novel by Kurt Tuchlosky, a German Jew, who, like Eisler, Heartfield, Grosz, and Brecht, was part of the satirical cutting edge scene in 1920s Berlin. After the Nazis came to power, he escaped to Sweden and settled near Castle Gripsholm, which became the title of his last novel. In 1935 he committed suicide.

14. In the 1990s an Independent Commission of Experts Switzerland–Second World War (ICE) (Unabhaengigen Expertenkomission Schweiz—Zweiter Weltkrieg) was established to examine various aspects of the nation's actions before, during, and after World War II. In December 1999 the commission presented a report known as the Bergier Report. It addresses Switzerland's refugee policy before and during the war, specifically criticizing two decisions by Switzerland that had a devastating impact on Jews attempting to find refuge there: in 1938, to stamp all passports with a "J," and in 1942, the sealing of Switzerland's borders. Recent years have witnessed a growing number of publications about the attitude of the Swiss authorities toward Jewish refugees that fled the Nazis. See for example Renata Broggini, *Frontier of Hope—Jews from Italy Seek Refuge in Switzerland 1943–1945* (Milano: Hoepli editore, 2003 [1998]).

15. Obviously the issues of migration, hospitality, and the Swiss state are very complex and sometimes present contradictory pictures. The following are some points that I would like to draw attention to in order to introduce a more comprehensive view of the issues. First of all, it should be mentioned that Switzerland has traditionally been a receiving/host country for political refugees, from the Russians to the Italian anarchists and communists (this is also the reason why the traffickers in *Journey of Hope* instruct the migrants to claim political asylum, as the Kurds are a persecuted minority in Turkey). For a discussion of the traditional Swiss hostility toward migrants and their attitudes toward their own "guest-workers," see Stephen

Castels, "Switzerland," in *Ethnicity and Globalization* (London: Sage, 2000), 68–69. According to an article by Luke Harding in the *Guardian,* the rise of Switzerland's far-right People's Party (SVP), whose leader is Christoph Blocher, signified growing xenophobia and anti-migration sentiments in the Swiss public. Blocher's anti-immigration party fought the most explicit foreigner-bashing campaign in Switzerland's history—and won 26.9 percent of the vote. See Luke Harding, "Far-right Rise Threatens Swiss 'Magic Formula,'" *Guardian* (December 8, 2003), 15. In 2004 there was a referendum in Switzerland that approved that children (third generation) of immigrants cannot become naturalized. Even tighter asylum rules and measures were backed by some 67.8 percent of Swiss voters in a national referendum in September 2006. Consequently, Switzerland is currently the worst place in Europe to be an asylum seeker.

16. Zygmunt Bauman, "The Making and Unmaking of Strangers," in *Postmodernity and Its Discontents* (New York: New York University Press, 1997), 17–34.

17. It is interesting in this context to quote the words of the narrator in Thomas Mann's *Doctor Faustus:* "In my experience there is in Switzerland much feeling for suffering, much understanding of it, which, more than in other places of advanced culture, for instance intellectual Paris, is bound up with the old civic life of the towns." See Thomas Mann, *Doctor Faustus,* trans. H. T. Lowe-Porter (Middlesex: Penguin Books, 1974 [1947]), 174.

18. Mann, with typical irony, asks: "European fortress—or shall I say our prison, our madhouse?" Ibid., 245.

19. Ibid., 174. In light of Mann's favorable view of Switzerland it is not surprising that he chose to live in Zurich and not in Germany when he had to flee also from American exile. Mann's novel *The Magic Mountain* can still be seen, even today, as a cultural document on Europe's view of itself in dialectical opposition to its own imaginary/imagined construct of "Asia" and the "East." The following quote from the novel could be ironically resurrected as a motto for the current debate on the so-called "clash of civilizations": "Two principles, according to Settembrinian cosmogony, were in perpetual conflict for possession of the world: force and justice, tyranny and freedom, superstition and knowledge; the law of permanence and the law of change, of ceaseless fermentation issuing in progress. One might call the first the Asiatic, the second the European principle; for Europe was the theatre of rebellion, the sphere of intellectual discrimination and transforming activity, whereas the East embodied the conception of quiescence and immobility." See Thomas Mann, *The Magic Mountain,* trans. H. T. Lowe-Porter (New York: Vintage Books Edition, 1969 [1924]), 157.

20. For a further discussion of hotels and motels see Naficy, *An Accented Cinema,* 248.

21. The famous song "Over the Rainbow" from Victor Fleming's *The Wizard of Oz* (USA, 1939) has been described by Salman Rushdie as "the anthem of all the world's migrants." See Salman Rushdie, *The Wizard of Oz* (London: BFI, 1992), 23.

22. For a further discussion of the Alps, see Fergus Fleming, *Killing Dragons: The Conquest of the Alps* (London: Granta Books, 2005).

23. On the dimension of fantasy in the process of migration (a neglected area in migration studies), see Leon Grinberg and Rebecca Grinberg, *Psychoanalytic Perspectives on Migration and Exile* (New Haven, Conn.: Yale University Press, 1989), trans. Nancy Festinger.

24. The film's humanization of the traffickers (especially the young protagonist), showing them as victims of the new Europe, recalls Luc and Jean-Pierre Dardenne's *La promesse* (France, 1996).

25. Available at http://www.bfi.org.uk/sightandsound/2001_03/last_resort.html (accessed March 11, 2004).

26. The choice of the name Alfie is deeply indebted to the connotations embedded in this name within the context of the history of British cinema. Alfie was the name of the protagonist of the film *Alfie* (Lewis Gilbert, Britain, 1966), incarnated by Michael Caine as a working-class young man and tireless womanizer. The fact that Caine himself came from a working-class background and went on to become a famous star and Sir is invoked in *Last Resort* as an implicit comment on the "English Dream." It is not an accident either that Alfie, in *Last Resort,* works in "Dreamland" in the dreary resort town where the film takes place. Pawlikowski himself said that "as a kid I saw a lot of 1960s British films." Ryan Gilbey, "Pawel Pawlikowski: Another England," in "British Directors Special," *Sight & Sound* (October 2004): 38.

27. On the culture of the English resort town see John Uri, "Mass Tourism and the Rise and Fall of the Seaside Resort," in *The Tourist Gaze: Leisure and Travel in Contemporary Societies* (London: Sage Publications, 1990), 16–39. Gurinder Chadha's *Bhaji on the Beach* (Britain, 1994), a feminist film which celebrates the growing multicultural diaspora community in the city of Birmingham, takes place in the working-class seaside resort of Blackpool. In *Bahji,* the one-day bus trip that three generations of lower-middle- and middle-class Asian women (in Britain defined as women from India, Pakistan, and Bangladesh) take from Birmingham to the working-class seaside resort of Blackpool becomes an allegory of diasporic/exiled women's experience. The collective trip on the road thus becomes a filmic social critique of an Asian woman director who is deeply linked to her community while being critical of many of its values, particularly its authoritarian approach to marriage and its intolerance of blacks. Abdulrazak Gurnah, a former refugee from Zanzibar, describes Margate as "not quite an asylum-seekers' Gulag" but "a wreck, living up to its reputation as a decaying town." See Abdulrazak Gurnah, "Beside the Seaside," *New Statesman* (September 25, 2006), 67.

28. Turner lived in Margate and described the skies over the town as the loveliest in Europe.

29. In his *Sight & Sound* interview Pawlikowski said: "England is interesting because the landscape is more postmodern than anywhere else. I've just been in Spain where you can't escape the sense of continuity, but in Britain there is a spiritual vacuum and the fact that the meaningful aesthetics of family and religion have fallen by the wayside allows you to reinvent that." Gilbey, "Pawel Pawlikowski: Another England," 38.

30. Iain Sinclair, "The Cruel Seaside," *Sight & Sound* (March 2001): 16–18, available at http://www.bfi.org.uk/sightandsound/2001_03/last_resort.html (accessed March 11, 2004). According to Les Roberts, *Last Resort* "provides a key exemplar of a cinema of non-places, in its study of asylum and detention in contemporary Britain." See Les Roberts, "'Welcome to Dreamland': From Place to Non-Place and Back Again in Pawel Pawlikowski's *Last Resort,*" *New Cinemas: Journal of Contemporary Film* 1, no. 2 (2002): 80. In the same issue, see also Les Roberts's interview with the director ("From Sarajevo to Didcot: An Interview with Pawel Pawlikowski," 91–97).

31. John Frow, "Tourism and the Semiotics of Nostalgia," *October* 57 (Summer 1991): 144.

32. The child's initiation into Britishness and Englishness is through the Tikka Masala chicken offered to him by Alfie, an Indian dish which has become the most popular food in Britain, signifying the changing face of Britain and its transformation into a multicultural society. When they first eat fish and chips, the iconic traditional working-class English food, the child complains (and rightly so) that the fish has no fish.

33. *The Wizard of Oz* is about the return journey of Dorothy from Dreamland with the realization that "there is no place like home," a realization referenced and invoked in Tanya's journey of return.

34. Andrew O'Hagan in http://news.telegraph.co.uk/arts/main.jhtml?xml=/arts/2001/03/16/bflast16.xml, filed on March 16, 2001 (accessed November 3, 2004).

35. This enthusiasm was also shared by the British academic community, which invited him to participate in plenary sessions in some film studies conferences.

36. David Walsh, "Nothing to Boast Around Not: *Last Resort* & When Brendan Met Trudy," World Socialist website. See http://www.wsws.org/articles/2001/mar2001/film-m23_prn.shtml (accessed March 11, 2004).

37. Quoted in ibid.

38. Ibid.

39. In June 2005 Amnesty International published a report which criticized the British government for its policy of detaining asylum seekers, saying it breaches their human rights. The study came barely a fortnight after a report from the European Commissioner for Human Rights criticized Britain over the same issue. For further details see Vikram Dodd, "Amnesty Report Questions Legality of Detaining Asylum Seekers," *Guardian* (June 15, 2005), 5. At the time of writing the first draft of this chapter (July 2006) Panopticon Britain has been further fortified. On July 23, 2006, the Labor government announced that it would start using uniform border control at ports of exit to Britain to catch illegal immigrants.

40. Available at http://www.fucine.com/archivio/fm60/eng_kozole.htm (accessed September 23, 2004).

41. Rudi is also astonished to find out that Hitler was Austrian and not German. "Yes, 100% Austrian," Ludvik assures him. The comment about the Austrian origins of Hitler is very significant in the context of defining the boundaries of Europe and its inside and outside others. Those in Slovenia who want to dissociate the country from the "Barbaric Balkan" emphasize its geographical and cultural proximity to Germanic/European Austria. By illuminating his "pupil" about the Nazi past of Austria, Ludvik questions the high moral ground taken by Europe with regard to Slovenia and the Balkans. Slovenia's request to join the EU was rejected in 2000. In response, two big signs were installed on one of the bridges along the Sava River which crosses Ljubljana. One side of the bridge was designated for "EU members" and the other as "Others," mockingly replicating the spatial/bureaucratic division of most airports in the EU.

42. On the other hand, one of the traffickers, while trying to persuade the Macedonian girl whose boyfriend is desperate to have sex with him (what actually amounts to a rape that later drives her to commit suicide) offers/promises her "antibiotics." In an effort to be more convincing he says, "Very good antibiotic, American."

43. Miriam Cooke, "Journeys Real and Imaginary," *Edebiyat: The Journal of Middle Eastern Literatures* 4 (1993): 151.

44. For a discussion of *Les Princes* see Carrie Tarr, "Representation and Memory in *Les Princes,*" *Framework: The Journal of Cinema and Media* 44, no. 2 (Fall 2003): 120–26 (special issue, "Cinematic Images of Romanies," guest editor Dina Iordanova).

45. *Latcho Drom* itself is a journey film, a journey through time and space that traces the grand historical migration of the Gypsies from Rajasthan, India, to the Middle East, North Africa, and Europe. It is a music-and-dance odyssey that spans the centuries as it follows the westward migration of Gypsies from northern India to Spain. This journey is also a musical journey tracing the different musical traditions of the Roma that developed in different geographical/cultural regions. Gatlif's most recent film, *Transylvania* (France/Romania, 2006), is a sort of sequel to *Gadjo Dilo*. The female protagonist of the film, who starts her journey as a "modern" Western French woman, ends it as a traditional "crazy" Gypsy mother. With *Transylvania*, Gatlif said, "I wanted to write the story of a person who is lost and then rediscovers herself in an unfamiliar world." Cited in Michael Brooke "An Innocent Abroad," an interview with Tony Gatlif, *Sight & Sound* 17 (June 2007): 12. For an analysis of *Gadjo Dilo,* see Andrew McGregor, "French Cinema in Exile: Trans-national Cultural Representation in Tony Gatlif's *Gadjo Dilo,*" *New Cinemas: Journal of Contemporary Film* 6, no. 2 (2008): 75–83.

46. Goran Gocic, *The Cinema of Emir Kusturica: Notes from the Underground* (London: Wallflower Press, 2001), 93.

47. Dina Iordanova, *Cinema of Flames: Balkan Film, Culture and the Media* (London: BFI, 2001), 214, 215.

48. The Gypsies of Romania have suffered persecution more than the Gypsies of another country since the fall of the Eastern bloc. The collapse of the communist regimes of Eastern Europe has rekindled anti-Roma sentiment in Eastern and Western Europe. Violent attacks and pogroms against the Roma were particularly severe in Romania, with little or no restraint from government authorities. For a report on some of the atrocities committed against the Romanies in Romania before and during the release of *Gadjo Dilo,* see Veronika Leila Szente, "Sudden Rage at Dawn: Violence against Roma in Romania" (European Roma Rights Center: Country Reports Series 2 [September 1996]). It is safe to speculate that Gatlif chose Romania as the location of the third film in his Gypsy trilogy in response to these pogroms in an attempt to show the transnational solidarity among the Romanies.

49. Max Weber discussed the Jews and the Gypsies as "pariah-people" who "had lost their territories, were confined to particular occupations and were endogamous in respect of dietary prohibitions, religious practices and social intercourse. . . . The Jews developed a form of 'pariah-capitalism,' which started with money lending and built on speculative investment and thence to banking and high finance. The caste-like attributes of these groups provided the basis for complete trust inside the group and an acute need to create some security against the threatening outsider." Quoted in Robin Cohen, *Global Diasporas: An Introduction* (London: UCL Press, 1997), 101.

50. Isabel Fonseca, *Bury Me Standing: The Gypsies and Their Journeys* (New York: Vintage Books, 1995), 271. Gypsies and Jews are the two oldest minorities of Europe whose remote and foreign Oriental origin, lack of attachment to "host" countries,

"nomadic character," "strange" language, dress code, customs, strict dietary practice, and taboos voluntarily isolate them from the *Gadjo* and/or the *Goy,* while their darker complexion and "different" physical features cast them visually as "the other within Europe." Unlike the Jews, however, the Gypsy identity does not incorporate a religious identity as well. For a further discussion see Yosefa Loshitzky, "Quintessential Strangers: The Representation of Romanies and Jews in Some Holocaust Films," *Framework* 44, no. 2 (Fall 2003): 57–71.

51. Anikó Imre, "Screen Gypsies," *Framework* 44, no.1 (Fall 2003): 17. See also Anikó Imre, "Play in the Ghetto: Global Entertainment and the European 'Roma Problem,'" *Third Text* 20, no. 6 (November 2006): 659–70 (special issue, "Fortress Europe: Migration, Culture and Representation," guest editor Yosefa Loshitzky).

52. Imre, "Screen Gypsies," 17.

53. Peter Baxter, "Putting Characters in Place: From *Le Bonheur* to *La Vie de Jésus* and *Western,*" *Studies in French Cinema* 2, no. 2 (2002): 68. Although I agree with Baxter about the film's shift toward post-national identity, my understanding of this shift is not toward transnationalism but, as my discussion shows, toward regionalism.

54. Philippe Gajan, "Entretien avec Manuel Poirier," *24 Images,* no. 90 (Winter 1998): 32.

55. I am indebted to Jocelyne Tinestit for drawing my attention to this point. Indeed, the two lonely migrant men, in search of love and belonging (woman's love in the framework of this film is a prerequisite to acquiring a sense of belonging), replicate the old model of late nineteenth-century immigration to France when single men mostly from Belgium, Poland, and Italy came to work as miners.

56. It is not an accident that the name of the blonde Breton woman with whom Paco falls in love is Marinette (Elisabeth Vitali), recalling the name Marianne, a symbolic and recurrent female figure in French cultural life, expressing the idea of France as a woman. For a further discussion see *La France: Images of Woman and Ideas of Nation 1789–1989,* exhibition catalogue (London: South Bank Centre, 1989). In her book *Stars and Stardom in French Cinema* (New York: Continuum, 2005), Ginette Vincendeau discusses how Brigitte Bardot and Catherine Deneuve have modeled for Marianne, the effigy of the Republic.

2. Cities of Hope

The epigraph is from Zygmunt Bauman, "The Stranger Revisited—and Revisiting," in *Life in Fragments: Essays in Postmodern Morality* (Oxford: Blackwell, 1995), 126.

1. See Saskia Sassen, *Guests and Aliens* (New York: New Press, 1999), and Saskia Sassen, "Europe's Migrations: The Numbers and the Passions are Not New," *Third Text* 20, no. 6 (November 2006): 635–44 (special issue, "Fortress Europe: Migration, Culture and Representation," guest editor Yosefa Loshitzky).

2. Mike Davis writes: "Cities, indeed, have absorbed nearly two-thirds of the global population explosion since 1950 and are currently growing by a million babies and migrants each week. The present urban population (3.2 billion) is larger than the total population of the world in 1960." Mike Davis, "Planet of Slums: Urban Involution and the Informal Proletariat," *New Left Review* 26 (March–April 2004): 5.

3. Michael Hardt and Antonio Negri, *Empire* (Cambridge, Mass.: Harvard University Press, 2000), 364.

4. Tamara subverts ethnic stereotypes, looking more like a "typical" Bosnian Muslim rather than a Serbian "Slav." When they listen to news about the war in Bosnia, Jasmin says, "Damn Serbs," to which Tamara responds, "I'm Serb."

5. See Martin Reisgl and Ruth Wodak, *Discourse and Discrimination: Rhetorics of Racism and Antisemitism* (London: Routledge, 2001). The authors indicate that today several different groups of foreigners and minorities live in Austria: autochthonous minorities (Slovenes, Croats, Hungarians, Jews, Roma and Sinti, Czechs and Slovaks); migrant workers (mainly Turks and ex-Yugoslavs who began arriving in the 1970s); political refugees of all stripes (including Iranians, Vietnamese, Albanians, Bosnians); and since 1989, the so-called "economic refugees" (predominantly Hungarians, Poles, Czechs, Romanians, and Russians). Each of these groups has a different legal status. The years 1989–1990 witnessed a significant rise in "anti-foreigner" discourse on the so-called "foreigner and refugee problem." The Vienna chapter of the FPÖ (the Freedom Party, Jörg Haider's party, whose aim is to "protect the German culture" against a potential "multicultural society") put out a campaign poster declaring that "Vienna must not be allowed to become Chicago." This was an allusion to the fact that Chicago is the city with the largest concentration of people of Polish heritage outside Poland.

6. Another Austrian film on migrants is *I Love Vienna*, by Houchang Allahyari (Austria, 1991), a comedy made by a Tehran-born filmmaker (and psychiatrist). It is about the relationship between Ali Mohammed and a Viennese woman. Mohammed is a German teacher from Iran who moves to Vienna with his sister and son in order to get away from a new, frightening war. They move into a run-down hotel for immigrants and refugees in the Second District of Vienna. The film evolves around a "clash of cultures" between the Iranian immigrant and Viennese society. An interesting recent addition to migrant and diasporic cinema in Austria is Ulrich Seidl's *Import Export* (Austria, 2007) a bleak view on two-way migration between East and West (a Ukrainian nurse ends up as a cleaning woman in a geriatric ward in Vienna and in the opposite direction, Paul, an unemployed security guard from Vienna, seeks out a new life in Ukraine).

7. Adolf Hitler's notorious impressions of early twentieth-century "mongrel" Vienna were documented in *Mein Kampf* where, using medical imagery, he describes the constant attack on the national "host" body by the "parasite," the "noxious bacillus" and the "foreign virus," i.e., the Jews. When describing prewar Vienna, Hitler writes that "if the old hereditary territories were the heart of the Empire, continually driving fresh blood into the circulatory stream of political and cultural life, Vienna was the brain and will in one." Adolf Hitler, *Mein Kampf,* trans. Ralph Manheim (London: Hutchinson of London, 1980 [1930]), 63.

8. It is interesting to note that the film's politically subversive dimension was, according to the director of the film, unrecognized by the international community and the American Jewish community in particular. Alexander Horwath, the former director of the Viennale (Vienna International Film Festival) and a freelance writer, curator, and festival consultant, wrote: "When the anti-government demonstrations started in Vienna on February 4 [1999], Barbara Albert was there, marching and chanting with the crowds, next to a large number of other artists and filmmakers.

How strange it must have been when she heard that in Hollywood, a group of Jewish Academy members had called for a boycott of *Nordrand*'s L.A. screenings—as Austria's official entry in the Foreign Language Oscar nominations. . . . At the Berlin Film Festival, which opened five days after the new government was installed, Austrian filmmakers were already present with a strong indictment, published in all festival media. In Vienna, Paris, and L.A., people like Klaus Maria Brandauer, Michael Haneke and even Arnold Schwarzenegger spoke out against the Freedom Party and its newfound respectability—and these three guys aren't exactly known as leftists." Alexander Horwath, "*Northern Skirts* Raises Austrian Politics and Artists' Concerns in the Age of Haider," Reel.com: New Directors/New Films, posted March 29, 2000 (accessed October 27, 2004).

9. The brutality and ugliness of Albert's Vienna recalls the portrayal of the city in Elfriede Jelinek's *The Piano Teacher* (1983).

10. For a sociopolitical-cultural history of the Danube see Claudio Magris, *Danube,* trans. Patrick Creagh (London: Harvill Press, 1989 [1986]).

11. Jasmin is a compulsive eater of rich cream cakes (for which Vienna is well known). Albert's Vienna is a subversion of anything that smells of "classical Vienneism," including its famous *cream schnitt* cakes. Jasmin's love of cakes is represented as lower-class "white trash" binge eating, an excessive consumption of junk food rather than imperial delight. It signifies lack of control (which also characterizes Jasmin's sex life) and low self-esteem.

12. The scene of the celebrating masses in the city center recalls the *Anschluss* of Austria by Hitler.

13. In fact, the ending of the film is very confusing. I have found this confusion is shared by many others (see below). See roundtable discussion with Albert, Vienna, November 21, 2000, http://sources2.de/filmmakers.html (accessed October 27, 2004). It can be argued that the confusion was not only a matter of misleading editing but also a result of the ignorance prevalent in Western Europe about the Balkans.

14. The Europe-America axis resonates also in the grander political scheme alluded to in the film. European impotence in the face of the war in Yugoslavia has been a topic of much criticism. The political resolution to the recent Balkan conflict was eventually achieved by an American peace plan (the Dayton accords).

15. In the same roundtable discussion Barbara Albert said: "There are some moments in this film where I wanted to go outside of the story, and this was such a moment when I wanted to tell more about the situation of the eastern countries. And I wanted to give a feeling of where these people come from. I like it very much to hear the music from there, and then this hip hop, this rap from Romania, which is so much the opposite for me. So it's really a very strange phenomenon to see that one person, who is now maybe twenty-five, had something like that in his childhood, and now he listens to this music. Maybe here you get a feeling of what lies between these two points."

16. One of the foundational stories of my own life narrative is my mother's recollection of her post–World War II experience of transit in Vienna as a Jewish refugee from Poland. Her most powerful memory of Vienna is the contemptuous and loathing looks of the elegant, fur-clad, long-sleeved, and gloved Viennese ladies on their way to the opera, directed at a group of shabby-looking Jewish women refugees.

17. See Reisgl and Wodak, Discourse and Discrimination.

18. For a discussion of the cultural and ideological/political relationship between "the Balkan" and "Europe/Europeaness," see Dina Iordanova, *Cinema of Flames: Balkan Film, Culture and the Media* (London: BFI, 2001).

19. A testimony to the neutral space that Austria constituted during the Cold War is the 1961 meeting between John F. Kennedy and Nikita Khrushchev at the East-West summit in Vienna and the 1979 East-West summit held between Leonid Brezhnev and Jimmy Carter.

20. Timothy Garton Ash, *History of the Present: Essays, Sketches and Dispatches from Europe in the 1990s* (London: Allen Lane, 1999), 205.

21. Robin Wood, "*Beautiful People,*" *CineAction,* no. 54 (January 2001): 30. On buses, see Naficy, *An Accented Cinema: Exilic and Diasporic Filmmaking* (Princeton, N.J.: Princeton University Press, 2001), 257–61.

22. On January 21, 2005, the *Guardian* published a special supplement entitled "London: The World in One City: A Special Celebration of the Most Cosmopolitan Place on Earth."

23. Wood, "*Beautiful People,*" 31. It is interesting to illustrate this transition from the humble London bus to the house of an upper-class family of a Tory MP with what David McKie writes: "Some people shun service buses: they don't like having strangers jammed up against them. The normally gregarious Conservative politician Steven Norris once declared his distaste for using the bus because of the kind of people he found himself sitting next to." See David McKie, "All Aboard!" *Guardian* (February 17, 2006), 8. See also his book *Great British Bus Journeys* (London: Atlantic Books, 2006).

24. Robert Lightning, "*Beautiful People:* In Praise of the Liberal State," *CineAction,* no. 58 (June 2002): 68.

25. Laura Barton, "On the Buses," *Guardian,* G2 (July 15, 2005), 2. The subheading of the article says: "Laura Barton rides a few of the 6,500 red buses that mirror the city they serve" (2). She writes: "There has always seemed something so fundamentally benign about the red London bus, the tube's poor, red-checked relation. The jovial double decker is, like red telephone boxes and the Queen's guards, regarded by the visitor as a photo-opportunity rather than an integral part of the city. 'A man who, beyond the age of 26, finds himself on a bus can account himself as a failure,' Margaret Thatcher once said, and to a large extent this has seemed a tangible truth—buses were the slow, dirty cattle trucks of the city: the seats mottled with chewing gum stains, the greasy prickly of the upholstery, the dirt and the dust and the graffiti-stained walls of these juddering contraptions in which one sits, pressed in intimate proximity to one's fellow travelers, breathed upon, sneezed upon, for the length of one's rumbling, meandering journey." As an adjunct to this article, on the same page the *Guardian* published a comment by Hassan (signed as Hassan [his only name], Bradford, July 14, 2005), with the introduction: "Beginning in late April 2001 in Bradford, riots involving 'Asians' (mainly second-generation Pakistani immigrants), white youth and the police spread to Oldham, Leeds and Burnley." The title of the comment is: "Hassan, a young Muslim born and raised in Yorkshire, offers a heartfelt response to last week's attacks on London, 'A Letter to the Terrorists,'" *Guardian* (July 15, 2005), 5. The theme of public transport as a democratic, multicultural space exists also in *La Haine,* where

the Paris metro is a meeting place for Paris's others: migrants, second-generation immigrants, the homeless, and the poor.

26. It is very apt in this context to quote Michael Ignatieff: "Freud once argued that the smaller the real difference between two peoples the larger it was bound to loom in their imagination. He called this effect the narcissism of minor difference. Its corollary must be that enemies need each other to remind themselves of who they really are. A Croat, thus, is someone who is not a Serb. A Serb is someone who is not a Croat. Without hatred of the other, there would be no clearly defined national self to worship and adore." Michael Ignatieff, *Blood and Belonging: Journeys into the New Nationalism* (London: Chatto and Windus, 1993), 14.

27. For a further discussion of these issues see Lightning, *"Beautiful People:* In Praise of the Liberal State." Lightning's brilliant article is a polemic aimed at Robin Wood's celebratory review of the film. See Robin Wood, *"Beautiful People."*

28. Dizdar's choice of the Dutch as representatives of the "Europe" hated by white English supremacists is not accidental. The Dutch played a notoriously shameful role in the Balkan war. When Serb forces seized the UN "safe haven" of Srebrenica, marching about 8,000 Bosnian Muslims to the killing fields, Dutch soldiers did not interfere. There is even a controversy about whether or not Dutch peacekeepers helped the Serbs to separate Muslim men from the women (see Iordanova, *Cinema in Flames,* 282n3). The UN's highest court cleared Serbia, on February 26, 2007, of direct responsibility for genocide (the 1995 massacre at Srebrenica). The criticism expressed here against Europe creates a symbolic bond between the English barbarians and the Bosnian barbarians. The silence of the European bystanders in the face of the Balkan tragedy has created much bitterness in Bosnia, especially during the siege on Sarajevo.

29. It is also a latent criticism of the BBC's refusal to support Dizdar's film.

30. For a further, by now classical, discussion of this duality, see Edward W. Said, "Reflections on Exile," *Granta* 13 (Winter 1984).

31. Emir Kusturiça and Dusan Makavejev are two of the better-known masters of the genre of the crazy Balkan comedy. The popularity of this genre in the international market sphere suggests, in my opinion, that it is impossible to refer to the Balkan in "normal" terms, as if the Balkan and its "tribal barbarism" are beyond civilized comprehension and rational discourse. Content, in this respect, corresponds to form.

32. In a review of a book by (woman) war correspondent Janine di Giovanni, *The Place at the End of the World* (London: Bloomsbury, 2006), Adam Thorpe writes: "Her [Janine di Giovanni's] memoir of Kurt Schork, the legendary Reuters reporter killed in Sierra Leone, includes his observation, during the siege of Sarajevo, that 'his job was "the closest approximation of happiness."' Happiness comes from fulfillment, from fleshing out one's ideals, but hers (and Schork's) must also have a counterpart in the potential of war psychosis to create anticipation and excitement in impressionable young men." "Like many others in her line of work," Thorpe continues, "the country that haunts her most is neat, pretty Bosnia." See Adam Thorpe, "War Disease . . . and Plumbers," review of Janine di Giovanni, *The Place at the End of the World* (London: Bloomsbury, 2006), Review Saturday, *Guardian* (January 14, 2006), 9.

33. As in *La Haine* (see chapter 4), the skinhead is played by a Jewish actor (Danny Nussbaum).

34. It is worth quoting in this context the following anecdote: "Laslo Moholy-Nagy, one of the leading figures in the Bauhaus, arrived to work in England in 1935, two years after that experimental school of art and design was closed down by the Nazis. His English was not fluent. Taken to a party in London by John Betjeman, he said smilingly to his hostess: 'Thank you for your hostilities.'" Quoted in Fiona MacCarthy, "The Fiery Stimulator," Review Saturday, *Guardian* (March 18, 2006), 12. MacCarthy continues: "The remark was not entirely inappropriate: Moholy-Nagy's reception in this country was not an open-armed one."

35. The doctor in *Beautiful People,* like the doctor in *Journey of Hope* and *Dirty Pretty Things,* is a good doctor, a nurturing hospitable doctor. On the symbolic significance of the representation of doctors in the history of cinema, particularly in *Beautiful People,* see Lightning, *"Beautiful People:* In Praise of the Liberal State."

36. It is quite interesting that Dizdar chose a "Welsh" rather than IRA terrorist, which would have been a more realistic choice in the context of British politics. A more "realistic" choice of a Muslim terrorist, of course, would be highly problematic in the post 9/11–7/7 era.

37. For a very interesting debate about the film and its reading as a progressive or reactionary film see Lightning, *"Beautiful People:* In Praise of the Liberal State," 68–72. Lightning's very elaborate and well-sustained argument is that the film is deeply reactionary. It subscribes to an essentialist racial view by setting up and reinforcing, in the name of political neutrality, the dichotomy of Britain/Bosnia as connoting civilization/barbarism. Furthermore, he argues that the film celebrates British sensitivity and hospitality and opposes it to essentially Bosnian/Balkan brutality and violence. "The plethora of political positions given voice in the name of 'fairness'" helps, according to Lightning, "to disguise the text's more reactionary aspects" (72).

38. Similar questions regarding the moral vision offered by the use of "beautiful" in their titles are raised by the highly controversial films *Seven Beauties* (*Pasqualino Settebellezze*) by Lina Wertmuller (Italy, 1975) and *Life Is Beautiful* (*La Vita e Bella*) by Roberto Benigni (1998, Italy), which preceded *Beautiful People.* For further discussion of this issue, see Yosefa Loshitzky, "Forbidden Laughter? The Politics and Ethics of the Holocaust Film Comedy," in *Re-presenting the Shoah for the Twenty-First Century,* ed. Ronit Lentin (New York: Berghahn Books, 2004), 127–38.

39. The expression "two hybrid nations" is quoted in Lightning, *"Beautiful People:* In Praise of the Liberal State," 69. Lightning borrows the term from a letter published in response to Wood's article (Vadislav Mijic, "Nationalism and the Zizek Syndrome: More Beautiful People," *CineAction,* no. 55 [July 2001]: 72). One of the guests in the film tells Pero at his wedding, "You see, here in Britain we are mixed too. You see. I believe that all sides are equally guilty."

40. Wood, *"Beautiful People,"* 30.

41. Ian Cobain, a *Guardian* reporter who went undercover to explore the secretive part of the British National Party (BNP), writes: "Several young men, for example, talked about how uncomfortable they felt in central London, because there were so many non-white people around them. 'We're all being pushed out to the fringes', said one." Ian Cobain, "Special Report: Racism, Recruitment and How the BNP Believes It Is Just 'One Crisis Away from Power,'" *Guardian* (December 22, 2006), 4. I should mention that I have heard the same sentiment expressed by many people in almost identical words, including one of my students (a middle-aged white male Londoner)

who stressed that he feels like a "stranger" in central London for the same reason listed by the BNP member. Ironically, the title of my course in which this student participated was "The 'Other' and the 'Stranger' in European Cinema."

42. Salman Rushdie, "Divided Selves," *Guardian* (November 23, 2002), 13.

43. One cannot but recall in this context Hannah Arendt's painful words on the status of German Jewish refugees during the Third Reich: "If we are saved we feel humiliated, and if we are helped we feel degraded." Hannah Arendt, *The Jew as Pariah: Jewish Identity and Politics in the Modern Age,* ed. with an introduction by Ron H. Feldman (New York: Grove Press, 1978), 60. Arendt's original article was already published in January 1943 in *Menorah Journal,* 69–77, and was reprinted as "We Refugees" in *The Jew as Pariah,* 55–66. Giorgio Agamben notes that "the paradox from which Arendt departs is that the very figure who should have embodied the rights of man par excellence—the refugee—signals instead the concept's radical crisis." Giorgio Agamben, *Homo Sacer: Sovereign Power and Bare Life,* trans. Daniel Heller-Roazen (Stanford, Calif.: Stanford University Press, 1998 [1995]), 126. Some prominent Jewish refugees, like Walter Benjamin and Stefan Zweig, even committed suicide. Exhausted by their exile in Brazil, Zweig and his wife took overdoses of barbiturates together. In a *Cineaste* interview, Stephen Frears commented: "The influx of the migrants has all happened in the last ten years. Asylum is a huge political issue and the government doesn't handle it very well. In multicultural London it's OK, but the government sort of whips up the fears in the rest of England, as though these people have two heads or something. There's no attempt made to explain the problem, to explain that these people are serious. It's just assumed that they're crooks or terrorists or somehow feckless; whereas, it seems to me that casting the world to get a decent living for your family is not something you do casually." Cynthia Lucia, "The Complexities of Cultural Change: An Interview with Stephen Frears," *Cineaste* (Fall 2003): 9.

44. For an interesting discussion of the film, see Charlotte Brunsdon, *London in Cinema: The Cinematic City since 1945* (London: BFI, 2004), 117–19. The publicity material quoted is from the 46th Regus London Film Festival (London: BFI, 2002), 8.

45. Philip French, "Frears Finds the Heart of London's Underground," *Observer Review* (December 15, 2002), 7. Frears is not a newcomer to the British multicultural scene/debate. His collaboration with Hanif Kureishi on films such as *My Beautiful Laundrette* (1985) and *Sammy and Rosie Get Laid* (1987) constituted a significant intervention during the years of Margaret Thatcher's Britain. For further reading, see John Hill, "'Race' and Cultural Hybridity: *My Beautiful Laundrette* and *Sammy and Rosie Get Laid,*" in his *British Cinema in the 1980s* (Oxford: Clarendon Press, 1999), 205–18; Karen Alexander, "Black British Cinema in the 90s: Going, Going Gone," in *British Cinema of the 90s,* ed. Robert Murphy (London: BFI, 2000), 109–14; and Christine Geraghty, *My Beautiful Laundrette* (London: I. B. Tauris, 2004). For an interesting discussion of *Dirty Pretty Things* and *In This World* see Kevin Foster, "New Faces, Old Fears: Migrants, Asylum Seekers and British Identity," *Third Text* 20, no. 6 (November 2006): 683–92.

46. Screen Talk, December 12, 2002, Barbican Centre, with director Stephen Frears in conversation with film critic Nigel Floyd following a preview screening of *Dirty Pretty Things*. It is interesting that in this brochure the writer refers to the tourist gaze and not the Londoner's gaze. In Monica Ali's *Brick Lane,* there is an interesting

description of Chanu, the Bangladeshi migrant to London, who is transformed from a postcolonial migrant to tourist after he makes the decision to return to Bangladesh, to relocate to his own home: "Thirty or so years after he arrived in London, Chanu decided that it was time to see sights. . . . 'I've spent more than half my life here,' said Chanu, 'but I hardly left these few streets.' He stared out of the bus window at the grimy colours of Bethnal Green Road.' . . . 'It's like this,' said Chanu, 'when you have all the time in the world to see something, you don't bother to see it. Now that we are going home, I have become a tourist.'" Monica Ali, *Brick Lane* (London: Black Swan, 2004 [2003]), 289–90. According to Manchu, "Immigration is a tragedy" and, indeed, the whole novel can be seen as confirming and challenging this assertion. Ali both mocks and celebrates the tourist gaze or perhaps reclaims it for the non-welcome immigrant (the city welcomes tourists but not refugees/economic migrants).

47. Virginia Crisp, December 2, 2004, in my M.A. course at University College London on "Ethno-Diasporas in European Cinema."

48. Robert Young writes: "With each passing decade London has been ever more successful in living up to its officially proclaimed heterogeneous identity." Robert J. C. Young, "Hybridity and Diaspora," in *Colonial Desire: Hybridity in Theory, Culture and Race* (London: Routledge, 1995), 1.

49. Stephen Frears said: "The peaceful, picturesque London of the past is alive only in the romantic yearnings of an older generation." Quoted in Cynthia Lucia, "The Complexities of Cultural Change: An Interview with Stephen Frears," 8.

50. French, "Frears Finds the Heart of London's Underground," 7.

51. On claustrophobia and migration see Hamid Naficy, "Chronotopes of Life in Exile: Claustrophobia, Contemporaneity," in *An Accented Cinema*, 188–221.

52. Paul Coates, *The Gorgon's Gaze: German Cinema, Expressionism, and the Image of Horror* (Cambridge: Cambridge University Press, 1991), 48.

53. Ibid., 48.

54. For a further discussion of London and the service economy in *Dirty Pretty Things,* see Sarah Gibson, "'The Hotel Business is about Strangers': Border Politics and Hospitable Spaces in Stephen Frears's *Dirty Pretty Things*," *Third Text* 20, no. 6 (November 2006): 691–700.

55. Coates, *The Gorgon's Gaze*, 5.

56. Although Juliette is British, she is black and thus a "foreigner," though not in the sense of being a migrant. Her status as a second-generation member of an ethnic minority deliberately challenges her "Englishness" or "Britishness" and her sense of belonging, which echoes the scene in *Beautiful People* where a black man is beaten by the white gang. In a question-and-answer session following a preview screening of *Dirty Pretty Things* at the Barbican Centre in London, one of the members of the audience asked Steven Frears if Juliette is a foreigner. "No," he said. "How can she be a foreigner? She lives in Crouch End." As I am myself both a migrant and a resident of Crouch End, I found Frears's comment ambiguous and hilarious at the same time. Implicitly, his reply suggests that one cannot be more "English" than a Crouch Ender, a suggestion which, for obvious reasons (as I disclose in the afterword), I fiercely contest.

57. One can safely assume that his name is an ironic reference to Sergei Eisenstein's last film, *Ivan the Terrible* (1943–46).

58. In *My Beautiful Laundrette,* the laundrette is a metonym of Thatcher's London, a multicultural theatrical space in which sexual desires and social tensions are negotiated and performed and "Englishness" and "Britishness" are constantly constructed, reconstructed, and deconstructed.

59. This is a reference to Chaplin's *City Lights* (1931) and its blind heroine. Senay, until her rape, is as blind and naïve as Chaplin's protagonist.

60. In the *Cineaste* interview (11), Frears was asked, "What promise does England hold for people like Senay, whose dream ultimately is moving to New York? What greater promise does America hold?" Frears's answer (11–12) was that "America has always been the dream that people want to realize, but at a certain point people realize it is a dream, an illusion, as Senay does. But the Statue of Liberty is there welcoming people."

61. Alexander, "Black British Cinema in the 90s," 112.

62. Ibid., 113. A recent case in point is Richard Curtis's film *Love Actually* (UK, 2003).

63. On the psychoanalytic level his relationship to her is very fatherly-maternal. She is the substitute for his daughter in Nigeria.

64. Alexander, "Black British Cinema in the 90s," 111.

65. The many references in *Dirty Pretty Things, Besieged* (see chapter 3), and other migrant and diasporic films about Africans in Europe to the themes of disease and cure not only enhance the symbolic association between Africa and health/sickness but also foreground (though in a very subtle way) many debates in Europe about migration from Africa. Shandurai, the heroine of *Besieged,* like Okwe, the African protagonist of *Dirty Pretty Things,* is in the medical profession. Despite popular and official anti-immigration sentiments the British NHS (National Health Service), for example, relies heavily on the professional medical force of immigrant doctors and nurses from Africa and (in the 1950s) it relied on migrant Indian physicians and nurses. In fact there are more Ghanaian doctors in Manchester than in Ghana. Europe, particularly the British NHS, is benefiting from African (but not only African) health professionals in whose education Africa invested its meager resources, exacerbating Africa's brain drain.

66. Jim Pines, "British Cinema and Black Representation," in Murphy, *British Cinema of the 90s,* 177.

67. The *Cineaste* interviewer (12) told Frears, "The performance of Ejiofor puts me in the mind of Sidney Poitier in his early roles in the 1960s America when the rare African-American protagonist had to be almost excessively noble in order to be accepted by white audiences." In response Frears said, "I was quite aware of that and thought there was wisdom in drawing upon that, because, as far as I know, *Dirty Pretty Things* is the first film of substance made in Britain that's starred an African actor. There hasn't been a film about an African. The world hasn't become that wonderful all of a sudden."

68. "Foreigners" exploit other more vulnerable foreigners. The sweatshops constitute a traditional diasporic space of exploitation of immigrants, from the Jews of Manhattan's Lower East Side to the Jews of East London and the waves of the Pakistani/Bangladeshi migration to East London that came after them. In Monica Ali's *Brick Lane* the traditional patriarchal space of exploitation of migrant women

is transformed into a space of self-emancipation when the women build their own collective and communal business where they produce and sell their own creations, trendy variations on traditional South Asian clothes. Frears's and Kureishi's film collaborations also depicted exploitation of migrants and other ethnic minorities by other migrants. It is not surprising, therefore, that they attracted criticism from the respective migrant and ethnic communities.

69. When the porter Ivan prepares a room-service sandwich, adding a sprig of parsley, he tells Okwe: "It's the little touch that makes a difference—that's capitalism." For obvious reasons this ironic remark is made by a migrant from the former USSR. In the *Cineaste* interview (12), Frears was asked: "Are those 'little touches' corrupting for immigrants seeking a better way of life?" to which he answered: "Well, they have come to a capitalist country. The truth is, nowhere is utopia."

70. Ross Forman, "Picking on Portugal, or the Fortress at the Final Frontier: Immigration and the Reversal of the Diasporic Gaze in *Terra Estrangeira*," paper presented at the international conference "Fortress Europe and Its 'Others': Cultural Representations in Film, Media and the Arts," Institute of Germanic and Romance Studies, School of Advanced Study, University of London, April 4–6, 2005. The paper interrogates some of the assumptions and problems of the Fortress Europe film genre through an examination of Walter Salles's *Terra Estrangeira* (1995). Financed from Brazil, *Foreign Land* tells the story of reverse diaspora: young immigrants who leave São Paulo for Lisbon after the currency crisis instigated by the Fernando Collor de Mello government in 1989, and with it the collapse of the Brazilian middle class's dream of democracy and peaceful prosperity. Set partly in Brazil and partly in Portugal, the film offers an important "insider's" perspective on the travails of immigration. For a further discussion of *Foreign Land* see Caroline Overhoff Ferreira, "The Limits of Luso-Brazilian Brotherhood: Fortress Europe in the Film *Foreign Land*," *Third Text* 20, no. 6 (November 2006): 731–42.

71. Liza Schuster, "The Origins of Fortress Europe," plenary paper presented at the international conference on "Fortress Europe and Its 'Others.'"

72. R. L. Rutsky, "*Metropolis*: Between Modernity and the Magic," in *Film Analysis: A Norton Reader*, ed. Jeffrey Geiger and R. L. Rutsky (New York: W. W. Norton, 2005), 188.

73. Hardt and Negri, *Empire*, 297.

74. See Gibson, "'The Hotel Business is about Strangers,'" 691–700.

75. For a further discussion of how the migrants can help Europe resolve its "demographic problem," see Sassen, "Europe's Migrations: The Numbers and the Passions are Not New," 635–44.

76. In Samura's autobiographical documentary *Exodus*, he recounts his experience as a migrant in London, keeping four jobs around the clock and hardly sleeping at all. For an emphatic photo diary that accompanies the journey of a young Cameroonian migrant to Europe and his subsequent "settlement" there, see Olivier Jobard, "Promised Land: How One Young African Risked His Life Crossing Desert and Sea to Reach Europe," *Guardian* (December 9, 2006), 26–39.

77. Benedict Anderson, *Imagined Communities* (London: Verso, 1983).

78. The irony is that Senay, played by the French actress Audrey Tautou—who became famous during the shooting of *Dirty Pretty Things* due to the success of *Amélie* (*Le Fabuleux destin d'Amélie Poulain*, Jean-Pierre Jeuent, 2001), which was released at

the same time and where she was cast as the major protagonist—could hardly speak any English at the time of the shooting.

79. Bauman, "The Making and Unmaking of Strangers," 22. It is also worth quoting in this context Saskia Sassen's powerful (though less harsh than Bauman's) words: "Are the immigrants and refugees who have lived here for so long the settlers of today? Is postcolonial history, broadly understood, being enacted partly in these, the former metropolitan nations, and our immigrants and refugees part of postcolonial settlement? . . . Are the low-paying, hard and dangerous jobs that immigrants still disproportionately hold today's frontier in the midst of our prosperous societies? Have we created a new frontier zone in the heart of our advanced economies, especially our large cities in the United States and in Western Europe?" Saskia Sassen, *Guests and Aliens,* 156.

3. The White Continent Is Dark

The epigraph is quoted in Paul Gilroy, *The Black Atlantic: Modernity and Double Consciousness* (Cambridge, Mass.: Harvard University Press, 1993), 221.

1. In Britain mixed race is the fastest growing ethnic minority group. Laura Smith writes: "It was only in the 2001 census that mixed-race people were finally given an ethnic category of their own—and then only in the face of opposition from black groups who feared it would reinforce a color hierarchy that has its roots in slavery." Laura Smith, "Absent Voices," Society *Guardian* (September 6, 2006), 1.

2. See "Creolization: Towards a Non-eurocentric Europe," special issue of *Culture, Theory and Critique* 48, no. 1 (April 2007) (guest editors Mireille Rosello and Murray Pratt).

3. Richard Dyer, *White* (London: Routledge, 1997), 44.

4. Bill Ashcroft, Gareth Griffiths, and Helen Tiffin, *Key Concepts in Post-Colonial Studies* (London: Routledge 1998), 142. It is estimated that at least 5 percent of the population of the European Union—25 million and rising—is nonwhite. This figure does not include the eight million Roma in the EU. There are 785 members in the European parliament and only nine of them are not white. See Patrick Barkham, "Minority Report," *Guardian* (February 14, 2007), 4–7.

5. Ashcroft, Griffiths, and Tiffin, *Key Concepts in Post-Colonial Studies,* 142.

6. For a discussion of miscegenation in Hollywood cinema, see Susan Courtney, *Hollywood Fantasies of Miscegenation: Spectacular Narratives of Gender and Race 1903–1967* (Princeton, N.J.: Princeton University Press, 2004). See also Daniel Bernardi, ed., *The Persistence of Whiteness: Race and Contemporary Hollywood Cinema* (London: Routledge, 2007).

7. This recalls nineteenth-century pseudo-scientific racial theories about hybridity and its association with infertility. For a discussion of this association see Robert J. C. Young, *Colonial Desire: Hybridity in Theory, Culture and Race* (London: Routledge, 1995). Fassbinder was one of the prominent filmmakers of the New German Cinema who treated issues related to "guest workers," xenophobia, and racism. In the years following the Second World War, West Germany adopted liberal asylum policies and also invited *gastarbeiter* from Southern and Eastern European countries such as Turkey, Italy, Portugal, Greece, and Poland. For a further reading

see, among many other critical analyses of this much-discussed director, Thomas Elsaesser, *Fassbinder's Germany: History Identity Subject* (Amsterdam: Amsterdam University Press, 1996).

8. Enrica Capussotti and Liliana Ellena explain that in Italy "the term 'refugee' itself is absent from public debate, or at least it flows between different and ambivalent meanings: a person without a regular visa, an asylum seeker, an illegal migrant, in other terms a Non-Persona." See Enrica Capussotti and Liliana Ellena, "The Way of Oblivion: Refugees in Italy," *Feminist Review,* no. 73 (2003): 149.

9. For a discussion of the first two films of this Orientalist trilogy see Yosefa Loshitzky, "The Quest for the Other: Bertolucci's *The Last Emperor* and *The Sheltering Sky*," in *The Radical Faces of Godard and Bertolucci* (Detroit: Wayne State University Press, 1995), 100–134.

10. The notion of accented cinema was first explored by Hamid Naficy. It is a style of cinema typical of diasporic filmmakers, a majority of whom are from third world and postcolonial countries "who since the 1960s have relocated to northern cosmopolitan centers where they exist in a state of tension and dissension with both their original and their current homes." These filmmakers are presumed "to be more prone to the tensions of marginality and difference." Hamid Naficy, *An Accented Cinema: Exilic and Diasporic Filmmaking* (Princeton, N.J.: Princeton University Press, 2001), 10.

11. I am not arguing here, necessarily, that *Besieged* is the most important film made about migration to Italy. There is quite a wide range of contemporary Italian films that deal with this issue. See for example *Un'altra vita* (Carlo Mazzacurati, 1992), *La bionda* (Sergio Rubini, 1992), *L'Articolo 2* (Maurizio Zaccaro, 1993), *Teste rasate* (Claudio Fragasso, 1993), *Da qualche parte in citta* (Michele Sordillo, 1993), *Comincio tutto per caso* (Umberto Marino, 1993), *Alullo Drom* (Tonino Zangardi, 1993), *Sarahsara* (Renzo Martinelli, 1994), *Portami via* (Gianluca Maria Tavarelli, 1994), *Gli occhi stanchi* (Corso Salani, 1995), *Vesna va veloce* (Carlo Mazzacurati, 1996), *Intolerance* (film collettivo, 1996), *Terra di mezzo* (Matteo Garrone, 1997), *Torino Boys* (Marco e Antonio Manetti, 1997), *Lestate di Davide* (Carlo Mazzacurati, 1998), *Elvjs e Merilijn* (Armando Manni, 1998), *La Ballata dei lavavetri* (Peter del Monte, 1998), *Aprile* (Nanni Moretti, 1998), *Ospiti* (Matteo Garrone, 1998), *Rom Tour* (Silvio Soldini, 1999), *Occidente* (Corso Salani, 2000), *Zora la vampire* (Marco Manetti, 2000), *Pane e Tulipani* (Silvio Soldini, 2000), *Un posto al mondo* (Mario Martone e Jacopo Quadri, 2000), *Brucio nel vento* (Silvio Soldini, 2002), *L'ospite segreto* (Paolo Modugno, 2003), and *Genti di Roma* (Ettore Scola, 2004).

12. All the above quotations are taken from the introduction by the editors of *Cineaste* to the interview of Bertolucci by Bruce Sklarew. See Bruce Sklarew, "Returning to My Low Budget Roots," *Cineaste* 24, no. 4 (1999): 16–27.

13. James Lasdun, *The Siege,* in James Lasdun, *Besieged* (New York: W. W. Norton, 2000 [1985, 1992]).

14. Bertolucci's not so latent pleasure at gazing and filming the young bodies of the protagonists of *The Dreamers* did not escape the eyes of the *Guardian's* film critic. "It may be an old man's sentimental reminiscence, but this is still an intense, passionate, stimulating drama—judging by the copious nudity, Bertolucci found it pretty stimulating to make, too." See "Film in London Listings, Pick of the Week, The Guide," *Guardian* (February 14–20, 2004), 2.

15. Lasdun, *The Siege*, 55.

16. Ibid., 63.

17. Teshome H. Gabriel argues that "awe for the old in the Third World culture is very much in evidence." Several films from the third world which reflect it present "the old or the aged as repositories of Third World history." Teshome H. Gabriel, "Towards a Critical Theory of Third World Films," in *Cinemas of the Black Diaspora: Diversity, Dependence, and Oppositionality*, ed. Michael T. Martin (Detroit: Wayne State University, 1995), 81.

18. Shandurai's gay friend Agostino tells her jokingly: "You Africans don't know even what time is . . . you don't know who invented the clock," thus recalling popular Western stereotypes about Africa and Africans which imply that Africa is beyond not only history but also beyond change. Agostino's words recall the motto of Bertolucci's early film *Before the Revolution* (*Prima della rivoluzione*, 1964): "He who did not live in the years before the revolution cannot understand what the sweetness of life is." This motto, taken from Stendhal's *Charterhouse of Parma*, echoes, to a certain extent, Tancredi's words to Don Fabrizio (the Leopard) in Luchino Visconti's *The Leopard* (*Il Gattopardo*, 1963): "Things have to change in order to remain the same." This belief in the dialectic relationship between progress, change, and the future on the one hand, and decadence, destruction, pessimism, and nostalgia for the past on the other, was typical of these two Italian filmmakers during their Marxist heydays. It is not incidental that Visconti's *The Leopard* (based on Giuseppe Tomasi di Lampedusa's novel) takes place in Sicily, Italy's African "other."

19. The British Royal Family is well known for its love of everything African. Diana's legacy was carried on by Prince William, who continued his mother's charity work with AIDS-infected children in Africa. In recent years, the West (and particularly Britain) has shown more interest in Africa. The campaign "Make Poverty History" is the prime example of this renewed interest. Up to twenty million Britons were expected to participate in this campaign as part of the biggest mobilization against global inequality ever seen. However, the July 2005 G8 summit at Gleneagles in Scotland, which put this global campaign at the top of its agenda, was overshadowed by the 7/7 bombing attack in London, which again pushed Africa into the margins of global interest. Gordon Brown, Britain's prime minister, has put Africa again on the top of his international agenda. When he was Britain's chancellor and the Labor Party's candidate for prime minister, however, he stated clearly in a lecture to the Fabian Society on January 13, 2007, that delivering prosperity and stability to Africa is not only an issue of justice but of stopping migration from Africa to Europe; in his words, it is, like terrorism, "a very big concern for Europe." Oprah Winfrey's opening of a school for 152 poor South African girls outside Johannesburg on January 2, 2007, is yet another example of the growing attempts to revive Western interest in Africa.

20. The education theme, called by Robert Kolker the *padre/padrone* theme, epitomizes the dialectics of the political Oedipal complex in Bertolucci's work. The father figure in all his films is perceived as either a good tutor/educator (*padre*) or a tyrannical boss (*padrone*), and the quest for the father involves a process of growth in which the protagonist defines himself through identification but also differentiation from the father. See Robert Philip Kolker, *Bernardo Bertolucci* (New York: Oxford University Press, 1985). Shandurai's husband, Winston, is an African school teacher. He is brutally arrested by the military authorities of his country's dictatorial regime

after asking his pupils what the difference is between a leader and a boss. Within the Bertoluccian ideological scheme, which synthesizes a Marxist and antifascist stance with psychoanalytic thinking, Winston's question implies a choice between a good father (a role model, leader, educator) and a fascist, repressive dictator.

21. Yoweri Museveni, the president of Uganda, in an interview on BBC Radio 4 (September 29, 2004). It is interesting to note that the Balkans, which poses a more immediate "threat" to "Europe," has been traditionally named "the sick man of Europe."

22. Sorious Samura, a documentary filmmaker from Sierra Leone who made *Exodus* (2000) about African immigrants to Europe, said: "There is a strange media double standard as far as Africa is concerned. It's only the big disaster stories that interest: earthquake, famine, illness, outbreaks." "Sorious Samura, Documentary Maker, 40, London: Up Front This Much I Know," *Observer Magazine* (December 14, 2003), 6. One poignant example is the Kosovo conflict, which, unlike the Sierra Leone conflict that played out at the same time, was a highly visible media event. Moreover, in 1999 the United Nations Refugee Council managed to secure only 60 percent of the budget required to manage the crisis created by the six million refugees in Africa, while it obtained a full 90 percent of the funds necessary for improving the lot of Kosovo's refugees during this same year. The council also has not managed to obtain the money needed to transfer refugees in Sierra Leone to the border with Guinea and to provide their children with a basic education. The double standard revealed in the attitude of the international community toward European and African refugees seems to conform to the prevailing opinion in many European countries at the time, namely, that an influx of refugees from Kosovo was more worrisome than a refugee problem from relatively remote Africa. Incidentally, since 1999 many African refugees have been smuggled into Europe, mostly through Spain and Italy, the two main countries currently used by traffickers and "illegal immigrants" as entrance points into Fortress Europe.

23. It should be noted, however, that the concept of miscegenation has different histories and meanings in different ethno-national contexts. In Brazil, for example (perhaps the most racially mixed country in the world), the idea of miscegenation is encouraged and is based on the idea of homogenization as the foundation of the Brazilian national project. As such, it is a nationalist idea. In Brazil, there is a suspicion toward the idea of Black Diaspora, which as a transnational entity betrays the idea of nationalism. I am indebted to Lucia Villares for this information, which I came across in her work in progress through a seminar, "Reading Clarice Lispector's Novel *O Lustre* after Having Read Toni Morrison and Bessie Head," given at the Institute of Romance Studies, School of Advanced Study, University of London, July 3, 2003. The Brazilian paradigmatic work on miscegenation is Gilberto Freyre's book *The Masters and the Slaves,* published in Brazil in 1934. See Gilberto Freyre, *The Masters and the Slaves,* trans. S. Putnam (New York: Knopf, 1946). For a discussion of this book in the context of hybridity see Nikos Papstergiadis, "Tracing Hybridity in Theory," in *Debating Cultural Hybridity: Multi-Cultural Identities and the Politics of Anti-Racism,* ed. Pnina Werbner and Tariq Modood (London: Zed Books, 1997), 260–62.

24. John Dickie discusses a map which he sees as typical of the attitudes to the South current at the time of the emergence of the *Lega/Lombarda/Lega Nord* in which the *Mezzogiorno,* beginning just below Florence, would be renamed "The Island of

'New Africa'" (Isola "Nuova Africa"). The channel, which divides the north from the south, is protected by an electronic or electric border that operates automatically when an "African islander" approaches. See John Dickie, "Fantasy Maps," in *Italian Cultural Studies: An Introduction,* ed. David Forgacs and Robert Lumley (Oxford: Oxford University Press, 1996), 103.

25. To define Italy as civilized, John Dickie writes, "one has to have a sense . . . of where that civilization fades at its boundaries into the barbarous. The South was one of Italy's most important banks of images of Otherness. The barbarous, the primitive, the violent, the irrational, the feminine, the African: these and other values, negatively connoted, were repeatedly located in the *Mezzogiorno* as foils to definitions of Italy." John Dickie, "Stereotypes of the Italian South: 1860–1900," in *The New History of the Italian South: The Mezzogiorno Revisited,* ed. Robert Lumley and Jonathan Morris (Exeter: University of Exeter Press, 1997), 119. "'Europe ends at Naples and ends badly. Calabria, Sicily and all the rest belong to Africa', wrote Creuze de Lesser in 1806. The South was considered a frontier dividing civilized Europe from countries populated by savages from Africa. . . . After Naples one fell into an abyss, an inferno, an outpost of Africa." Gabriela Gribaudi, "Images of the South: The *Mezzogiorno* as Seen by Insiders and Outsiders," in Lumley and Morris, *The New History of the Italian South,* 87.

26. For the origin of this quote on *Last Tango in Paris,* see Gideon Bachmann in an interview with Bernardo Bertolucci, "Every Sexual Relationship Is Condemned: An Interview with Bernardo Bertolucci apropos *Last Tango in Paris,*" *Film Quarterly* 26, no. 3 (1973): 6.

27. Lasdun, *The Siege,* 56.

28. On the displacement of the Jew and Jews and blacks in the Italian context see "Gender, Historiography, and the Interpretation of Fascism," an interview with Luisa Passerini by Ara H. Merjian, *Qui Parle* 13, no. 1 (Fall/Winter 2001): 157–64. Passerini argues that "Italian historiography . . . has not paid enough attention to the racial implications of Italian colonialism. We must remember that 'race' in Italy still bears the connotations linked to the Fascist use of the term, especially in reference to Jews. . . . The recognition of a racial or ethnic aspect to the discourse on Fascism is appearing only now, as the result of the recent wave of immigration into Italy of people from Africa and Asia. . . . Some scholars (for example, Karen Pincus) have indicated how the Fascist view of Jews and Blacks was gendered: both were either deprived of virility or attributed an excessive and perverse sexuality" (162). Frantz Fanon makes many connections between blacks and Jews as well as between antisemitism and negrophobia in *Black Skin, White Masks* (London: Pluto Press, 1993 [1952]), trans. Charles Lam Markmann.

29. Young, *Colonial Desire,* 25. Young's argument that racial theory was never simply scientific or biologistic but always culturalist is dominant in contemporary critical discourse on racism and miscegenation. This discourse problematizes the origins of the concept of hybridity as a biological grafting of different "races" and reconceptualizes it as cultural synthesis and diaspora. See for example Werbner and Modood, *Debating Cultural Hybridity,* and Avtar Brah and Annie E. Coombes, eds., *Hybridity and Its Discontents: Politics, Science, Culture* (London: Routledge, 2000).

30. Lola Young, *Fear of the Dark: 'Race', Gender and Sexuality in the Cinema* (London: Routledge, 1996), 84.

31. For a discussion of Bertolucci's ambivalence toward miscegenation, see Loshitzky, "The Quest for the Other."

32. Bertolucci himself said in the interview that Shandurai "is the muse and he is inspired by her" (see Sklarew, "Returning to My Low Budget Roots," 18). Bertolucci's problematic "negrophilic" attitude has its earlier seeds in *Last Tango in Paris,* which plays with clichés about black Paris. The images of blacks in this film are quite disturbing. They include the black saxophone player in the Paris flat seen with his open fly being attended by a kneeling black woman who may be sewing or perhaps pleasuring him. The black concierge of the Paris flat is a huge, rather monstrous-looking woman with a vicious and sinister laugh. The heroine, Jane (Maria Schneider), has black-like (and childish) stereotypical features, long curly hair (which before her first act of "liberating sex" with Paul [Marlon Brando] she keeps in a tight bun), full sensual lips, and large bosom.

33. One of the artifacts in Kinsky's mansion is an African "primitivist" miniature nude statue on whose huge penis Shandurai, in one scene, spits in order to dust and clean it while an expression of amazement spreads on her face. Allegorically, this can be read as an expression of contempt on her part (as well as a latent critical comment implicitly made by Bertolucci himself) on the exploitation, appropriation, and commodification of "authentic" tribal works by Western European art (especially by the so-called "Modernist Primitivism") and its vogue for "l'art nègre," which fetishized black African culture, appropriating it, in Stuart Hall's words, "as an exoticized 'support' to the West's inventiveness." Stuart Hall, "Black Diaspora Artists in Britain: Three 'Moments' in Post-War History," *History Workshop Journal,* no. 61 (Spring 2006): 16.

34. See Bertolucci's interview in Sklarew, "Returning to My Low Budget Roots," 17–18.

35. See ibid. One of my students, who was very critical of what she read as the film's reactionary vision, argued that only a privileged white man who has never cleaned his own living space could have romanticized domestic work.

36. Shandurai's otherness, both seductive and threatening, is constituted by the film through, among other things, her different skin color, "mysterious" background, eating habits (the exotic fruits that she indulges in, eating the papaya and the mango with her hands, not using fork and knife, and her evident, erotic-like enjoyment of these exotic fruits), her music, and her friends (both homosexual and other foreigners).

37. The complete dialogue of this scene reads as follows. He: "We can go anywhere. I'll go anywhere with you. We can go to Africa." She: "What do you know about Africa?" He: "May I ask you why he is in jail?" Shandurai does not reply but bursts into tears of frustration. How can she explain to him what Africa is? How can a white European grasp what Africa is "really" like? Similarly, in *Dirty Pretty Things,* when Okwe, the African protagonist, is asked to explain his situation, he switches to another subject, sighing (in a sort of silent despair), "It's an African story."

38. In all of Bertolucci's films, particularly his early ones, dance scenes epitomize rare moments of true liberation. For a discussion of this motif in Bertolucci's early films, see Marsha Kinder and Beverle Houston, "Bertolucci and the Dance of Danger," *Sight & Sound* 42, no. 4 (Autumn 1973): 186–91. It is interesting to note that

Agostino (Allen Midgette) is the name of the best friend of Fabrizio (Francesco Barilli), the hero of Bertolucci's *Before the Revolution* (1964). Agostino, who acts as a sort of double to Fabrizio, commits suicide to escape the suffocation of his bourgeois home and his deep pessimism regarding any hope of solving his personal anxieties through political action.

39. The portrayal of natives and "savages" as children is typical of colonial and racist discourse. For a survey of the evolution of these prejudices, see Gustav Jahoda, "Why Savages Are Child-Like: 'Arrested Development' and the 'Biogenetic Law,'" in *Images of Savages: Ancient Roots of Modern Prejudice in Western Culture* (London: Routledge, 1999), 152–63.

40. Because Thandie Newton is of mixed race (born in London to a Zimbabwean mother and British father), Shandurai's black beauty is closer to the standard white beauty, to what Partha Mitter, in his excellent discussion of Western cultural constructions of beauty, perceptively calls "the Western canon of beauty." See Partha Mitter, "The Hottentot Venus and Western Man: Reflections on the Construction of Beauty in the West," in *Cultural Encounters: Representing 'Otherness,'* ed. Elizabeth Hallam and Brian V. Street (London: Routledge, 2000), 35–50.

41. Fanon, *Black Skin, White Masks*, 58.

42. John Dickie, "Imagined Italies," in Forgacs and Lumley, *Italian Cultural Studies*, 25.

43. Saskia Sassen, "Rebuilding the Global City: Economy, Ethnicity and Space," *Social Justice* 20, nos. 3–4 (1993): 32.

44. Dickie, "Imagined Italies," 25.

45. According to this reading, *Besieged* suggests that not only does the mansion need to share its wealth, but it needs to invite others inside. Hence it exposes the ironic incongruity in the desire for population growth versus the rejection of the "wrong" kind of blood. One of Italy's current problems is its declining birth rate. See Will Hutton, "An Italian Lesson for Europe: The Declining Birth Rate in Italy Offers a Harsh Warning to Economies which Fail to Cater for the Needs of Families," *Observer* (September 26, 2004), 30: "Italy is suffering a baby bust; in 2004, its population is starting to decline. Even if Italian men and women start to form more families earlier and have more babies in the immediate future, Italy's population is set to drop from today's 58 million to some 44 million by 2050. If there is no recovery in the birth rate, its population will fall even further." "Europe as we know it is dying," so Sophie Arie opens a recent report in the *Observer* [see Sophie Arie, "Italian Town Where the Mayor Pays You to Have a Baby," *Observer* (November 9, 2003), 24]. "Italy is leading the way. It has the lowest birthrate in Europe.... Experts predict that Italy's population will fall by 15 million by 2050 and would be shrinking already were it not for the immigrant population keeping figures up."

46. Sklarew, "Returning to My Low Budget Roots," 18.

47. *Besieged* can be seen as (not necessarily deliberately or consciously) raising the same question posed by Frantz Fanon in his discussion of the relationship between the woman of color and the European. See Fanon, *Black Skin, White Masks*, 42. For Fanon, "authentic" love can exist only between a black man and white woman because the master, the white male, "can allow himself the luxury of sleeping with many women," whereas when "a white woman accepts a black man there is auto-

matically a romantic aspect. It is a giving, not a seizing." Fanon, *Black Skin, White Masks*, 46n5.

48. For a further discussion of race relationships in *The Sheltering Sky*, see Yosefa Loshitzky, *The Radical Faces of Godard and Bertolucci*.

49. Sklarew, "Returning to My Low Budget Roots," 18.

50. On Bertolucci's hostile attitude toward television, see Loshitzky, *The Radical Faces of Godard and Bertolucci*, 203–6. On the role played by television in contemporary Italy, see Tobias Jones, "The Means of Seduction," in *The Dark Heart of Italy* (London: Faber, 2003), 109–30. Ironically, *Besieged* was made for a television format. In his *Cineaste* interview, Bertolucci spoke about television as a miniature "in comparison with cinema, which is like a big fresco." Sklarew, "Returning to My Low Budget Roots," 17.

51. The latest chapter in Italy's ongoing "immigration crisis" was (at the time of writing this chapter) the arrival of an aid agency ship carrying thirty-seven shipwrecked African men to Sicily in July 2004. "A relief worker and two crew members were later arrested, and officials claimed that some immigrants had lied about coming from Darfour in Sudan, which is in a humanitarian crisis. The ship passed Malta and headed for Sicily, but once there the Italians blocked it from landing. For days, Italy, Germany, Malta and aid groups debated who should take in the men." Aidan Lewis, "Aid Worker Held as Italy Lets Refugee Land," *Guardian* (July 13, 2004), 9. As Capussotti and Ellena argue, the "first Italian state body confronted by the asylum seeker is the border police" ("The Way of Oblivion: Refugees in Italy," 9). *Spare Parts* indeed demonstrates this point (see chapter 1).

4. Intifada of the *Banlieues*

The first epigraph is from Jean-Paul Sartre, *Anti-Semite and Jew* (New York: Grove Press, 1960), 95. The second epigraph is from Frantz Fanon, *Black Skin, White Masks* (London: Pluto Press, 1993 [1952]), trans. Charles Lam Markmann, 115.

1. Evidence of the huge impact that *La Haine* had in France, even prior to the 2005 riots, is the fact that the prime minister, Alain Juppé, called for a special screening for his cabinet so they could understand "reality." The *banlieues* were built between the 1950s and the 1970s at the periphery of French cities and today connote urban, social, and cultural marginality.

2. Mireille Rosello, *Declining the Stereotype: Ethnicity and Representation in French Culture* (Hanover, N.H.: University Press of New England, 1998), 2. For another interesting discussion of the black/blanc/beur metaphor in the French context see Elizabeth Ezra, *The Colonial Unconscious: Race and Culture in Interwar France* (Ithaca, N.Y.: Cornell University Press, 2000), 145–53. For some major analyses of the *beur* and *banlieue* film and *La Haine* in particular, see among others Carrie Tarr, *Reframing Difference: Beur and Banlieue Filmmaking in France* (Manchester: Manchester University Press, 2005); Ginette Vincendeau, "Designs on the Banlieue: Mathieu Kassovitz's *La Haine* (1995)," in *French Film: Texts and Contexts*, ed. Susan Hayward and Ginette Vincendeau (London: Routledge, 2000), 310–27; Ginette Vincendeau, *La Haine: French Film Guide* (London: I. B. Tauris, 2005); Will Higbee, "The Return of the Political, or Designer Visions of Exclusions? The Case for Mathieu Kassovitz's

'*fracture sociale*' Trilogy," *Studies in French Cinema* 5, no. 2 (2005): 123–25; Will Higbee, *Mathieu Kassovitz* (Manchester: Manchester University Press, 2006), esp. chapter 2, "Social Struggles in the Popular Sphere" (49–94, on *Métisse* and *La Haine*); Thomas Bourguinon and Yann Tobin, "Entretien avec Mathieu Kassovitz," *Positif,* no. 412 (June 1995): 8–13; Dominique Bluher, "Hip-Hop Cinema in France," *Camera Obscura* 17, no. 4 (2001): 77–97; Erin Schroeder, "A Multicultural Conversation: *La Haine, Rai,* and *Menace II Society*," *Camera Obscura* 17, no. 4 (2001): 143–79; Tom Conley, "A Web of Hate," *South Central Review* 17, no. 3 (Fall 2000): 88–103; Bérénice Reynaud, "Le 'hood: Hate and Its Neighbors," *Film Comment* 32, no. 2 (March–April 1996): 54–58; Kevin Elstob, "Hate" (movie review), *Film Quarterly* 51, no. 2 (Winter 1997): 44–46; Myrto Konstantarakos, "Which Mapping of the City? *La Haine* (Kassovitz, 1995) and the *cinéma de banlieue*," in *French Cinema in the 1990s: Continuity and Difference*, ed. Phil Powrie (Oxford: Oxford University Press, 1999), 160–71; Carrie Tarr, "Questions of Identity in Beur Cinema," *Screen* 34, no. 4 (1993); Carrie Tarr, "Ethnicity and Identity in the *cinéma de banlieue*," in Powrie, *French Cinema in the 1990s*, 172–84; Jill Forbes, "La Haine," in *European Cinema: An Introduction*, ed. Jill Forbes and Sarah Street (New York: Palgrave, 2000), 171–79; Karen Alexander, James Leahy, and Keith Reader, "*La Haine*," *Vertigo* 5 (Autumn/Winter 1995): 45–46; James Leahy, "The Children of Godard and 90s TV," *Vertigo* 5 (Autumn/Winter 1995): 42–43; Reader Keith, "After the Riot: *La Haine*," *Sight & Sound* 5, no. 11 (November 1995): 12–14; Sanjay Sharma and Ashwani Sharma, "'So Far So Good . . .': *La Haine* and the Poetics of the Everyday," *Theory, Culture & Society* 17, no. 3 (June 2000): 103–16. For sources on France and postcolonial culture (particularly in the context of cinema) see among others *CinémAction*, no. 56 (July 1990), a special issue on "cinéma métis de Hollywood aux films beurs"; Michel Cadé, "Du côté des banlieues, les marques d'un territoire," *CinémAction*, no. 91 (1999): 172–80; Alec G. Hargreaves and Mark McKinney, eds., *Post-Colonial Cultures in France* (London: Routledge, 1997); Dina Sherzer, ed., *Cinema, Colonialism, Postcolonialism: Perspectives from the French and Francophone Worlds* (Austin: University of Texas Press, 1996); Susan Hayward, *French National Cinema* (London: Routledge, 1993); Guy Austin, *Contemporary French Cinema: An Introduction* (Manchester: Manchester University Press, 1996); and Petrine Archer-Straw, *Negrophilia: Avant-Garde Paris and Black Culture in the 1920s* (London: Thames and Hudson, 2000).

3. See, for example, Sharma and Sharma, "'So Far So Good,'" 104.

4. Ibid.

5. For a discussion of these films, see Carrie Tarr, *Reframing Difference*.

6. Quoted in Sharma and Sharma, "'So Far So Good,'" 114n1. This recalls Gayatri Spivak's essay "Can the Subaltern Speak?" where she states that the subaltern has no voice and that any undertaking to provide a voice involves speaking for or "representing" the marginalized subject. Gayatri Spivak, *Can the Subaltern Speak?* (Urbana: University of Illinois Press, 1988). A similar awareness of the complications involved in representation is echoed by Hanif Kureishi, as his notes on the making of *Sammy and Rosie Get Laid* (Stephen Frears, 1988, UK) indicate: "Is the quality of work irrelevant to the social issue, which is that of middle-class people (albeit dissenting middle-class people) who own and control and have access to the media and to money, using minority and working-class material to entertain other middle-class people? In one part of me I do believe there is some anger in the film; and it does deal

with things not often touched upon in British films. In another part of me when I look at the film industry run by the usual white middle-class public-school types, with a few parvenu thugs thrown in, I can see that the film is just a commercial product." Hanif Kureishi, *The Rainbow Sign* (New York: Penguin, 1992), 165.

7. Sander Gilman, *The Jew's Body* (New York: Routledge, 1991), 4.

8. Ibid., 5.

9. It is also both significant and interesting to note in this context that it was Peter Kassovitz, Mathieu's father, who made *Jakob the Liar* (1999), a remake of the 1974 film *Jakob the Liar,* directed by Frank Beyer from a film script by the child-survivor author Jurek Becker, and produced by DEFA (*Deutsche Film-Aktiengesellschaft*), the state-owned studio of the German Democratic Republic (GDR). Mathieu Kassovitz plays one of the ghetto Jews in his father's film. In *La Haine,* Peter Kassovitz plays the owner of the art gallery who, after the expulsion of the trio from this upper-middle-class arty space, refers to them as "troubled youth." There is no indication for the "innocent spectator" in this scene that he is a Jew. Mathieu Kassovitz also played a young Jesuit priest, Father Riccardo, attached to the Vatican during the Second World War, in *Amen* (2002), Constantin Costa Gavras's controversial film which tackles the role played by the Catholic Church during the Holocaust, asking why the Church remained silent while the Jews were sent to death.

10. Jonathan Webber, "Introduction," in *Jewish Identity in the New Europe,* ed. Webber (London: Littman Library, 1994), 13.

11. René Prédal, "François, David et les autres dans le cinéma hexagonal des années soixante-dix," in *CinémAction* 37 (1986): 144–57 (special issue, "Cinéma et Judéité," guest editors Annie Goldmann and Guy Hennebelle). This reflects the change in the status of Jews in France as a result of May '68. Before May '68, polite people did not use the word "Jew" (*Juif*) in France—it was considered an insult; the polite term was "Israelite." In 1968, one of the leaders of the student movement was Dany Cohn-Bendit. His political role was haughtily dismissed by the president, General Charles de Gaulle, who called him "a German Jew." The next day, students and strikers demonstrated in the street, screaming, "We are all German Jews" (*Nous sommes tous des Juifs allemands*). This proved to be cathartic, and in the deep cultural revamping that followed May '68, it became possible to somehow discuss issues of Jewish cultural identity, particularly in philosophical/literary publications initiated by Sephardim who were interested in pursuing a dialogue with Arab intellectuals or artists. Issues of racial and ethnic identity are usually not discussed in France the way they are in the United States and the United Kingdom. Even now the word *communautarisme* (communitarism) is close to being an insult, something akin to narrow-minded parochialism. As Ineke Van der Valk explains: "The French model of integration is consciously constructed and opposed to the British-American multi-cultural model that is based on the recognition of ethnic groups as communities. . . . Notions of 'community,' 'cultural pluralism,' or any concept that emphasizes the importance of the immigrants' culture of origin are rejected because they are assumed to reflect an immigré's state of non-integration. This state is believed to engender social problems between émigrés and French society, and therefore threaten social cohesion which, in turn, would favor the development of racism. 'Communitarism,' in the dominant vision, is considered a danger." Ineke Van der Valk, "Right-wing Parliamentary Discourse on Immigration in France," *Discourse & Society* 14, no. 3 (May 2003): 312. The concept of

"integration" as a policy goal addressing the issue of legal immigrants' cultural differences became dominant after the "headscarves affair" in 1989, writes Van der Valk: "It then gained victory over two competing concepts, 'insertion' (which presupposes the protection of differences) and 'assimilation' (which presupposes the suppression of differences) and was imposed as a compromise by the Socialist government" (311).

12. Rosello, *Declining the Stereotype*, 8.

13. Ezra, *The Colonial Unconscious*, xiv. The history of French Jews is indeed intimately linked to both the history of French colonialism (hence the necessity to link that history of Jewish identity to the history of West and North African immigration into France) and the sequels of the Holocaust in France, but its roots are much more ancient. Without even going back to the flourishing Sephardic communities of southern France in the Middle Ages and Renaissance, the fact that the Jews of France were the first in Europe to be granted citizenship (by Napoleon), the scars left by the Dreyfus Affair, and the role played by a Jewish intellectual like Bernard Lazare in theorizing antisemitism and the militant antisemitism of right-wing groups in the 1930s have all influenced the way the Jew is still perceived in French society.

Another major factor that was to play a seminal role later was the way French colonization used the Jews in its colonies in North Africa. While Jews and Arabs had coexisted peacefully for generations in Algeria, Morocco, and Tunisia, only the Jews were granted French citizenship, while the Arabs were considered second-class residents. The animosity thus created was to become part and parcel of the problems affecting the relationships between Jews and Arabs in the Middle East. After 1945, two major sets of events changed the perception/identity of the French Jew. The first was the decolonization of French North Africa. Tunisia was decolonized by a French Jewish politician, Pierre Mendes-France, giving rise to a new surge of antisemitism among right-wing nationalist groups, who mourned the loss of the French colonial empire. Later, Algeria was freed in 1962 after a bitter war of liberation.

Non-Arab refugees from the former colonies started to flock into France. There were people of Spanish, Italian, and Portuguese origin who were second- and third-generation settlers and who had also been granted French citizenship, as well as Sephardim. These refugees became known as *"pieds-noirs"* (black feet). They were, culturally speaking, more "Mediterranean" and "Oriental" than "French," they had lost everything, and their assimilation was problematic. Among them, the fate of the Jewish *pieds-noirs* was the worst. Shortly after independence, a number of antisemitic measures had been taken in Morocco, for example, where Jews were forbidden to own a business unless they had an Arab partner and co-shareholder (even in the case of a small grocery). The established French Jewry did not recognize themselves in these loud-speaking immigrants. The Jews living in the cities were more likely to be newly arrived Sephardim than long-assimilated Ashkenazim, which is why the identity of the ethnic origin of Vinz's grandmother is problematic. Shortly after Algeria gained independence, the two governments decided together to organize a semi-illegal immigration of laborers, especially to work on construction sites to contribute to the major urban renewal that France was undergoing. The influx of these underpaid, often non-documented working-class men, who lived in harrowing conditions and had left their families at home, created racial tension and became a major social issue. As they worked under conditions inferior to these negotiated by the French unions, the latter considered them no better than "finks," generating a deep split and long-lasting animosity within the French working class. As West African countries won independence at the same time, another wave of immigrants also flocked to the metropolis in search of better jobs. Therefore, working-class immigration from West and North Africa was concurrent with the immigration of *pied-noir* Sephardim and they were likely, as the film shows, to live in the same *banlieue*.

14. A famous example is Jean-Paul Gautier's use of Hasidic folklore in one of his fashion shows. The exoticization of the Jew can also be seen as part of the emergence of global commodified ethnicization. Hamid Naficy notes, ironically, that "the new beur is part of the French 'beur-geoisie,' no longer a threat to the dominant culture." Hamid Naficy, *An Accented Cinema: Exilic and Diasporic Filmmaking* (Princeton, N.J.: Princeton University Press, 2001), 100. More recent examples of the assimilation of the *banlieue*'s culture into chic French culture are the appropriation of *banlieue* fashion (in itself an imitation of the Anglo-Saxon fashion icons—hoodies and sweats, sport labels, and so on—influenced by youth and urban ghetto culture) by the Paris fashion scene; a first novel by Faiza Guene, a 19-year-old writer of Algerian parentage, the surprise hit of 2004, about her run-down, high-rise *banlieue;* and Luc Besson's film *Banlieue 13* (2005), set in an unnamed *banlieue* outside a big French city, which was the country's number-two box office hit for weeks.

15. For an interesting discussion of *Métisse* and its invocation and linkage of the Holocaust and slavery against the backdrop of postcolonial France, see Dina Sherzer, "Comedy and Interracial Relationships: *Rommuald et Juliette* (Surreau, 1987) and *Métisse* (Kassovitz, 1993)," in Powrie, *French Cinema in the 1990s: Continuity and Difference* (Oxford: Oxford University Press, 1999), 148–59. *La Haine* creates intertextual references to *Métisse,* particularly in relation to the link that both films establish between the Holocaust and the postcolonial.

16. Notable among these is the Jewish Defense League, founded in the United States, and the Israeli political movement Kach (renamed Kahane Hai after the murder of its leader, Meir Kahane), whose anti-Arab racist ideology is based on a belief in the superiority of "Jewish power." It should be mentioned that this newly growing obsession with Jewish power, particularly among French Jews, is not exclusive to marginal, extremist organizations. It is no accident that Claude Lanzmann, the director of *Shoah* (1985), who was in Israel during the First Gulf War, spoke out against the Likud government's policy of *havlaga* (restraint) precisely because of the memory of the Holocaust. In fact, *Shoah* is Lanzmann's second film in his trilogy on "Jewish power" (or lack of it). The first was *Pourquoi Israël?* (1973). The third, *Tsahal* (1994), is a glorifying documentary about the Israeli army. *Tsahal* signified for Lanzmann the reappropriation of force by Jews, specifically Israeli Jews. For a further discussion of this issue, see Yosefa Loshitzky, "Holocaust Others: Spielberg's *Schindler's List* versus Lanzmann's *Shoah,*" in *Spielberg's Holocaust: Critical Perspectives on Schindler's List,* ed. Loshitzky (Bloomington: Indiana University Press, 1997), 104–18.

17. I am indebted to Jocelyne Tinestit for drawing my attention to this point.

18. All the references to this scene in the literature completely missed the point. Although the elderly Jew says very clearly that the train was on its way to a labor camp in Siberia, critics referring to this key scene (out of a limited knowledge of the history of Polish Jews during the Holocaust) took it for granted that the train was en route to an extermination camp, resulting in a misinterpretation of its significance.

The irony is that Grunwalski actually missed his chances to survive by missing his train. Most of the Polish Jews who survived the Holocaust were those who escaped to the Soviet Union after the German invasion to Poland. Many of them, under Stalin's orders, were sent by trains to labor camps in Siberia because they refused to give up their Polish citizenship and accept Soviet papers. Although some of the forced Jewish laborers died in the Soviet camps, for most Polish Jews these camps were their only chance for survival (as was the case with my father).

19. For a further discussion of these fears, see Janet Lungstrum, "Foreskin Fetishism: Jewish Male Difference in *Europa, Europa,*" *Screen* 39, no. 1 (Spring 1998): 53–66.

20. Babylonian Talmud, Ethics of the Fathers 3:1. For drawing my attention to this point I am indebted to Ruti Efroni, "To Represent the Non-Place: Reflections on *La Haine,*" seminar paper, Department of Communication, Hebrew University, 2000.

21. Perhaps there is an ironic critical reference here to Israeli racist discourse which coined the phrase "the only good Arab is a dead Arab."

22. *La Haine* is inscribed with a cinephilic context through a sophisticated use of quotations and allusions to American cinema. However, its representation of blacks is indebted to the different history of representation of blacks in French cinema, due in part to Jean Rouch's seminal *Moi un Noir* (1958), and in part to the large presence of an African and West Indian population and the ready availability of African or West Indian movies (produced or co-produced with French money within the context of the Ministere de la Cooperation by the likes of Ousmane Sembène, Idrissa Ouedraogo, Souleymane Cissé, Euzhan Palcy, and others) that propose a much more complex image of the black man. Hubert's characterization is quite congruent with this image.

23. Sharma and Sharma, "'So Far So Good,'" 107.

24. Ibid.

25. The *cinéma de banlieue,* as many critics, notably Reynaud and Tarr, suggest, positions at its narrative, thematic, and ideological center the figure of the young angry man. Masculinity, according to these authors, is always in crisis in these films.

26. Sharma and Sharma, "'So Far So Good,'" 107.

27. For a further discussion of this displacement, see Ella Shohat, *Israeli Cinema: East/West and the Politics of Representation* (Austin: University of Texas Press, 1989), and Yosefa Loshitzky, *Identity Politics on the Israeli Screen* (Austin: University of Texas Press, 2001).

28. Sharma and Sharma, "'So Far So Good,'" 107.

29. For a discussion of the narrative and ideological significance of the series, see Rosello, *Declining the Stereotype,* 168–71.

30. See, for example, Leahy, "The Children of Godard and 90s TV." The *banlieues* riots were called "un petit Mai-68 des banlieues" by French commentators. See, for example, Patrick Jarreau, "Un petit Mai-68 des banlieues," *Le Monde* (November 5, 2005), 15.

31. Shmuel Trigano, "The Notion of a 'Jewish Community' in France: A Special Case of Jewish Identity," in Webber, *Jewish Identity in the New Europe,* 185.

32. Reynaud, "Le 'hood: Hate and Its Neighbors."

33. Elisabeth Mahoney, "'The People in Parentheses': Space under Pressure in the Post-Modern City," in *The Cinematic City,* ed. David B. Clarke (London: Routledge, 1997), 168–85.

34. Konstantarakos, "Which Mapping of the City? *La Haine* (Kassovitz, 1995) and the *cinéma de banlieue*," 160–71.

35. In the scene in which we learn that they cannot drive, we also learn that Vinz lied to his friends in the past, telling them that he took an American girl on a cross-country tour through Israel in a Mercedes.

36. The metro is represented in *La Haine* as the democratic space of the other France, belonging to the homeless, the poor, the immigrants, and the ethnic minorities. It is a space of equality (unlike the privately owned car), accessible even to the poorest.

37. The issue of "importing" and recruiting young professional immigrants from the third world, particularly India to Germany, so that the tax that they pay on their income will cover the pensions and retirement fees of old Germans, has recently been a subject of heated public debate in Germany. Similar issues and concerns have been raised in Italy where the phenomenon of childless or one-child families has become a national problem.

38. See, for example, Gilman, *The Jew's Body,* and Ann Pellegrini, "Whiteface Performances: 'Race,' Gender, and Jewish Bodies," in *Jews and Other Differences: The New Jewish Cultural Studies,* ed. Jonathan Boyarin and Daniel Boyarin (Minneapolis: University of Minnesota Press, 1997), 108–49. In the realm of representation, Richard Dyer's interesting discussion of the political problems arising from the use of categories such as "white" and "black" is of prime significance. See Richard Dyer, *White* (London: Routledge, 1997).

39. For a discussion of the Jewish community in France, see Trigano, "The Notion of a 'Jewish Community' in France."

40. See Paul Gilroy, *The Black Atlantic: Modernity and Double Consciousness* (Cambridge, Mass.: Harvard University Press, 1993), 217.

41. Sharma and Sharma, "'So Far So Good,'" 106.

42. According to Carrie Tarr, "Kassovitz claimed that he wanted to use a Jewish character for its folkloric interest, to please his grandmother, and also to prevent the story turning into a story of 'clans', but that a Portuguese character would have done as well." Carrie Tarr, "Ethnicity and Identity in *Métisse* and *La Haine* by Mathieu Kassovitz," in Tony Chafer, ed., *Multicultural France: Working Papers on Contemporary France,* vol. 1 (Portsmouth: University of Portsmouth Press, 1997), 40–47.

43. Talal Asad (whose own exceptional life story is a rare and unique "life narrative" that both exemplifies and challenges the notions of Jewish identity, Muslim identity, and "Europe") argues that until just "after the Second World War, European Jews were marginal too, but since that break the emerging discourse of a 'Judeo-Christian tradition' has signalled a new integration of their status into Europe." Talal Asad, "Muslims and European Identity: Can Europe Represent Islam?" in *Cultural Encounters: Representing "Otherness,"* ed. Elizabeth Hallam and Brian V. Street (London: Routledge, 2000), 16.

44. Although my premise is that Vinz comes from an Ashkenazi family, I am aware that there are alternative readings, given that *pied-noir* Sephardi Jews are more likely to live in the cities than the more assimilated Ashkenazi Jews, as I explained before. According to an alternative reading, Kassovitz is very careful not to assign a specific origin to Vinz's family, and even manages to "mix and match" his actors. Grandma is played by Ryvka Wasjbrot (more than probably an Ashkenazi), but Sarah, the sister, is Heloise Rauth (who could be anything) and the aunt is played by Olga Abreco, a

clearly Mediterranean name. And the plate that Grandma brings for breakfast seems covered with pita bread more than with blinis.

45. For elaborations on the Zionist body (the new Jew) versus the diasporic body (the old Jew), see, among others, Daniel Boyarin, *Unheroic Conduct: The Rise of Heterosexuality and the Invention of the Jewish Man* (Berkeley: University of California Press, 1997); Gilman, *The Jew's Body*; David Biale, *Eros and the Jews: From Biblical Israel to Contemporary America* (New York: Basic Books, 1992), esp. chapter 8, "Zionism as an Erotic Revolution"; Judith Doneson, "The Image Lingers: The Feminization of the Jew in *Schindler's List*," in Loshitzky, *Spielberg's Holocaust*, 140–52.

For a comparison between the construction of the Sabra image and the New American Adam, see Ella Shohat, "Columbus, Palestine and Arab-Jews: Toward a Relational Approach to Community Identity," in *Cultural Readings of Imperialism: Edward Said and the Gravity of History*, ed. Keith Ansell Pearson, Benita Parry, and Judith Squires (London: Lawrence and Wichart, 1997), 88–105, and Ella Shohat, "Taboo Memories and Diasporic Visions: Columbus, Palestine and Arab-Jews," in *Performing Hybridity*, ed. Jennifer Fink and May Joseph (Minneapolis: University of Minnesota Press, 1999), 131–56.

46. For drawing my attention to this point, I am indebted to Efroni, "To Represent the Non-Place: Reflections on *La Haine*."

47. For an interesting discussion of the use of music in *La Haine*, see Sharma and Sharma, "'So Far So Good.'"

48. Dina Iordanova, *Cinema of Flames: Balkan Film, Culture and the Media* (London: BFI, 2001), 235.

49. Webber, "Introduction," 13.

50. The September 11 attack on the United States further destabilizes the ostensible calm of post-Holocaust Europe. For an excellent (pre–September 11) discussion of this topic see Asad, "Muslims and European Identity: Can Europe Represent Islam?" 11–27. Asad argues in this article that the ideological construction of Europe ("Europe" as conceptualized by Europeans) both includes and excludes Muslim immigrants, consequently turning them into present/absent.

51. In Godard's *La Chinoise* (1967), which may be seen as a preview of May 1968, the revolutionary students learn how to prepare a Molotov cocktail. The opening scene of *La Haine* is juxtaposed to a voiceover narration which tells about a man falling from a fifty-story building who, as he falls, repeats, "jusqu'ici tout va bien" (so far so good). This story is an allusion to Godard's film *Tout va bien* (1972). For a discussion of the contradictions inherent in Godard's revolutionary (?) film, see Yosefa Loshitzky, *The Radical Faces of Godard and Bertolucci* (Detroit: Wayne State University Press, 1995), 32–48. Kassovitz's father was a militant of May 1968 and worked with Godard and Chris Marker.

52. Webber, "Introduction," 10. Trigano argues that the idea of a "Jewish community" in France "was invented only after the Second World War, as a way of designating the Jewish population as a whole rather than simply the *landsmanschaften* of Jewish immigrants of common geographical origin that had banded together to organize self-help and cultural activities and to defend their common interests." Trigano, "The Notion of a 'Jewish Community' in France," 179.

53. Trigano, "The Notion of a 'Jewish Community' in France," 186. The concrete political trigger to this debate was that, as Trigano describes it, the embrace of communitarianism, which threatens the ideal and model of French Republicanism, was

severely criticized by many intellectuals (including Pierre Bourdieu), who claimed that it was a manifestation of "racist communitarianism of the Jews." In reaction to these accusations, the advocates of Jewish communitarianism equated the "Jewish community" with "the immigrant community" and "the Muslim community." It should also be pointed out that since the outbreak of the Al-Aqsa Intifada in October 2000, the relationships between Jews and Muslims in France (particularly Arabs from North Africa) have dramatically worsened. This new situation positions the trio of *La Haine* in an even more utopian light.

54. Trigano, "The Notion of a 'Jewish Community' in France," 179.

55. See ibid., 184.

56. Sharma and Sharma, "'So Far So Good,'" 111.

57. *La Haine* is also part of a new wave of films on the other France and it signifies, among other things, the return of the political to French cinema. See Serge Toubiana, "Retour du politique (suite)," *Cahiers du Cinéma* 511 (1997): 28–29. This return includes not only the ethnic and the immigrant but also the poor, the homeless, and the unemployed in films such as *L627* (1992) and *Ça Commence Aujourd'hui* (1998), directed by Bertrand Tavernier; *Rosetta* (1999) by Jean-Pierre and Luc Dardenne; and *La ville est tranquille* (2000) by Robert Guédiguian. The new films deal with France's major social problems: unemployment, immigration, and crime.

58. See Kim Willsher, "French Celebrities Desert Sarkozy in Wake of Attack on Urban Poor," *Guardian* (December 23, 2005), 13.

59. See http://www.mathieukassovitz.com/blognews2, November 8, 2005 (accessed November 11, 2005).

60. "Back in November," writes Angelique Chrisafis, "when the forests of tower blocks in the Paris suburbs were lit by rioters torching cars, Floreal Mangin woke each morning to count the blackened metal wrecks outside her bedroom window. She watched the gangs of boys in tracksuits and hoods who were setting light to all they could find. They had grown up with her and some were in her class at school. 'They were on self-destruct,' she says. 'They were destroying their own neighbourhood, smashing their families' cars, but they had no other way of telling the world they existed.'" Angelique Chrisafis, "'The 1968 Crowd Had Dreams—We Are Dealing with Reality,'" *Guardian* G2 (March 30, 2006), 11. Her description fits also the representation of the riots in *La Haine*. Prime minister Dominique de Villepin's decision to invoke a law not used since the Algerian war deepened the anger. "'Ninety per cent of the people who live here are Arabs. What does that tell them? Fifty years later, you're still different? We're not allowed outside, and everyone else is?' said Djoued, 21, on the Chene Pointu Estate in Clichy-sous-Bois, where the riots began on October 27." Jon Henley Sevran, "'We Hate France and France Hates Us,'" *Guardian* (November 9, 2005), 17.

61. Arendt, *The Jew as Pariah: Jewish Identity and Politics in the Modern Age* (New York: Grove Press, 1978), 77.

62. See Rana Kabbani, "Bible of the Muslim Haters," *Guardian* (June 11, 2002), 14. Kabbani writes: "White Western Europe sees itself—wrongly, as research illustrates—as besieged by 'hooded hordes' in the guise of thieving immigrants or asylum seekers. The recent, well orchestrated campaign alerting opinion to the rise of anti-semitism in Europe camouflages the fact that Jews are not the foremost victims in the carnival of hatred. That dubious honour goes to Muslims, Europe's largest religious minority, numbering over 20 million. They are the continent's poorest and most badly housed

citizens. . . . It is also the result of neglect . . . of injustice among the young in Muslim ghettos." The debate about current antisemitism in Europe is beyond the scope of this chapter. For a further discussion of this issue and its relationship to the so-called "Palestinian question" see Yosefa Loshitzky, "Pathologising Memory: From the Holocaust to the Intifada," *Third Text* 20, nos. 3/4 (May/July 2006): 327–35.

5. The Camp Trilogy

The epigraph is from Giorgio Agamben, *Homo Sacer: Sovereign Power and Bare Life,* trans. Daniel Heller-Roazen (Stanford, Calif.: Stanford University Press, 1998 [1995]), 181.

1. Sarkozy's likening of the rioters in the *banlieues* to "scum" still rankles with France's North African community, including the *beur* filmmakers. Abdellatif Kechiche, who made the highly successful *La Graine et le mulet* (*Couscous,* France, 2007), and who grew up in a *banlieue* in Nice, said, "As long as France refuses to realise how lucky it is to have a young population so rich and diverse, as long as it insists on seeing that diversity and difference as a problem, France will miss out on the abundance of energy, culture and possibility." Cited in Angelique Chrisafis, "Migrant Movie Brings Hopes of French Cultural Revival," *Guardian* (December 14, 2007), 25.

On Tuesday, November 27, 2007, while I was revising this chapter, nearly eighty French police officers were injured, six seriously, during a second night of riots by youths in the Villiers-le-Bel *banlieue* north of Paris. The youth said they were avenging the two teenagers of Algerian origin, 15-year-old Moushin and his friend, Larami, age 16, killed in a motorcycle accident involving a police car on Sunday, November 25, 2007. The resemblance to the event which triggered *banlieue* riots throughout France in 2005 is significant. The 2005 unrest (see chapter 4), sparked by the accidental deaths of two youths, spread from the nearby Clichy-sous-Bois *banlieue* of Paris to other cities and continued for three weeks, during which more than 10,000 cars were set ablaze and 300 buildings firebombed.

2. The 7/7 attack was hailed by the French media as an example of the collapse of the British model of integration. This was in response to previous pre-7/7 British criticism of the color blindness of the French Republican model of integration, which has traditionally resisted multiculturalism and communitarianism.

3. Ryan Gilbey, "British Directors Special: Michael Winterbottom," *Sight & Sound* (October 2004): 31.

4. Ali Jaafar, *Sight & Sound* (October 2007), cited in program notes and credits compiled by the Filmographic Unit, BFI National Library, for a special preview of *A Mighty Heart* at NFT1, September 11, 2007.

5. Winterbottom's "capitulation" to American capitalist modes of production and representation recalls Jean-Luc Godard's and Jean-Pierre Gorin's *Tout va Bien* (1972), made with American money and American stars. For a discussion of the contradictions and ambiguities embedded in Godard's capitulation, see Yosefa Loshitzky, *The Radical Faces of Godard and Bertolucci* (Detroit: Wayne State University Press, 1995), 32–48.

6. I am indebted to Haim Bresheeth for drawing my attention to the fascinating idea about the symbolic space that the camp occupies in contemporary western popular culture.

7. Fiachra Gibbons, "Afghan Boy Turns Movie Role into Real Life," *Guardian* (November 6, 2002), 8. *In This World* shares some similarities with the film *Kandahar* (Moshen Makhmalbaf, 2001, France/Iran). That film deals with the treatment of women under Taliban rule. An Afghan woman who has left Afghanistan, Nafas (Nelofer Pazira, an exiled Afghan working as a television journalist in Canada), goes back home and embarks on a journey to find her troubled sister in Kabul. It also resonates with the play *Homebody/Kabul* by Tony Kushner, which premiered on December 5, 2001, directed by Declan Donnellan and designed by Nick Ormerod. The play was written prior to the September 11 attacks and was perceived therefore as prophetic by some critics.

8. This review by Richard Kelly appeared in the April 2003 issue of *Sight & Sound*. See http://www.bfi.org.uk/sightandsound/2003_04/inthisworld.php (accessed October 20, 2004).

9. The death from suffocation in a lorry in Italy recalls another similar real incident. On October 18, 2000, the corpses of six illegal migrants, presumed to be Kurds, were found along a road inside trash bins in one of the suburbs of Puglia in southern Italy, having suffocated in the cargo of a lorry.

10. Another interesting artistic treatment of the Sangatte camp is Théâtre du Soleil's *Le Dernier Caravansérail* (The Last Caravanstop). The theater used conversations with migrants in Sangatte, Lombok, and other camps to create the theatrical performance. *Le Dernier Caravansérail* used physical theater, live music, voiceover, and projected images to relate the experiences of migrants from around the world, showing them at their point of origin, on international borders, and in transitional zones such as Sangatte. Theorist, novelist, and playwright Hélène Cixous was involved in the creative process. The interviews with asylum seekers and migrants, conducted by director Ariane Mnouchkine and the company, were originally meant to be the raw material for a new play by Cixous. Eventually a decision was made to abandon the play, letting the migrants' words and languages speak for themselves to avoid the risk of theatricality. The production's main theatrical device was of company members wheeling the migrant characters around the stage on skateboard-like rollers. The originality of this metaphor injected complexity into stories too often reduced to simplistic media clichés, and subverted the power of the people traffickers featured in the production. The Théâtre du Soleil's venue, the Cartoucherie, itself played a significant role as a space of hospitality, generosity, and openness in shaping *Le Dernier Caravansérail's* reception.

11. See http://www.bfi.org.uk/sightandsound/2003_04/inthisworld.php (accessed October 20, 2004).

12. See http://www.bbc.co.uk/films/2003/02/21/in_this_world_2003_review.shtml (accessed October 20, 2004).

13. On Winterbottom's affinity with Godard, see Gilbey, "British Directors Special: Michael Winterbottom," 31–32.

14. Gibbons, "Afghan Boy Turns Movie Role into Real Life," 8. See also the reply of Marcel Zyskind (the film's cinematographer) to Manu Anand, http://www.cinematography.com/forum2004/lofiversion/index.php?t1039.html (accessed October 20, 2004): "Regarding Jamal. He is living in a Pakistani foster family in London. After we made the film, he went home with Enayatollah, but with the money he

earned and a visa he still had he then made a trip to Paris and took the eurostar to London and seeked asylum. He was granted to stay until the day before his 18th birthday. . . . It will be interesting to see what happens when he turns 18. Will he be sent back to Afghanistan, which is his nationality, but he has never lived there."

15. Winterbottom expressed his admiration for Fassbinder's work in many interviews. Winterbottom said: "I don't like films where you feel you're being forced into emotion—where you have a sentimental scene and the score swells up underneath it in case you haven't got the point. I like films where if I go with someone they might feel one thing and I might feel another." *Guardian,* "Unlimited Film | Interviews | A Winterbottom's tale," http://film.guardian.co.uk/interview/interviewpages/0,6737,1136149,00.html (accessed October 20, 2004); Geraldine Bedell, "A Winterbottom's Tale," *Observer,* February 1, 2004.

16. The 2004 Silk Road exhibition at the British Library did not make any mention of the use of the Silk Road today for trafficking refugees to the West. Ironically, one of the educational/research brochures given to visitors asks, "How did people travel from one country to another, across the deserts and tall mountains around the Silk Road a thousand years ago? How much time do you think it took? Was it dangerous? What did they have to do to prepare for their journey?"

17. What is emerging at the outset of the twenty-first century in response to the growing forces of globalization, according to Dauvergne, "is encapsulated by the idea of people 'being illegal'" (87). This allows talk of "illegals," "as though the term had some fixed meaning besides being an adjectival description" (92). The category of global "illegal" defines its bearers solely through their relationship to the law. The label itself is empty of content—"illegals are transgressors—and nothing else—by definition" (92). See C. Dauvergne, "Making People Illegal," in *Critical Beings: Law, Nation and the Global Subject,* ed. P. Fitzpatrick and P. Tuitt (Aldershot: Ashgate, 2004). This helps neutralize the political and economic causes of migration, masking deep global divisions, just as it does the causes of terrorism.

18. One of the examples of Jamal's linguistic competence is the following joke, which he repeatedly tells. An Afghan man sees a British guy lying on the ground. He gives him a hand to help him and the British guy says, "Thank you." The Afghan man says, "So you are going to send a tank you after me?" and pushes him back to the ground.

19. Zygmunt Bauman, "Refugees in a Full World," in *Society under Siege* (Cambridge: Polity Press, 2003), 114.

20. Chris Darke, "The Underside of Globalization: On Michael Winterbottom's *In This World,*" *Open Democracy* (April 3, 2003), http://www.globalpolicy.org/globaliz/cultural/2003/0403refugee.htm (accessed October 20, 2004).

21. Paul Smethurst, "A Revolutionary from Venice: Marco Polo's Travels Changed Forever the Way Europe Beheld Asia," *Time* (August 7–August 14, 2006, special issue: "In the Steps of Marco Polo: How East Meets West Today").

22. Zhang Longxi, "The Myth of the Other: China in the Eyes of the West," *Critical Inquiry* 15 (Autumn 1988): 110.

23. Smethurst, "A Revolutionary from Venice."

24. Ibid.

25. Darke, "The Underside of Globalization."

26. William Dalrymple, "Return to Xanadu: The World Today Is Not So Different from the Way It Was in Marco Polo's Time," *Time* (August 7–August 14, 2006), 91.

27. Darke, "The Underside of Globalization."

28. The question of "refugee numbers is a vexed issue," as Philp Marfleet observes (14). For a further discussion of this issue, see Philip Marfleet, "The Problem of Numbers," in *Refugees in a Global Era* (New York: Palgrave, 2006), 14–16.

29. *Guardian*, "Unlimited Film | Interviews | A Winterbottom's tale," http://film .guardian.co.uk/interview/interviewpages/0,6737,1136149,00.html (accessed October 20, 2004). The idea of a "protected zone" applies also to the Green Zone, the "walled city within a city that housed the U.S.-run government of Iraq, the Coalition Provisional Authority (CPA), and now houses the U.S. embassy." Naomi Klein, *The Shock Doctrine: The Rise of Disaster Capitalism* (London: Allen Lane, 2007), 341–42. The Green Zone ("Emerald City"), inside Saddam's former conference center, was also, as Klein explains ironically, the site where a small group of influential Iraqis were given lessons in capitalist transformation.

30. Quoted from interviews extracted from film production notes by the Cornerhouse Film Theatre in Manchester as part of the Crossing Borders season, September 16–30, 2004, and in conjunction with the conference "Crossing Borders: Images of Immigration in European Cinema," September 15–16, 2004, Manchester Metropolitan University.

There are other allusions to *In This World*. The peddlers who harasses William on his way to the airport, for example, look like the refugees we see in Shamshatoo, the Afghan refugee camp at the beginning of *In This World*. In an interview with Ian Berriman for SFX, it becomes apparent that this visual similarity (evident also in other parts of the film) is far from accidental and that Winterbottom drew much of his inspiration for *Code 46* from his experience of making *In This World*. "Having had the basic idea for the film we then went away and made *In This World*, and then yeah, we consciously borrowed quite a lot of the texture of the world of *Code 46* from *In This World*. We took the idea that outside of the cities, there'd be deserts. We'd done a lot of filming in desert on *In This World*, a lot of the refugee camps were in very arid areas and there was just something visually about the harshness of that, how hard it is to survive in that context that seemed good for the film." Ian Berriman, "Interview: Michael Winterbottom on *Code 46*, 1 September 2004," http:// www.futurenet.com/sfx/features/default.asp?pagetypeid=2&articleid=31684&subsec tionid=1201 (accessed October 20, 2004).

31. The genetic component of the papelle is also a reference to the new biometric passports and ID cards introduced, particularly by the United States and the United Kingdom, as part of their policy of tightening border controls in their "war on terror."

32. There are numerous intertextual references to Godard's work in *Code 46*. As an independent semi-militant filmmaker, Winterbottom shares many affinities with the radical Godard. Winterbottom's film production company is called "Revolution." He works with light, hand-held cameras and uses the same crew in most of his productions. His collaboration with cameraman Marcel Zyskind has been compared to that between Godard and Raoul Coutard. In *Code 46*, Samantha Morton (particularly her short hair cut) recalls Jean Seberg in Godard's *Breathless* (1960). When she first appears in a Shanghai subway, she is wearing a Mao-style hat resembling that worn

by Juliet Berto in Godard's *La Chinoise* (1967), an almost prophetic film in its anticipation of the May '68 events and their political aftermath (in particular the growth of urban terrorism).

33. Agamben, *Homo Sacer.*

34. Film production notes from the Cornerhouse Film Theatre in Manchester.

35. David Desser, "Race, Space and Class: The Politics of Cityscapes in Science-Fiction Films," in *Alien Zone II: The Spaces of Science Fiction Cinema*, ed. Annette Kuhn (London: Verso, 1999), 84.

36. According to Zygmunt Bauman, "Refugees have become, in a caricatured likeness of the new power elite of the globalised world, the epitome of extraterritoriality." Zygmunt Bauman, *Society under Siege* (Cambridge: Polity Press, 2002), 112.

37. Virginia Crisp, "Amalgamation and Separation: *Code 46,* the Generic City and the Refugee," paper submitted to Yosefa Loshitzky, module leader of "The Representation of Ethno-Diasporas in European Cinema," offered by the M.A. Programme in Film Studies, University College London (UCL), 2004.

38. Wendy Mitchell, "Michael Winterbottom on 'Code 46'; A Typical Love Story in an Atypical World," http://www.indiewire.com/people/people_040806winter.html (accessed by Crisp on March 7, 2005). I am indebted to Virginia Crisp for bringing this source to my attention.

39. Crisp, "Amalgamation and Separation."

40. Mitchell, "Michael Winterbottom on 'Code 46.'"

41. Crisp, "Amalgamation and Separation."

42. Muhammad Asad writes in his biography on the Bedouin desert Arabia (which Jabel Ali is part of) that it "became the soil and matrix of a way of life which was destined to express itself, in the course of time, in a great spiritual movement and thereafter in a civilization which extended its influence, directly and indirectly, over almost the whole world: the religion of Islam and the civilization engendered by it. The human and social prerequisite of this development was what may be described as 'Bedouin culture'—a way of life which will soon belong to the past and of which history offers no other example." Muhammad Asad, *The Road to Mecca* (London: Muslim Academic Trust, 1998 [1954]), 178–79. Muhammad Asad, né Leopold Weiss, was a European Jew who converted to Islam and whose own exceptional life story encompasses the major grand narratives of the twentieth century—including, among others, the heydays of central European culture (e.g., psychoanalysis, European avant-garde), the Holocaust, the colonization of the Middle East by Britain, the partition of India, and the establishment of the Islamic state of Pakistan (of which he was one of the founding fathers).

43. Maria is originally from Jabel Ali, the desert. When she tells William her family story she says that her father loved Jabel Ali from where he was expelled but she has always hated the desert.

44. Obviously the terms "Near East" and "Far East" are ideologically laden for their alleged Eurocentrism. I am using them deliberately in order to further problematize the Orientalist binarism that the film constructs.

45. Mike Davis, *Planet of Slums* (New York: Verso, 2006).

46. Western women's disappearance in the desert is a prevalent motif in colonial narratives. Of particular interest in relation to the last image of Maria in the desert

is the last image of Amy Jolly (Marlene Dietrich) in Joseph von Stenberg's *Morocco* (1931). Following her lover, the legionnaire Tom Brown (Gary Cooper), to the heart of the Sahara desert, she covers her head with a white veil and kicks off her high-heeled gold sandals as she vanishes into the sand dunes. For a discussion of this trope as well as its associated "veiling" and "unveiling" motif, see Yosefa Loshitzky, "The Tourist/ Traveler Gaze: Bertolucci and Bowles' *The Sheltering Sky*," *East-West Film Journal* 7, no. 2 (July 1993): 110–32.

47. By posing this question, I do not ignore the economic reality of this film and the need and desire on Winterbottom's side to use white Anglo-American actors. The contradictions embedded in producing "political" films within the framework of a capitalist system are fully acknowledged by Winterbottom in many interviews, though they are not always inserted or referred to in the films themselves (a practice for which Godard was famous).

48. The image of Maria in the desert bears not only biblical associations but also mythological ones. Oedipus was also expelled to the desert/wilderness in order to evade the prophecy of the Sphinx, a plot which is prominent in Pier Paolo Pasolini's *Edipo re* (1967), inspired by Sophocles' *Oedipus Rex* and *Oedipus at Colonus*. Pasolini's film also takes place in a mythical desert. Maria is the name of the female protagonist of Lang's futuristic *Metropolis* (see chapter 2). Her clone, the robot, the "bad Maria," is a predecessor of *Code 46*'s bio-technological clone.

49. The word *Hagar* in Hebrew derives from the word *hagira,* which means both immigration and emigration. *Ger* in Hebrew means foreigner, stranger. In Arabic, the word for migration is *hijrah*. According to Islam, in 622 God gave the Muslim community the command to emigrate. This event, the *hijrah* or migration, in which they left Mecca for the city of Medina, marks the beginning of the Muslim calendar.

50. The association with issues of fertility and reproduction through "primitive" premodern "methods of cloning" connects Hagar to the post-human world of cloning depicted in *Code 46*. The film can also be read, according to Debra Shaw, "as suggesting that clones themselves have become scapegoats for a social order that is maintained through the management of sexuality and reproduction." Debra Shaw, Seminar, School of Social Sciences, Media and Cultural Studies, University of East London, January 24, 2007.

51. For a study of Hagar as a postcolonial feminist icon see, for example, Janet Gabler-Hover, *Dreaming Black/Writing White: The Hagar Myth in American Cultural History* (Lexington: University Press of Kentucky, 2000).

52. According to Islamic tradition and the Qur'an, Abraham (Ibrahim in the Qur'an and other Muslim texts) was neither a Jew nor a Christian but a Hanif who rebelled against polytheism and thus became the original Muslim. A fundamental tenet of Islam is that Abraham and Ishmael (Ismail in the Qur'an) laid the foundations of the Kaaba in Mecca. For a discussion of the historical roots and debates regarding this tradition, see Irving M. Zeitlin, "The Role of Abraham, Hagar, and Ishmael," in *The Historical Muhammad* (Cambridge: Polity Press, 2007), 36–45. For an interesting account of the outstanding place that Abraham occupies in the Muslim and Arab tradition, see Asad, *The Road to Mecca*, 353–56.

53. Howard Feinstein, "Michael Winterbottom Talks about His Tragic Road Movie, 'In This World,'" http://www.indiewire.com/people/people_030918winter.html (accessed October 20, 2004).

54. Agamben, *Homo Sacer,* 137. Agamben discusses this issue in relation to National Socialism's biopolitics. He argues that the "fundamental biopolitical structure of modernity—the decision on the value (or nonvalue) of life as such," started with the euthanasia program (137).

55. Fran Cetti, personal communication. According to Agamben, we should regard the Nazi concentration camp not only as a historical fact "and an anomaly belonging to the past . . . but in some way as the hidden matrix and *nomos* of the political space in which we are still living" (166). This is the reason, he argues, that we "find ourselves virtually in the presence of a camp every time such a structure is created." Among the examples that he gives: "The stadium in Bari into which the Italian police in 1991 provisionally herded all illegal Albanian immigrants before sending them back to their country" and "the zones d'attentes in French international airports in which foreigners asking for refugee status are detained" (174). Obviously we can think of many more examples existing in today's "New Europe." *Last Resort,* discussed in chapter 1, deals with a detention center that fits into Agamben's understanding of the camp as existing in the "materialization of the state of exception and in the subsequent creation of a space in which bare life and the juridical rule enter into a threshold of indistinction" (174).

56. Agamben, *Homo Sacer,* 3.

57. Ibid., 122. It is worth quoting here in full Agamben's concluding paragraph of his book, which seems to both theorize about and capture the ideological significance of the end of *Code 46:* "Today's democratico-capitalist project of eliminating the poor classes through development not only reproduced within itself the people that it excluded but also transforms the entire population of the Third World into bare life. Only a politics that will have learned to take the fundamental biopolitical fracture of the West into account will be able to stop this oscillation and to put an end to the civil war that divides the peoples and the cities of the earth" (180).

58. Agamben, *Homo Sacer,* 175.

59. Samuel P. Huntington, *The Clash of Civilizations and the Remaking of World Order* (New York: Simon and Schuster, 1996).

60. Riots involving "Asians" (mainly descendants of Pakistani migrants), white youths, and the police broke out in late April 2001 in Bradford and from there spread to Oldham, Leeds, and Burnley, cities with high proportions of Pakistanis living in segregated neighborhoods. The climax of the riots was on July 7 in Bradford, where 164 police officers were injured on a single day, dozens of shops were set on fire, and several streets turned into war zones. Most media commentators agreed that these were the worst race riots in Britain since Brixton in 1981. Some of the violence was provoked by the British National Party (see chapter 2).

The riots came as a shock to the British public and the political establishment and put into crisis the notions of multiculturalism and race relations in Britain. Monica Ali's *Brick Lane* (see chapter 2) reflects on some of these issues, particularly on the "Islamic turn" among Bangladeshi and Pakistani youth, which can be understood as a manifestation of an aftershock response to these riots. According to Robert Winder, "It wasn't only the Britons who put up walls. The Muslims themselves were reluctant to sever any ties with their homeland. Few previous immigrant communities had been quite so determined to cling to the culture they brought with them. Unlike many West Indians, who idealised Britain and had to swallow much humiliation when they arrived, the Pakistanis had no false hopes: they arrived with the warnings of their elders ringing in their ears." Robert Winder, *Bloody Foreigners: The Story of Immigration to Britain* (London: Little, Brown, 2004), 297.

61. The Tipton Three is the collective name given to three men (Ruhel Ahmed, Shafiq Rasul, and Asif Iqbal) from Tipton, England, who were held in extrajudicial detention for two years at Guantanamo Bay. For an interesting discussion of the significance of the trio's experience in Guantanamo, see Klein, *The Shock Doctrine,* 338–39. See also Andy Worthington, *The Guantanamo Files: The Stories of the 774 Detainees in America's Illegal Prison* (Ann Arbor: University of Michigan Press, 2007), and Clive Stafford Smith, *Bad Men: Guantanamo Bay and the Secret Prison* (London: Phoenix, 2007). In *Torture Team: Deception, Cruelty and the Compromise Law* (London: Allen Lane, 2008), Philippe Sand, professor of law at University College London, reveals that the American TV drama *24,* featuring counterterrorism agent Jack Bauer (Kiefer Sutherland), inspired lawyers at Guantanamo to come up with new interrogation (i.e., torture) techniques. Lieutenant Colonel Diane Beaver, a military lawyer at the American "black hole," said that Bauer "gave people lots of ideas." Cited in Richard Norton-Taylor, "Top Bush Aids Pushed for Guantanamo Torture," *Guardian* (April 19, 2008), 1.

62. Quoted in Bruce Bennett, "Making public(s): *The Road to Guantanamo* and Film as Political Practice," paper presented at "Disunited Nations: Cinema Beyond the Nation State," conference at the University of Birmingham, April 27–28, 2007.

63. See BBC News, http://newsvote.bbc.co.uk/mpapps/pagetools/print/news.bbc .co.uk/1/hi/world/america . . . (accessed March 9, 2007). It should be noted that Peter Hain, who was the Northern Ireland cabinet minister in Tony Blair's government, said that the Guantanamo Bay camp should be closed. He followed Blair, who defined the camp as an anomaly and said that if the United States wants to preserve its moral superiority it had to abolish the camp.

64. The U.S. naval base at Guantanamo was established in 1903 following the Spanish-American War on land Cuba leased to the United States. Later, the de facto U.S. protectorate backed the military dictator Fulgencio Batista in Cuba until his overthrow in 1958. It is also interesting to note that the first appearance of concentration camps anywhere in the world was in Cuba in 1895, when the Spanish tried to suppress a new uprising of local plantation owners. On January 22, 2009, on Barack Hussein Obama's second full day in the White House, the president gave an executive order to abolish the CIA's secret detention centers at Guantanamo. At this writing, President Obama continues to struggle to fulfill his campaign promise to close the Guantanamo military prison within a year of taking office. Negotiations to transfer some of the detainees to other countries have proved difficult, especially given the United States' own unwillingness to receive detainees. Congress, including Democrats, has rejected Obama's request for funding to close down Guantanamo, expressing strong opposition to bringing detainees to the United States.

65. Bennett, "Making public(s)." See also Bruce Bennett, "Cinematic Perspectives on the 'War on Terror': *The Road to Guantanamo* (2006) and Activist Cinema," *New Cinemas: Journal of Contemporary Film* 6, no. 2 (2008): 111–26.

66. Klein, *The Shock Doctrine,* 45.

67. Bennett, "Making public(s)," notes that "*The Road to Guantanamo* appeared on British screens in an exceptional way as the first film ever to be released simultaneously in cinemas, on broadcast television, on DVD and over the internet for

streaming or downloading, and it has been suggested that this release strategy marks the emergence of a new business model for film distribution, exploiting growing consumer demand for choice with regard to modes of access to films."

68. BBC News, http://newsvote.bbc.co.uk/mpapps/pagetools/print/news.bbc .co.uk/1/hi/world/america.

69. Quoted in Philippe Sands, "The Dangerous Distraction of Guantanamo," review of Clive Stafford Smith's *Bad Men: Guantanamo Bay and the Secret Prison* (London: Weidenfeld & Nicolson, 2007), *Guardian Review* (June 16, 2007), 8.

70. Agamben, *Homo Sacer*, 171.

71. Quoted in "Window on Their World," *Time* (European edition), March 31, 2003, http://www.time.com/time/europe/magazine/article/0,13005,901030331-435935,00 .html (accessed October 20, 2004).

72. See Klein, *The Shock Doctrine.*

73. In the global context, the three major "zones of exclusion" are the U.S./Mexico border, the Australia/South East Asian rim, and the European Union or "Fortress Europe." These zones mirror the major trading blocs and spheres of influence, and the erection of physical barriers follow the mapped patterns of these sites of white power and wealth.

74. Davis, *Planet of Slums*, 201.

75. It is perhaps ironic, but certainly in accord with the current zeitgeist, that on the day that I wrote this section—November 14, 2007—a new package of national security measures was unveiled by British Prime Minister Gordon Brown. These measures include searches of rail passengers at Britain's largest stations and screening of their bags and the building of new concrete anti-car bomb barriers and vehicle exclusion zones outside airport terminals, shopping centers, and the 250 busiest rail stations. New guidelines are also to be sent to thousands of cinemas, theaters, restaurants, hotels, sporting venues, hospitals, schools, and places of worship, advising them to train staff to carry out searches. "At the same time the Home Office announced it had awarded the main contract for its £1.2bn 'e-borders' programme to ensure that the personal details of everyone who travels into and out of Britain are logged in advance so they can be tracked against U.S.-style 'no fly' lists. Immigration airline liaison officers posted abroad are to be given the on-the-spot power to cancel visas to prevent travel. The £650m contract with a consortium led by U.S. defense company Raytheon will involve up to 90 separate pieces of information being supplied to the security services before a passenger flies to or from Britain. The programme aims to achieve 100% coverage by 2014. Mr. Brown also confirmed an intention to set up a single, 25,000-strong border force, merging the immigration service with customs and some visa staff. He indicated that legislation would be introduced to ensure that its officers have police-style powers to detain and investigate criminal and terror suspects for up to nine hours." Alan Travis and Patrick Wintour, "Rail Passengers Face Anti-terror Searches," *Guardian* (November 15, 2007), 4.

This packet was introduced while the debate about the need to hold terror suspects longer than twenty-eight days was still going on. I have quoted this item at length because it exemplifies both Klein's argument regarding what she calls "the security bubble" (whose prime exporter is fortress Israel) and Agamben's more philosophical concerns regarding the "state of exception" claimed by the sovereign. Timothy Garton Ash (like many others) argues that "Britain has the most watched society in Europe. The country that invented habeas corpus now boasts one of the longest periods of detention without charge in the civilized world." Timothy Garton Ash, "The Threat from Terrorism Does Not Justify Slicing Away Our Freedoms," *Guardian* (November 15 2007), 33.

76. Giorgio Agamben, *State of Exception,* trans. Kevin Attell (Chicago: University of Chicago Press, 2005 [2003]).

77. Hannah Arendt, *The Origins of Totalitarianism* (New York: Harcourt, Brace and World, 1951).

78. Davis, *Planet of Slums,* 201. Davis argues: "With a literal 'great wall' of high-tech border of enforcement blocking large-scale migration to the rich countries, only the slum remains as a fully franchised solution to the problem of warehousing this century's surplus humanity" (200–201).

79. Agamben, *Homo Sacer,* 9.

80. Ibid., 123.

81. Davis, *Planet of Slums,* 205.

82. Cited in Emilie Boyer King, "Police Say Paris Rioters Are Armed as Clashes Escalate," *Guardian* (November 28, 2007), 20.

83. Naomi Klein, "Forget the Green Technology—The Hot Money Is in Guns," *Guardian* (November 30, 2007), 43.

Afterword

The epigraph is from Queen Elizabeth II, in her annual broadcast to the Commonwealth on Saturday, December 25, 2004.

1. "Fortress Europe and Its 'Others': Cultural Representations in Film, Media and the Arts."

2. Fohrenwald was one of the largest DP camps in post–World War II Europe and the last to close (in 1957).

3. I am indebted to Haim Bresheeth for coining this term, which perceptively captures the spirit of post-Imperial London.

4. I am indebted to my colleague Ashwani (Ash) Sharma for coining the term "the global classroom."

5. See Martin Hickman, Consumer Affairs Correspondent, "Films and TV Shows Prompt Britons to Buy Slice of Paradise," *Independent* (March 3, 2008), 15. Thirteen percent of buyers in the south of France were seduced by the television series *A Year in Provence,* based on Peter Mayle's diary of restoring a French farmhouse.

6. Homi Bhabha, "The Other Question: The Stereotype and Colonial Discourse," *Screen* 24, no. 6 (1983): 18–36.

7. See http://www.darkmatter101.org/site/2007/05/07/editorial-celebrity-big-brother-dialogues-the-global-pantomime-of-race.

8. Prior to its assimilation into corporate-driven youth fashion in Europe, the *kafiyah* was worn by the politically conscious youth, particularly those affiliated with the anti-capitalism, anti-globalization movement, as a gesture of solidarity with the Palestinians.

9. Ian Traynor, "EU Told to Prepare for Flood of Climate Change Migrants," *Guardian* (March 10, 2008), 6.

10. Ibid.

11. Ibid. The precedent, perhaps, has already been established by the Maldives. Mohamed Nasheed, the president of the Maldives, announced on November 10, 2008, that the Maldives are planning to buy a new homeland as an insurance policy against climate change that threatens to turn the 300,000 islanders into environmental refugees. Tom Picken, head of international climate change at Friends of the Earth, said, "The Maldives is left to fend for itself. It is a victim of climate change caused by rich countries." Randeep Ramesh, "Paradise Almost Lost: Maldives Seeks to Buy a New Homeland," *Guardian* (November 10, 2008), 1.

12. Traynor, "EU Told to Prepare for Flood of Climate Change Migrants," 6.

13. At the ABCDS (The Moroccan NGO, Association Beni Znassen pour la culture) conference, supported by the MRN (Migrants Rights Network, based in London) and titled "Migration & Human Rights: The War Against Migrants at EU New Borders," Amnesty International Human Rights Action Centre in London, April 1, 2008, Dr. Hein de Haas (Research Officer at the International Migration Institute, Oxford University) spoke on "The Myth of Invasion: The Inconvenient Realities of African Migration to Europe." He began with an assessment of the alarmist tone employed by the media in their treatment of migration, and the frequent use of overdramatic (frequently aquatic) metaphors to create the idea of a huge wave of immigrants about to crash on the shores of unwilling countries. This leads to the formation of a siege mentality, where politicians gain easy points by using strong, warrior-like language about "combating" the problems of migration in "Fortress Europe." Despite this image, de Haas said that there was no evidence of a net increase in migration from Africa, but rather a long-running phenomenon that must be seen against its historical background.

14. Renato Leys, "The Physiology of Feelings," in *The Sheltering Sky: A Film by Bernardo Bertolucci Based on the Novel by Paul Bowles,* ed. Livio Negri and Fabien S. Gerard (London: Scribners, 1990), 59.

15. Georges-Louis Bourgeois, "The Road from Parma," in *The Sheltering Sky,* 134.

16. Film production notes by the Cornerhouse Film Theatre in Manchester.

17. It should be noted in this context that the mostly Pakistani practice of marrying brides from the mother country (and bringing them to the UK) is the focus of a heated debate there, both in relation to issues pertaining to "social cohesion" and immigration.

18. Jacques Rancière, "Guantanamo, Justice and Bushspeak: Prisoners of the Infinite," trans. Norman Madarasz, *Counterpunch* (April 30, 2002), http://www.counterpunch.org/ranciere0430.html (accessed April 16, 2008). Rancière writes in this opinion piece: "Hegel had already sunk into the night of the Absolute in which 'all cows are grey.' The lack of ethical distinction, in which politics and the law drown nowadays, has transformed the prisoners of Guantanamo Bay into captives of the same type of infinite, with grey being switched to orange."

19. John Hooper, "Berlusconi Seeks to Woo Anti-Immigrant Party," *Guardian* (April 16, 2008), 16. These announcements were interpreted by analysts and political commentators as a reaction to the electoral success of the anti-immigrant *Lega Nord* (Northern League).

20. See, for example, the *Caché* dossier, *Screen* 48, no. 2 (Summer 2007): 211–50. Haneke's previous film, *Code Unknown* (*Code inconnu,* France/Germany/Romania, 2000), offers powerful images of the "other" France by linking the disparate

experiences of a Romanian economic migrant, a son of West African refugees, a Parisian couple, and a poor French peasant. This chronicle of contemporary Parisian life takes place against the backdrop of the violent conflict in Kosovo.

21. In October 1961, a confrontation on the Pont de Neuilly in Paris between demonstrating Algerians and police resulted in a riot that ended with 200 dead Maghrebi migrants. Their bodies were thrown into the Seine by the police under the orders of police chief Maurice Papon, who served in the Vichy government as a secretary-general of the Gironde *département* and was involved in the deportation of nearly 1,600 Jews (including over 200 children), who were sent first to the French camp of Drancy and then to Auschwitz. Papon was tried for his crimes only in 1997 in what was often referred to as "the trial of the century." Papon's trial, as Naomi Greene observes, plunged France "into a period of collective introspection concerning the Vichy years." See Naomi Greene, *Landscapes of Loss: The National Past in Postwar French Cinema* (Princeton, N.J.: Princeton University Press, 1999), 64.

22. See Andrew Hussey, "The Paris *Intifada*: The Long War in the *banlieue*," *Granta* 101 (April 15–June 29, 2008): 41–59. Hussey writes: "For many Parisians, the banlieue represents 'otherness'—the otherness of exclusion, of the repressed, of the fearful and despised. . . . The positions and tactics of the immigrants of the banlieue—their identification with Palestine, their hatred of France—reveal the struggle to be part of the Long War every bit as much as those caught up in the conflicts in Iraq and Afghanistan. . . . In the early twenty-first century, the ghosts of colonial and anti-colonial assassins, from Algeria to Beirut, from Congo to Rwanda, continue to be visible in the daylight of the banlieue" (59).

INDEX

Page numbers in italics refer to figures.

Yosefa Loshitzky is Professor of Film, Media, and Cultural Studies at the University of East London. She is author of *The Radical Faces of Godard and Bertolucci* and editor of *Spielberg's Holocaust: Critical Perspectives on* Schindler's List (Indiana University Press, 1997). Her most recent publication, *Identity Politics on the Israeli Screen,* was a *Choice* Outstanding Academic Book for 2002.